TWO CENTS MORE

Tis ⱽ always the season to proclaim the Good News!

Blessings —
Linda

TWO CENTS MORE

Confronting an Untethered Culture

by Living a Principled Life

LINDA C. ROWGO
with RUSTY JAMES ROWGO

Copyright © 2022 – Linda C. Rowgo and Rusty James Rowgo

All rights to this book are reserved. No permission is given for any part of this book to be reproduced, transmitted in any form or means; electronic or mechanical, stored in a retrieval system, photocopied, recorded, scanned, or otherwise. Any of these actions require the proper written permission of the author.

Scripture quotations marked (AMP) are taken from the amplified® Bible (AMP), Copyright © 2015 by The Lockman Foundation. Used by permission. www.lockman.org

Scripture quotations marked (ESV) are taken from the esv® Bible (The Holy Bible, English Standard Version®), Copyright © 2001 by Crossway, a publishing ministry of Good News Publishers. Used by permission. All rights reserved.

Scripture quotations marked (MSG) are taken from THE MESSAGE, copyright © 1993, 2002, 2018 by Eugene H. Peterson. Used by permission of NavPress, represented by Tyndale House Publishers. All rights reserved.

Scripture quotations marked (NKJV) taken from the New King James Version®. Copyright © 1982 by Thomas Nelson. Used by permission. All rights reserved.

Scripture quotations marked (NIV) are taken from the Holy Bible, New International Version®, niv®. Copyright © 1973, 1978, 1984, 2011 by Biblica, Inc.™ Used by permission of Zondervan. All rights reserved worldwide. www.zondervan.com. The "NIV" and "New International Version" are trademarks registered in the United States Patent and Trademark Office by Biblica, Inc.™

Scripture quotations marked (NLT) are taken from the Holy Bible, New Living Translation, copyright ©1996, 2004, 2015 by Tyndale House Foundation. Used by permission of Tyndale House Publishers, Carol Stream, Illinois 60188. All rights reserved.

Scripture quotations marked (TPT) are from The Passion Translation®. Copyright © 2017, 2018, 2020 by Passion & Fire Ministries, Inc. Used by permission. All rights reserved. ThePassionTranslation.com.

Cover design by Rusty James Rowgo

First Printing Edition, 2022
ISBN: 978-1-66788-087-7

To my mother, Christine—

Imparting *strength* through humbleness

a consistent *voice* through adversity

and an unwavering *vision* as the consequence of prayer

ACKNOWLEDGMENTS

Thank you to my son, Russ Rowgo, who challenged me to step up my game and consider there was more I could share through writing. Taking a simple draft, he composed a professional-grade project more significant than the sum of the parts. For this, I will always be grateful.

Special props to my favorite sister, Deborah Okamuro, for encouraging me to keep writing. Deb and I engaged in a good number of lengthy phone calls as this project was coming together. She was instrumental in reminding me of the many stories from our childhood as we meandered down Memory Lane. I shared some of them in this book. Thanks for the memories!

Two Cents More was inspired by my friends. If we know each other, you are likely in this category. A life-changing power is experienced when true friendships allow discussions to reach deep into the more hidden places. Our times of *being real* have fueled me to continue to write. Without you, I would not have the impetus even to explore—what is now clear to me—this precious and God-given outlet.

When writing a book based on the Word of God, there is already an implicit nod to the work of our Creator and Savior throughout. Because of this, one could eliminate a seemingly unnecessary thank you here. However, a personal acknowledgment is warranted.

> *Because of the weight of the words on these pages and how You have called me to convey them, heavenly Father, I appreciate that You have given me a unique level of insight into Your timeless words of truth and promise. And You provided a platform to reach where You have seen fit. I know You open a unique set of doors for every one of your children, and I want to thank You as I know I could not step through mine without Your powerful presence and guiding hand.*

TABLE OF CONTENTS

Foreword xxi
Introduction 1

MORE FOCUSED INWARD

The Pause That Refreshes 5
You Really Are Special 8
Free Choices and Mistakes 10
In Case You're Wondering 12
Whose Thought Is It? 13
About That Rejection 15
Still a Baby 16
Empty Information 18
What Do You Think About That? 19
Keep on Asking 21
"Impossible" People? 23
No Sloshing! 25
Personal Improvement 26
The Attack Is On! 27
Commercials for Crazy 29
Stomp Out Collateral Damage 30
No Worries, Mate! 31
Inside Out 33
When Bad Things Happen 34
Autobiography 35
Triggers Need Safety Locks 36
The Unabridged Version 38
Oh Well... Shake It Off! 40
You *Can* Help It! 42

The Four "H"s	43
To Be or Not To Be	45
About Trusting God's Grace	46
Not a Roll of the Dice	50
Permission Granted	51
Rocking the Boat	52
Get Off the Fence	53
Keep Blooming	54
The Ladder of Success	55
Don't Resist Change	56
Your Assignment	57
A Different Perspective	58
Victim Mentality	59
Dangerous Anger	61
The Love Container	62
A Million Reasons	63
This Is Love	64
Who Doesn't Want It?	66
Life Lessons	67
Change Your Focus	69
Start Moving	70
Character Signals	71
Spot the Difference	72
Negativity Sucks	73
Take a Walk	74
Trauma Responses	75
Time Limitations	77
Push "Pause"	78
Flat Squirrels	79
I Can't Hear You	80
When Enough Is Enough	82
Rebuild	84
"Should" Happens	85

Choice Versus Process	87
Intentionality	89
Failure	90
Flood Effects	91
Not a Spectator Sport	92
Grief Over Good Decisions	93
Wasteland Dwellers	94
Anxiety Sucks	95
I Decided Today Was the Day	97
Stuff	98
Step by Step	99
Puzzle Pieces	100
More Than Scratching the Itch	101
Say What?	103
Sticks and Stones	105
Zip Your Lip	106
Keep Scrolling	107
Change the Formula	108
Grow Up	109
Indulgence or Transformation	110
A Lack of Separateness	112

MORE FOCUSED OUTWARD

A Fair Fare	117
An Antique of Great Value	122
Ban the Blame Game	123
Moms Facing Difficulties	124
Trusting Hearts	126
Wired for Safety	128
The Best Reason to Change	129
The Lord Told Me...	131
Communication Mode	132
I Can See Clearly Now	134

Problematic Love 135
Root Canals 136
Two Sides to the Coin 138
Double Standards 139
On Craving Friendships 140
Demands Don't Do Diddly 143
Exit Stage Left 144
Let Kindness Reign 145
Seedtime 146
Go for Righteous! 147
Give and Take 149
Little Atlas 151
Let's Talk 152
What's the Difference? 153
F-R-E-E-D-O-M! 154
The Spectrum of Frustration 155
Mara Allin 157
Unconditional Conditions 158
Watch Your Mouth! 159
The Problem with Honesty 161
A Caring Heart 162
Sterilize Your Words 163
Domino Effect 165
Dream On! 166
Break the Rule… I Dare You 167
Patience 169
Major Test 170
Repetition Matters 172
To Be or To Do 173
Do as God Does 175
Predictors of a Long Life 176
Parent Alert 178
Born to Judge 179

Old Is Priceless	181
Forever Friends	182
Don't Put Up With It	184
Pretty Words	186
Staying Power	187
Skewed Point of View	189
Relationship Green Flags	190
Self-Destruction	191
Confrontation Conflicts	192
Intentions Don't Count	194
Sad but True	195
Appreciation	197
Change	198
Upward Mobility	199
Who Can I Call?	200
Who's Being Difficult?	202
The Dividing Factor	203
Blessed	205
Toxic Oxygen	206
Check Your Credentials	207
Gift Appreciation	208
Safety Tops People Pleasing	210
Speak Up	211
Excuses Kill Relationships	213
A Time for Pad and Pen	214
Knock It Off	215
Look Out for Pretense	217
Mini Me Woes	219
Motivated Deviants	220
Make Their Day	222
Black Holes	223
Pseudo-Love	225
Teaching Opportunities	226

Make Memories 227
Hold Onto the Straw 229
Take Your Voice Elsewhere 230
Offenses Galore 231
Running Stop Signs 232
A Toxic Equation 235
Look for the Main Messages 237
Safety Nets 239
Funny—Not Funny 241
Set the Bar High 243
My Favorite Home 245
Connecting in Person 246
Birds of a Feather 248
Ready or Not 249
Avoid Toxic Empathy 250
Home Schooling for Real 252
Mum's Note 253
Live Life with Gusto 255

MORE FOCUSED UPWARD

Read the Instructions 261
Coincidence? 263
The Big Black Spot 264
Delaying Gratification 266
Uncertainty 267
Be Aware 268
Evil Weaponry 270
Who Am I... Really? 273
Truth Be Told 274
Get to the Root 276
Rock-Solid Faith 277
Never Alone 279
I Can Only Imagine 280

Be Still And Know	282
Radical Living	284
What Really Matters	285
Christ-Like Internet Control	287
Conversations That Matter	289
Complacency	290
Cut to the Chase	291
Count the Cost	292
Yay or Nay	294
It Is Well with My Soul	295
Pick Your Lens	297
No Comfort Zone	299
For Such a Time as This	300
I Pray Because	303
Mind Renewal Is Critical	304
God Cares, But...	305
Bits and Pieces	306
Worn Out Bibles	308
Whose Will Be Done?	309
Spiritual Metabolism	310
Break the Cycle	312
The Yoke is on You	315
It is Finished!	316
Time to Choose	318
Hardened "Heart-eries"	320
Who's Talking?	322
This is Wrong!	323
Corrie ten Boom	324
Ask the Right Question	326
More Than Enough	327
Go in All the Way	328
Laying Bricks	330
God's Plan	331

Just Breathe	332
Balancing the Scale	334
Might as Well Take It	335
Walking on Logs	336
Blind Belief and Obedience	340
Convergence of Science and Scripture	341
A Great Interdependency	342
Trials Versus Warfare	343
Hold on Tight	345
Rev. Harper and the Titanic	346
Surrender Is the Key	348
Faith Has Different Directions	350
It's Called "Conviction"	352
Hope for Tomorrow	353
The Chase Is On	358
God Is an Overachiever	359
A Quaff for Atheists	360
One Life to Live	362
Do as You're Told	363
This Is So Not True!	364
Expand the Goal	365
Compulsive Christian Disorder	368
Finish Strong	369
I Hate Religion!	370
Faulty Thinking	372
Benefits for the Ages	373
No Substitute	374
There Is Another Option	376
Call Waiting	377
Hard Truths	378
Sing a New Song	380
Put on Your Listening Ears	382
Tell People the Truth	383

Citizenship 385
Voice Recognition 386
Who Needs to Be First? 387
Pray Like Elijah 388
Religion Versus Jesus 390
Does God Limit Himself? 392
Rambling Wee-Hour Tutorials 394
My Thoughts 397
The In-Between Place 401
Not Tomorrow, but Now 403

FINAL THOUGHTS

Afterword 409
Topical Scripture Reference 413
Index 419
Focused Forward Journal 424
About The Authors 464
Where It All Started 466

FOREWORD

WE ARE ENGAGED in a culture war—but not the one you're thinking of—the one relentlessly propagated through social media and news outlets on a daily basis. If it were, this war would be about race relations, economic inequalities, and political divisions, fueled by a genuine "us vs. them" disdain. No, the war we find ourselves battling is not *directly* related to any of these issues, real though they may be. They are merely artifacts stemming from the spiritual war that has raged since the days of Adam. A war not only among men but one initiated in realms unseen.

I once heard a story about a conspiracy perpetrated by a cadre of manufacturing companies. Like any business endeavor, this was to encourage purchasing their flagship product. Their pitch was simple: remind us of the unique importance of their product and that it alone would satisfy. So as unsuspecting consumers, we believed the hype and ran out and bought their product—*the ubiquitous hand drill.* We were absolutely convinced that we needed this when, in all truthfulness, we did not. We were sold a lie, and all the drill manufacturers were in on it. We didn't need a drill; we needed—a hole.

I think about this simple story and how its essence applies everywhere. We are bombarded with the sales pitch demanding what we need—freedom from oppression, freedom from rules, freedom from pain, freedom from shame, freedom from discipline, and freedom from responsibility—almost as though the only way we can get this is through buying something. Well, indeed. This then begs the question, "What is it that's actually being sold and what have we been willing to pay?"

Pundits from all sides have failed to properly address these questions, let alone find any feasible solutions. Attempting to do so is an absolute trap—a quagmire having no resolution, no utopia, no guiding principles, no ultimate purpose, and no "free at last, free at last" moment. Why? Because no consideration is given to anything beyond the limited potential of human effort. We are long due for a recalibration.

During our conversations leading up to writing this book, Linda has recognized that this cultural sales pitch has gotten it completely wrong. It's a non-starter. There is nothing to buy because the solution is already bought and paid for. Throughout the ages, there have never been adequate solutions to confront these issues from our limited human understanding. Like having a goal of a drill when a hole is needed, Linda implores us to step back and consider our true needs. God's perspective on the issues we face is timeless, truthful, and simply *will not fail.* Bear in mind this does not mean following His principles is easy. But living easy is how we got to this point.

Linda is aware of the highly polarized cultural shifts we are seeing play out but has long determined to seek after God's heart and the unchanging truth of scripture. Throughout this book, she encourages us to do the same. Gleaning a rich insight from the many generational and societal shifts she's witnessed throughout her lifetime, Linda has recognized how God's steadfast principles have continued to prevail undeterred. Regardless of our unique situation, Linda's heart seeks to draw our focus back to the grounded perspective of our heavenly Father and away from the wavering, unsubstantiated opinions of the day. As we focus on her words of encouragement and the Word they are based on, let's allow today's sales pitches to fade into the background and remember to keep the main thing, the main thing. Life starts making sense when we do.

Your brother in Christ—

Rusty James Rowgo
Host of *The Ride Podcast*

INTRODUCTION

When the final draft of my first book, *Two Cents,* was nearing completion, emotionally, I was in the final ascent to my long-awaited summit. Hitting this goal would afford me some rest. Upon handing it off to my son to put it all together, I informed him that he needed to wait as I had a few more entries to send to complete the draft. His response shocked me. "That's ok, but unless these final entries were pivotal, there was already more than enough material in this first book." Ok, but—*Wait?*—*The first book?* Clarifying, Russ instructed me to keep writing and add to this excess with a mind toward a sequel. After a bit of introspection and a deep cleansing breath, I knew he was right—I had more to say—much more. You are reading the result of his challenge right now.

This has been a difficult year. Many of us have lost friends and family—some due to age, some to illnesses or accidents. As I close in on eight decades, I suppose this is how things will continue. The trials of life seem to be creating more significant hurdles than ever before. The world is often in chaos, with people running in all directions trying to figure out what directions to take, problems to fix, and the proper methods to address them. Because of this, I am writing with more passion and urgency about the things that matter most. If you've already read *Two Cents*, I believe that, as you read *Two Cents More*, you will be able to sense this urgency stemming from my deep desire to help reveal timeless truths that have been obscured by the lies so prevalent in the culture of the day.

Once again, here's the bottom line: Facebook fed me posts, just like it did in *Two Cents*. Many of the posts stand alone without any indication of their origin. I've identified and credited most posts where I could (check out the index for a list of all references). Although it was quite rare in my first book, I have included more of my original thoughts and personal disclosures in this sequel. As I did in the first book, I wrote comments about each of these posts that rose up in my spirit. I am deeply convinced that God inspired me to write what appears on these pages. Also, keep in mind that there may be a few random posts that I chose to include because they contain half-truths or outright lies that have been propagated throughout our modern culture. I included these to provide a well-reasoned and Godly rebuttal.

Both books in this series contain sections focusing inward (self), outward (others), and upward (God). As you make your way through the sections, you will discover that, although these help direct your actions, all three focal areas are inextricably intertwined. Ample journaling room is provided to capture your valued memories and opinions— "a penny for your thoughts," so to speak. *Note the additional "Focused Forward" journal pages in the Final Thoughts section at the end of the book.*

For such a time as this, God has a word for every one of us—and I have included many of them in these pages. I pray that His Word and His desire and love for you will resonate with your spirit and that the power of His Word will deeply penetrate the deepest part of you—that special place that genuinely yearns to become all He created you to be. Enjoy the journey, and know you'll never have to walk it alone. You matter, and you are loved.

Blessings!

Linda

1

MORE FOCUSED INWARD

THE PAUSE THAT REFRESHES

The whole world paused this morning.

Do you know why? Because an 8-year-old's tank was empty.

The boys had already started their school day at their desks, and I was preparing to leave for work when I noticed my littlest standing in the bathroom wiping his face.

I paused at the door and asked if he was okay. He looked up with tears silently dripping and shook his head. When I questioned if something happened, again he shook his head.

So I sat on the side of the tub and pulled him in my lap. I told him sometimes our heart tanks feel empty and need to be refilled.

He cried into my chest, and I held tight. I asked if he could feel my love filling him up. A nod, and tears stopped.
I waited a minute—

"Has it reached your toes yet?" He shook his head no—

"Okay, man. We will take as long as you need. Work doesn't matter right now. School isn't important either.
This right here is the most important thing today, okay?
Filling you back to the top. Is that good?" *nods*

One more minute—
"Is your heart full of mama's love now?"
"Yeah—"
Looks into his eyes. "I saw it shining in there,
you're full to the top, and you're smiling!"

Y'all. You may not be 8—you may be 28, 38, 48 or whatever—

but ALL of us run on empty just like he did. His weekend was so busy and so full and his little soul was just dry!!

We all have to pause and take a moment to refill with the good things. Scripture, prayer, sunshine, worship, song, laughter, friends, hugs. Refill your empty (tank), or you'll find those emotions (tears, anger, snappy words) overflowing with no reason why.

Take a moment. Refill. It's the most important part of your day!

Justin Nutt

Trying to run on fumes is the absolute worst. Take the time to top off your tank with whatever it is missing. You cannot function well by trying to run on empty. Self-care is essential, but if you ever happen to see someone struggling like this young lad, it is important to slow down, stop, listen, and provide the grace that is needed to bring restoration to someone running on the faintest of fumes. High-octane fuel to fill up an empty love tank might be just the thing needed to help someone begin to function—firing on all cylinders once again. You might find that focusing on others helps to fuel you too.

On a personal note, whenever I begin to feel like I'm running low on emotional fumes, leaving me sad, empty, and lonely, I have learned how to snap out of the blahs rather quickly. My solution involves other people. I have a friendly neighborhood café filled with "regulars" who come in to fill up their empty days. Many of them are older and live alone, just like me. There is a special large table where people come and go at will, engaging in lively conversations covering many subjects and life events. These special moments are full of caring and sharing and top off my love tank. Once I've spent time with these precious people, all is well with the world once again.

MORE FOCUSED INWARD

May you experience the love of Christ, though it is too great to understand fully. Then you will be made complete with all the fullness of life and power that comes from God.
EPHESIANS 3:19 NLT

True to your word, you let me catch my breath and send me in the right direction.
PSALM 23:3 MSG

_____
_____
_____
_____
_____
_____
_____
_____
_____
_____
_____
_____
_____
_____
_____
_____
_____
_____
_____
_____
_____
_____
_____

YOU REALLY ARE SPECIAL

Sometimes a children's book can have so much to say about my grown-up life. One of my favorite stories is *You Are Special* by Max Lucado. At the end of the story, the main character is learning to deal with the dots people have stuck to him. The dots are symbolic of the labels people tend to put on each other.

The "aha" moment comes when the boy is told, "The dots only stick if you let them."

I know it's a kid's story, but as an adult these words were an epiphany to me. It was a moment of complete revelation to understand the simple principle of not letting other people's opinions and comments define me.

Over the years I've learned to embrace the mantra, "Don't let other people's compliments go to your head nor their criticisms go to your heart."

It's not easy, but it is quite the start to embracing who I'm meant to be.

Lysa TerKeurst

I also appreciate this Max Lucado story and have given copies to some of the younger members of my family. I love how Lysa "connected the dots." Nothing can or will stick to you unless you let it. That seems like a no-brainer, yet there are many walking along with their tell-tale dots affixed—impeding their ability to live a quality and successful life. Remember that you *are* who God *says* you are. Let Him define your identity. It's perfectly OK for you to let that truth stick to you. Meditate on this knowledge often. With it, you will be able to walk tall, with the great confidence you'll need.

MORE FOCUSED INWARD

*Seek the Kingdom of God above all else, and live righteously,
and he will give you everything you need.*
MATTHEW 6:33 NLT

FREE CHOICES AND MISTAKES

*You can never make the same mistake twice—
because the second time you make it, it's not a mistake—
it's a choice.*

I didn't know what I didn't know, but now—*no excuses!* I was so upset when I saw a couple of verses in James 4 for the first time. I could no longer claim ignorance—it wasn't bliss anymore. Personal responsibility was the order of the day from then on.

Some might say that even making a mistake the first time is a choice—no argument there. Whatever we do *is* a choice, but sometimes we don't realize it's a mistake until after the fact. Those are called "honest mistakes," and grace must be extended here.

Here's what gets me though: When counsel is asked for and given in the form of a warning that doing something will wind up with feelings of regret (perhaps because the counselor has already experienced it in their own life), the person, fully warned, but ignoring the counsel, says, "I'm going to do it anyway—I want to make my own mistakes." *Why* are people so arrogant and hell-bent on doing things that they know in their heart of hearts will end up in heartbreak and regret? I get *why* it happens—it's all laid out in the Bible, but it still breaks my heart to see people who know better sitting on the throne and governing their lives in such self-destructive ways. They have created a god in *their* image, refusing to do things God's way. If this is what total independence looks like, no thank you! Fully depend on God to steer you in the right direction and give you the route that will best lead you to the place He wants you to go.

Those who find themselves in a crisis repeatedly due to poor choices have become conditioned to being the "victim" and have had their "friends" feel sorry for them and bail them out of the messes they created. When that happens, the problem is perpetuated. Commiseration is never helpful in cases like this. It simply enables the mistake-makers to stay stuck and not grow into maturity. This leaves the enabler also trapped in their ungrounded notion that what they are doing is actually helping, causing maturity in the errant one. Nope and nope! These behaviors of giving and taking doubles the trouble.

A phrase I have used often is "You don't know what you don't know," but oh my goodness, once you know and put into practice what you've learned, lives can be forever changed. Doing things God's way will *always* be beneficial. The Father knows best! ""

Below are the two verses from James that hit me hard when I saw them for the first time many years ago. I have never been able to shake them out of my memory when I am tempted to do the wrong thing. God has convinced me and, quite often, convicted me with these verses when I'm faced with choices.

> *As it is, you are full of your grandiose selves.*
> *All such vaunting self-importance is evil. In fact, if you know the*
> *right thing to do and don't do it, that for you, is evil.*
> JAMES 4:16-17 MSG

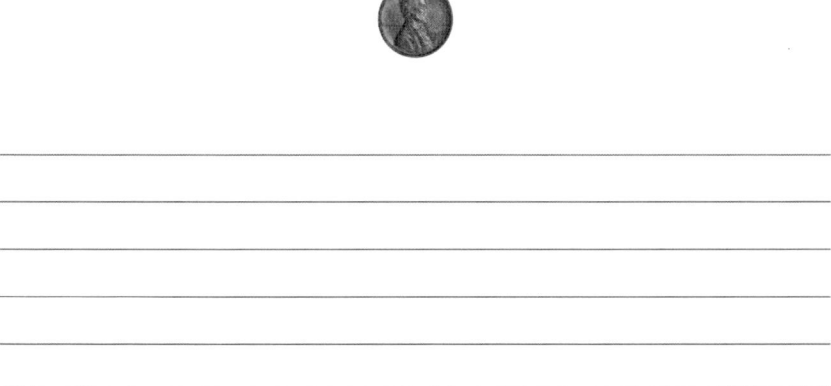

_____
_____
_____
_____
_____

TWO CENTS MORE

IN CASE YOU'RE WONDERING

*Nothing ever goes away
until it teaches us what we need to know.*

Pema Chodron

Just in case any of us are wondering why the same issues keep coming up like a playlist on repeat, this might be the reason. There are things we *need* to know, but sometimes we don't *want* to know them and stubbornly refuse to learn. It might require a different perspective and changing the way we think and the choices we make. It might also involve one of my grandson's favorite and frequently-used words—*surrender!*

*Give instruction to a wise man, and he will be still wiser;
teach a just man, and he will increase in learning.*
PROVERBS 9:9 NKJV

WHOSE THOUGHT IS IT?

We can't afford to have a thought in our head that isn't His.

No matter which way we turn these days, it seems like everything and everyone is offering their "two cents" about how things are and how things need to be—me included. The "truth" is being expounded through a myriad of channels. Certainly, we are being inundated by social media opinions and "fact-checked truths" 24/7. Conversations around the water cooler and meeting up for coffee to catch up on the latest news trend or hot story have become commonplace. So many thoughts and opinions have been offered up by the "experts" that make it difficult to discern what is accurate or what is a long-held belief and something that fits an adopted agenda. What we think matters. It drives our talk and the way we behave.

It is imperative to get our facts straight and become aware of what is really going on. Who are we going to believe? And how will we proceed living our lives responsibly and with a high level of integrity? This is the perfect time to look at Romans 12:1-2. For people who look to the Bible for direction, it seems like it would be prudent to check out what God has to say about our thoughts. If we begin to think the way He thinks, much confusion will dissipate, and clear thinking would prevail. I don't know about you, but here's what I want more than anything: The truth—the whole truth—and nothing but the truth.

> *So here's what I want you to do, God helping you.*
> *Take your everyday, ordinary life—your sleeping, eating,*
> *going to work, and walking around life—and place it before God*
> *as an offering. Embracing what God does for you is the*
> *best thing you can do for him.*
> ROMANS 12:1 MSG

TWO CENTS MORE

Don't become so well-adjusted to your culture that you fit into it without thinking. Instead, fix your attention on God. You'll be changed from the inside out. Readily recognize what he wants from you, and quickly respond to it. Unlike the culture around you, always dragging you down to its level of immaturity, God brings the best out of you, develops well-formed maturity in you.
ROMANS 12:2 MSG

ABOUT THAT REJECTION

As I look back on my life, I realize that every time I thought I was being rejected from something good, I was actually being re-directed to something better.

Funny how that works! Kicking against it, but missing the point by a mile. I have experienced a great many disappointments and heartbreaks in my life. There were times when I really believed that I would never heal and return to living a happy life. Having a sense of loss or rejection can be so debilitating. At least, it always seemed to be like that for me. Life would be going along so well, and then the bottom would drop out. How could I possibly go on when everything fell apart? Sometimes it would take me a while to think about moving on, but eventually, I would remember who I was and Who had promised to never leave me or forsake me. Once I poured my final cup of tea at my lonely pity party for one, the cobwebs would start to get brushed aside, and hope for something better would begin to come into view. Was I hurting? *Yes!* Did everything seem hopeless at that moment? *Yes!* Was it the end of my life? *No!* Was there hope for the future? *Absolutely!*

And we know that all things work together for good to those who love God, to those who are the called according to His purpose.
Romans 8:28 NKJV

_____
_____
_____
_____

STILL A BABY

The attitude of "that's just how I am, take it or leave it" is still a sign of immaturity. As an adult, it's your responsibility to figure out which of your traits are toxic or negatively impactful towards other people and the ones you love, and to eventually learn how to fix them.
At some point, we all gotta start making ourselves better individuals. If you truly believe that you don't have to change anything about yourself, even at the very least the worst in you, and that people will just have to deal with it, then sorry, you are still a child.

This is the picture of a willful, spoiled brat who doesn't give a rat's patootie about how their childish behaviors and attitudes affect the people around them—especially the ones who have loved them, invested in them, and been in their life for a long time. There is no sign of an Empathy Chip anywhere to be found. You might ask, "Do these people really exist today?" Yes, they do! In fact, this approach seems more prevalent than ever. There seems to be a growing "que sera, sera" attitude. With so much uncertainty and chaos in the world today, some people seem to be quite content just to live life like there is no tomorrow. Don't bother with self-improvement—it is what it is.

Here's what "it is"—an enormous waste of time and a lack of appreciation for the precious life graciously given to each of us by a loving Father with a great plan. People are certainly free to live however they want, acting as if there is no tomorrow, but this is not reality. There will always be a tomorrow! How our tomorrow turns out will be determined by how we live today. It's time to make positive changes and *grow up!* God didn't plant you here to do *stupid!* Get in line for an Empathy Chip and deliberately begin caring about others, sensing how your behaviors and attitudes can affect them. Doing this will mature how you view and deal with yourself. Remember, your tomorrow hinges on what you actively do today.

MORE FOCUSED INWARD

*"For I know the plans I have for you," says the Lord.
"They are plans for good and not for disaster, to give you a
future and a hope. In those days when you pray, I will listen.
If you look for me wholeheartedly, you will find me."*
JEREMIAH 29:11-13 NLT

EMPTY INFORMATION

We can know the right words
yet never be changed.
This is the difference between
information and transformation.

A.W. Tozer

Actions speak much louder than words! Once we have receive clear and concise information about how change works, following the instructions and embracing the hard work brings transformation. Desiring actual change requires a concerted effort to bring it to pass. Words give definitions and meaning to issues; acting upon that information brings change.

> *By this we know that we love the children of God,*
> *when we love God and keep His commandments.*
> I JOHN 5:2 NKJV

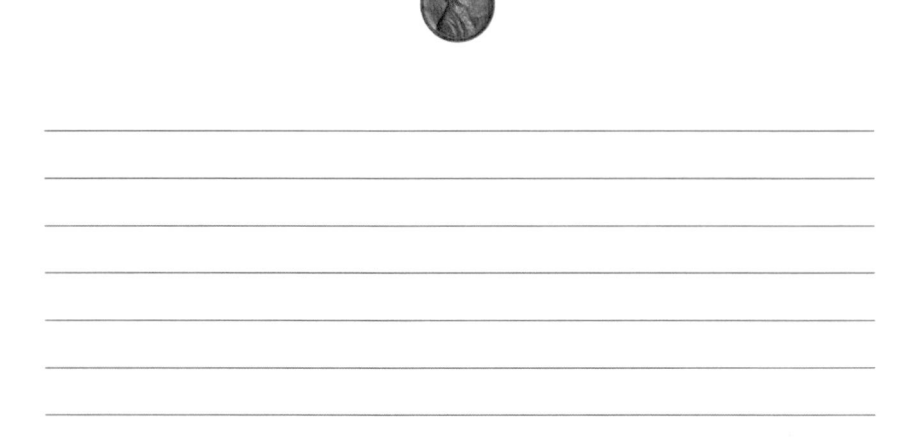

WHAT DO YOU THINK ABOUT THAT?

> We can't solve problems by
> using the same kind of thinking
> we used when we created them.
>
> Albert Einstein

Ya think? Problems are inevitable. Life is always going to challenge us one way or another. Sometimes we create our own problems by making bad choices or even doing things unwittingly that end up becoming problems. It is also true that issues outside our control can become trouble for us. Regardless of where they originate, problems creep into our space and must be confronted. We want to think that we can take on anything that comes into our environment, but experience shows that our way of thinking cannot always find the best solution. Look at the issues the prodigal son faced due to his choices in Luke 15.

Whether self-imposed or not, finding a resolution to the issues we face is best handled by applying the unfailing wisdom God provides.

> *Wise thinking leads to right living;*
> *stupid thinking leads to wrong living.*
> ECCLESIASTES 10:2 MSG

> *Oh, the depth of the riches both of the wisdom and knowledge of*
> *God! How unsearchable are His judgments and His ways past*
> *finding out! "For who has known the mind of the Lord?*
> *Or who has become His counselor?"*
> ROMANS 11:33-34 NKJV

TWO CENTS MORE

I have taught you in the way of wisdom;
I have led you in right paths.
PROVERBS 4:11 NKJV

KEEP ON ASKING

> I would rather have questions that cannot be
> answered than answers which cannot be questioned.
> Nobody ever figures out what life is all about,
> and it does not matter. Explore the world.
> Nearly everything is really interesting
> if you go into it deeply enough.
>
> Richard Feynman

Nobody knows everything, but we've all probably run into a few people who like to give the impression that they are omniscient. These are the people who hate to be challenged or questioned about anything. On the other hand, some know they still have a lot to learn, and are curious enough to ask questions. They are the "inquiring minds want to know" people. It would be so nice if everybody would be patient, compassionate, and kind enough to allow others to ask questions to gain knowledge and information. This is the key to learning.

Unfortunately, some have information that should be available to all, but they hate being questioned. In cases like this, valid questions deserve a response, but many are unwilling to provide one. And if they respond at all, their answers are often misleading or incomplete. Feynman calls this the "answers which can't be questioned" situation. A vague answer that doesn't even address the question may be given, and, upon further questioning for clarification, the person being questioned becomes angry or dismissive. They have adopted a non-disclosure stance. When non-answers or lies are the responses to sincere, fact-seeking questions, trust is gone.

If the answer to a question is unknown, just say so. But, if the answer to a question is unsatisfactory, it ought to be acceptable to seek further clarification. These days, there are many who will not be happy about being questioned further. When you encounter this remember to operate in the grace of God knowing that the truth we seek is ultimately found in Him.

We don't yet see things clearly. We're squinting in a fog, peering through a mist. But it won't be long before the weather clears and the sun shines bright! We'll see it all then, see it all as clearly as God sees us, knowing Him directly just as He knows us!
I CORINTHIANS 13:12 MSG

Anyone who claims to know all the answers doesn't really know very much.
I CORINTHIANS 8:2 NLT

"IMPOSSIBLE" PEOPLE?

Sheri Rose Shepherd wrote about praying for "impossible" people. "God knows those people in your lives, which is why He says 'if it is possible' (Romans 12:18). So, if you are beating yourself up because you can't get a breakthrough in an impossible relationship, then it may be time to stop fighting and leave the impossible in God's hands."

In situations like this, I have finally concluded that it is time to walk away and pray, realizing that it's not about me getting or not getting a breakthrough. As it has been said over the years, "You can lead a horse to water, but you can't make him drink." I'm leaving feelings of frustration behind. It's a relief to realize that it is often about the unwillingness of the other person to receive and respond—and besides, it's always about God's ability and desire to break down the barriers anyway.

Rowgo

The for-real friends and family in my corner for the long haul is secure. At my age, I have learned that relationships have different levels and degrees of connection. Many have come and gone over the years—I call them "crossroads friends." They have entered my life for a significant time, and I don't know what I would have done without them. But they have moved on due to a myriad of reasons, as have I. Sometimes it has been an acrimonious parting of ways, but not always. Most of the time, geographical moves, changing interests, and life events have caused harmonious and very amicable separations. It just happens.

My circle of safe friends—my "no matter what" friends—has been carefully selected for this stage of my life and is limited in numbers due to available time and opportunity. There is one cool thing though. Due in part to modern technology, my larger circle of friends is still very vibrant and flourishing. It's funny how there has been such an ebb and flow over the years. Friends have faded away, and contact has ended, and then, all of a sudden and out of the blue, there is a reconnection. After a short time of catching up, it's as if the gap of silence has been filled up with meaningful information.

Finally, although a couple of friends are miles away, they *are* in my little "no matter what" circle. Virtual visits are almost as good as physical face-to-face connections. We can sip coffee together from a distance and still share our lives and love with one another.

I am so thankful for the people who bring such joy into my life—so many Godwinks!

> *When you knock on a door, be courteous in your greeting.*
> *If they welcome you, be gentle in your conversation.*
> *If they don't welcome you, quietly withdraw.*
> *Don't make a scene. Shrug your shoulders and be on*
> *your way. You can be sure that on Judgment Day they'll be*
> *mighty sorry—but it's no concern of yours now.*
> MATTHEW 10:12-15 MSG

> *If it is possible, as much as depends on you,*
> *live peaceably with all men.*
> ROMANS 12:18 NKJV

_____
_____
_____
_____
_____

NO SLOSHING!

Once you carry your own water,
you will learn the value of every drop.

Taking personal responsibility for your own stuff and recognizing carelessness and waste will help you learn how to value what belongs to you and take care of your own business very well. It's important to remember that everyone has their own bucket of "water" to manage. Please don't interfere with how others choose to carry their load. You need to mind your own business and avoid as much spillage as possible. Everything you do and the way you carry yourself and your load matters.

Stay calm; mind your own business; do your own job.
You've heard all this from us before, but a reminder never hurts.
I THESSALONIANS 4:11 MSG

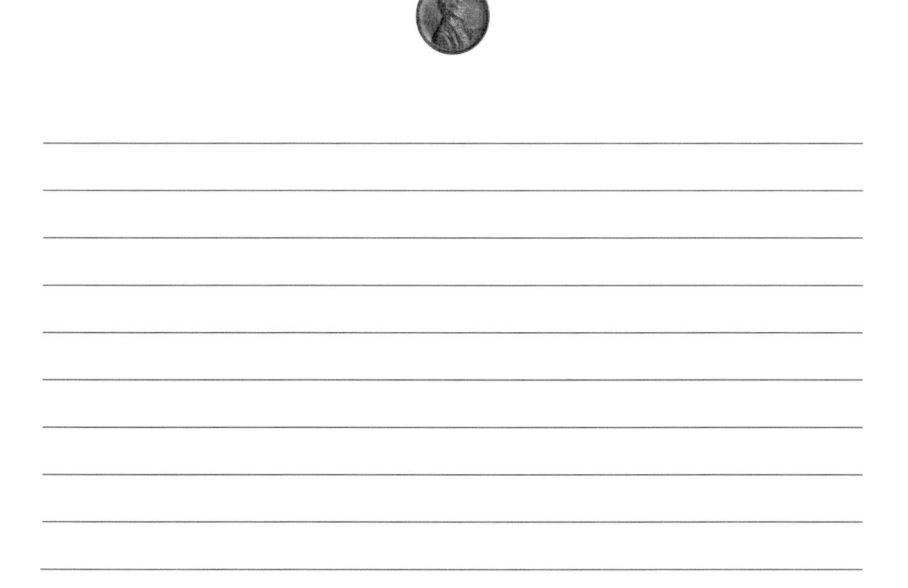

PERSONAL IMPROVEMENT

Being single isn't a time to look for love.
Use that time to work on yourself and grow as an individual.

Ditch the search! When beginning to focus on a new relationship, it takes time to pull back and work on necessary individual growth and make changes. It becomes all about another person and pleasing them. That's how people lose themselves as individuals over and over again. For a relationship to be healthy and last, it takes two people who have done the hard work to become as whole and complete as they can be. One person should never be expected to complete another. It must be all in—100% from each person. Going for 50/50 will be a Lose/Lose proposition—it never works. Don't rush the process!

And this I pray, that your love may abound still more and more in knowledge and all discernment, that you may approve the things that are excellent, that you may be sincere and without offense till the day of Christ, being filled with the fruits of righteousness which are by Jesus Christ to the glory and praise of God.
PHILIPPIANS 1:9-11 NKJV

THE ATTACK IS ON!

*Make sure your worst enemy is not
living between your two ears.*

Zig Ziglar

You'd better be very aware of what you're thinking about. If your thoughts are counterproductive and contrary to the way God has encouraged us to think about—well—everything, you may very well have invited the enemy to take up residence in your head space. Establishing boundaries is your responsibility, and when you allow negativity and wrong thinking into your thought processes, your peace and soundness of mind will be challenged big time. Put that enemy out forthwith and slam the door behind him.

This is my personal experience: There have been so many times that I have lost sleep by incessantly running thoughts through my head, especially on nights when I need and crave a solid block of sweet rest. Even during active, awake hours, conversations and just plain words and ideas run rampant. What is being said to and about me by others and my own thoughts and words become my inner dialogue. If I'm not careful, the content invading my thought life becomes harmful, debasing, and genuinely destructive. It's time to think about what I'm thinking about. Once I renew my mind and begin to think "God thoughts" over and above the other nonsense, my enemy is vanquished. I am well able to silence the chatterbox living between my own two ears. How about you?

*Incline your ear and hear the words of the wise,
And apply your heart to my knowledge.*
PROVERBS 22:17 NKJV

Summing it all up, friends, I'd say you'll do best by filling your minds and meditating on things true, noble, reputable, authentic, compelling, gracious—the best, not the worst; the beautiful, not the ugly; things to praise, not to curse. Put into practice what you learned from me, what you heard and saw and realized. Do that, and God, who makes everything work together, will work you into his most excellent harmonies.
PHILIPPIANS 4:8-9 MSG

COMMERCIALS FOR CRAZY

*I don't want my life to be so crowded
that I'm nothing more than a commercial for crazy.*

Lysa TerKeurst

That statement smacks of overly full and busy activities and schedules. My concern goes a little deeper. A crowded thought life, especially when many of the thoughts run contrary to God-thoughts, frequently manifests outwardly in words and actions. Big mistake! Now we're talking about a major, prime-time commercial for crazy!

Correct thinking and emotional stability are available to everyone. Every corner of the Bible contains antidotes for crazy thinking. In a nutshell, when we straighten up our thought-life, commercials for crazy will no longer exist.

> "For My thoughts are not your thoughts, nor are your ways My ways," says the Lord. "For as the heavens are higher than the earth, so My ways higher than your ways, and My thoughts than your thoughts."
> ISAIAH 55:8-9 NKJV

STOMP OUT COLLATERAL DAMAGE

Your kids watching you stay in a
toxic relationship does more damage
than you being a single parent.

Anyone who even considers entering a toxic relationship just to avoid being alone is a clear indication that there is something missing in them by settling for something so unhealthy and destructive. What are the messages stored up and carried with them for so long? Individual work and healing are needed first. Don't subject your kids to your bad decisions. They become collateral damage and wind up having to heal from your disastrous choices. That's so unfair and unloving. It's *not* all about you—think about them. Here's a thought: Work on the things that need healing in you so that you won't pick unhealthy relationships. That way, collateral damage is stomped out before it has a chance to rear its ugly head and damage your kids. Put a stop to the reign of terror that toxicity has done to destroy a healthy and peaceful family life. Stay single until you become whole and healthy. Remember Luke 10:5 declares: *But whatever house you enter, first say, "Peace to this house."*

*God-loyal people, living honest lives,
make it much easier for their children.*
PROVERBS 20:7 MSG

_____
_____
_____
_____

NO WORRIES, MATE!

*What you worry about the most shows what
you trust God with the least.*

This reminds me of a short phrase I hear fairly frequently these days. When people offer up excuses or reasons that something didn't happen as planned, I hear the words, "No worries." With this post, let us dig a little deeper.

It is early July 2021, and I have a friend who is possibly facing a dreaded diagnosis, and she is worried—and scared. And truth be told, I'm worried too. How often do we encounter uncertainties and feelings of dread that disasters might occur outside or even within our control? This is not a time to be flippant. That rock in our gut must be addressed.

When I'm about to crash and burn with worry, I only have one place of refuge and comfort where I can go—I run straight to the Lord and His Word. I change my focus. There is a problem, and I need a solution. Things don't always turn out the way I want them to, and I don't always understand why things happen the way they do, but I have learned one thing over the years—God is good *all* the time. I cannot imagine how people survive in this chaotic world without acknowledging Him and accepting His lovingkindness toward them. My hope is built on nothing less than Jesus' blood and righteousness.

When worries hit, I put my trust in God to manage what's going on. He knows the beginning from the end and will accomplish far more than I ever will with all my worrying. I'm looking forward to saying, without being flippant, "No worries—God has this."

Do not be anxious about anything, but in every situation, by prayer and petition, with thanksgiving, present your request to God.
PHILIPPIANS 4:6 NIV

INSIDE OUT

You cannot change what's going on around you
until you start changing what's
going on within you.

This is an inside-out procedure that is avoided way too often. Too many people tend to be reactionary to external forces. If only we would take care of the internal forces that drive our behaviors, attitudes, and words first, we would become healthier emotionally and spiritually to the people around us.

> *Now may the Lord direct your hearts into the
> love of God and into the patience of Christ.*
> II THESSALONIANS 3:5 NKJV

_____
_____
_____
_____
_____
_____
_____
_____
_____
_____

WHEN BAD THINGS HAPPEN

Sometimes the bad things that happen in our lives
put us directly on the path to the best things
that will ever happen to us.

This idea of bad things happening can be seen differently then. What appeared to be a difficult period of time or maybe even just a single incident wasn't entirely bad after all. The good may not have occurred until the disaster took place. Perhaps a relationship that looked promising in the beginning, fell apart and went sour. So much heartache, sorrow, and disappointment seem like the worst thing that could ever happen. And yet, this post suggests an intriguing perspective might be on the horizon. Not everything that happens in life *is* good, but according to Romans 8:28, *All things work together for good to those who love God.*

*For God is working in you, giving you the desire
and the power to do what pleases him.*
PHILIPPIANS 2:13 NLT

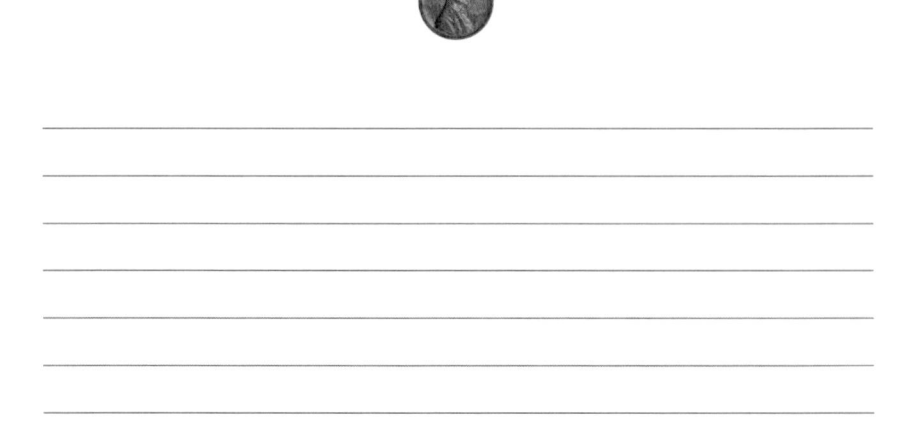

AUTOBIOGRAPHY

Every single day a new page unfolds for you to
write something new to your story. There's going to
be some good chapters and some bad ones, but
no matter how your story ends, make sure
that you are the one holding the pen.

Roger Lee Quotes

This is the epitome of self-control. Live your own life, and don't succumb to being controlled by others. Write your own story—an autobiography. You can even write your "Oughttobiography," if that play on words fits. That way, by taking full responsibility for your own life, you will also be able to take the credit.

If you are living your life as a Christian and desiring to live in a way that pleases God, you will consult Him as your story unfolds. Maybe your autobiography will have a ghostwriter—errr—Holy Ghost writer. If you lean on and trust God to direct your path, He will also direct your pen to write a masterpiece.

Only fear the Lord, and serve Him in truth with your whole heart;
for consider what great things He has done for you.
I SAMUEL 12:24 NKJV

TRIGGERS NEED SAFETY LOCKS

Finding The Cause of Your Triggers

Identify how your trigger made you feel
I felt unloved
I felt unheard
I felt judged
I felt controlled
I felt left out
I felt betrayed
I felt blamed
I felt unimportant
I felt uncared for
I felt disrespected
I didn't feel worthy
I didn't feel good enough

Narc-Wise

Feelings are fickle and based on emotions. People are often responsible for pulling the trigger that produces these feelings. You will need to identify the culprits and decide who or what you will believe. Triggers cannot *make* you feel anything unless you allow the message to hit the target and penetrate your emotions in a hostile, debasing way. Go deeper than the emotional level and get to the root of the problem. That's how a safety lock can be activated to disable the trigger.

Feelings are very changeable, mainly depending on external events and influences. God has very positive affirmations to circumvent and eradicate all of these emotional feelings that trigger the beliefs that continually destroy a person's sense of purpose and value. Start checking out what He has to say about you and go from there. God's right; people aren't—unless they say the same thing God says about you. All of the above triggers will be permanently disarmed and disappear if you believe what God has to say about you. You *are* who God says you are, and that's final!

> *Peace I leave with you; My [own] peace I now give and bequeath to you. Not as the world gives do I give to you. Do not let your hearts be troubled, neither let them be afraid. [Stop allowing yourselves to be agitated and disturbed; and do not permit yourselves to be fearful and intimidated and cowardly and unsettled.]*
> JOHN 14:27 AMP

THE UNABRIDGED VERSION

*We must allow the Word of God to correct us
the same way we allow it to encourage us.*

Like it or not, the Bible is the complete package, and it covers *everything*. If we go in with a black marker to cross out the parts we disagree with, we will construct our own set of instructions and rules. It doesn't work that way. God knew what He was doing and how everything would work best when He put the whole shebang together. If we pick and choose, avoid the warnings and the necessary corrections along the way, we will suffer the consequences of our disobedience. And we *can* be sure of one thing—God *will* have the final say.

The Bible is readily available to all, and we will never be able to say that living a good life was impossible because it didn't come with instructions. It's our responsibility to read and follow the directions step-by-step, not leaving out the hard parts. It all comes together for our good.

There is an acronym for the word "Bible" that I have heard over the years. It suggests that the Bible is a book filled with instructions: *Basic Instructions Before Leaving Earth*. Many people have said that the Bible is hard to understand, and while I agree that there are parts of it that can be confusing or even appear contradictory, there is good news. Many versions and translations are now available that can provide greater clarity. Check out the free online resources at the Blue Letter Bible, BibleGateway, or BibleHub websites—to name just a few—to access scores of translations and commentaries.

The key is to pray for understanding as you study His Word because our God has promised to illuminate your understanding. In Psalms 119:105, David writes, *"Your Word is a light unto my feet and a lamp unto my path."*

David affirmed that God's Word showed him how to live and where to go; this Word is for you as well.

> *God means what He says. What He says goes.*
> *His powerful Word is sharp as a surgeon's scalpel, cutting*
> *through everything, whether doubt or defense, laying us open to*
> *listen and obey. Nothing and no one can resist God's Word.*
> *We can't get away from it—no matter what.*
> HEBREWS 4:12-13 MSG

OH WELL… SHAKE IT OFF!

One day a farmer's donkey fell into a well. The animal cried piteously for hours as the farmer tried to figure out what to do. Finally, he decided the animal was old, and the well needed to be covered up anyway. It just wasn't worth it to retrieve the donkey. He invited all his neighbors to come over and help him. They all grabbed a shovel and began to shovel dirt into the well.

At first, the donkey realized what was happening and cried horribly. Then, to everyone's amazement, he quieted down. A few shovel loads later, the farmer finally looked down the well. He was astonished at what he saw. With each shovel of dirt that hit his back, the donkey was doing something amazing. He would shake it off and take a step up. As the farmer's neighbors continued to shovel dirt on top of the animal, he would shake it off and take a step up. Pretty soon, everyone was amazed as the donkey stepped up over the edge of the well and happily trotted off.

> MORAL: Life is going to shovel dirt on you, all kinds of dirt. The trick to getting out of the well is to shake it off and take a step up. Each of our troubles is a steppingstone. We can get out of the deepest wells just by not stopping, never giving up! Shake it off and take a step up. Remember the five simple rules to be happy:
>
> 1. Free your heart from hatred. Forgive.
> 2. Free your mind from worries. Most never happen.
> 3. Live simply and appreciate what you have.
> 4. Give more.
> 5. Expect less from people, but more from yourself.

When troubles like this come our way, we can either engage in a pity party and cry or get creative and rise to the challenge. What a great opportunity to do a little problem-solving and apply Godly solutions to become victorious when confronted with disastrous life events. Rising up and coming out on the other side is the best! Disasters do not always guarantee catastrophic results. Shake it off.

> *I waited patiently for the Lord; and He inclined to me and heard my cry. He also brought me up out of a horrible pit, out of the miry clay, and set my feet upon a rock, and established my steps.*
> PSALM 40:1-2 NKJV

TWO CENTS MORE

YOU *CAN* HELP IT!

Reminder:
A choice of behavior is always within our control.

Andy Andrews

How often have we heard somebody say emphatically, "but... but... but... I just couldn't help it!" That's a crock! The truth is that you could have done something differently, but you just didn't feel like it *or* it was too hard *or* you didn't think of it in time *or* you didn't want to upset anybody—*or...or...or*. Excuses are a dime a dozen. When you know the right thing to do, *do it!* Self-control is the order of the day, and it's on *you* to exercise it. Selah!

> *So eat your meals heartily, not worrying about what others say about you—you're eating to God's glory, after all, not to please them. As a matter of fact, do everything that way heartily and freely to God's glory. At the same time, don't be callous in your exercise of freedom, thoughtlessly stepping on the toes of those who aren't as free as you are. I try my best to be considerate of everyone's feelings in all matters; I hope you will be too.*
> I Corinthians 10:31-33 MSG

THE FOUR "H"S

Which do you want:
The pain of staying where you are
or the pain of growth?

Great question. This requires much careful thought. The pain is very real in both circumstances. Because of this, there are the four "H"s to consider— Hurt, Harm, Help, and Healing. They will all come into play. Staying stuck in a bad place is Harmful, chipping away at your very being. However, it will Hurt to do the hard work of moving forward, but it will no longer be Harmful. Change can be very challenging, but it will always Help to work on getting better and not staying stuck for a minute longer where you don't belong. It's time to experience a growth spurt—with the associated growing pains. You might even have to seek out trained Help to address the situation properly. Your decision to do whatever it takes to get better will bring healing that lasts.

The most essential ingredient needed when beginning to work through the four "H"s is asking God to be your main Helper. Surrender to His guidance and Help, and He will bring about total Healing, changing you from glory to glory!

Whenever, though, they turn to face God as
Moses did, God removes the veil and there they are—
face-to-face! They suddenly recognize that God is a
living, personal presence, not a piece of chiseled stone.
And when God is personally present, a living Spirit, that
old, constricting legislation is recognized as obsolete.
II CORINTHIANS 3:16-17 MSG

*We're freed of it! All of us!
Nothing between us and God, our faces shining
with the brightness of His face. And so we are transfigured,
much like the Messiah, our lives gradually becoming brighter and
more beautiful as God enters our lives and we become like Him.*
II CORINTHIANS 3:18 MSG

TO BE OR NOT TO BE

Instead of focusing so much on a To Do List, I'm starting a To Be List.
Things I Want To Be:
Happy
Calm
Loving
Healthy
Awesome

Be a human being, not a human doing. One is an internal development; the other is external activity. The things we do are important, but the core of who we are drives our lives. If we enjoy a fruitful life filled with outstanding achievements and recognition for jobs well-done, that is a worthy goal, but operating from an internal place of knowing who we are and Who directs our path far surpasses it. This is, after all, the basis of the only reward extending into eternity.

What marvelous love the Father has extended to us! Just look at it— we're called children of God! That's who we really are. But that's also why the world doesn't recognize us or take us seriously, because it has no idea who He is or what He's up to.
I JOHN 3:1 MSG

ABOUT TRUSTING GOD'S GRACE

A Revelation that Produced a Revolution

The revelation of strengthening grace Paul received from the Lord produced such a revolution in his life that he actually began to rejoice in his tests and trials! Following his joyful words in II Corinthians 12:9, he continued and expanded his response to the revelation Jesus delivered to him with these words:

> *"Therefore I take pleasure in infirmities, in reproaches, in necessities, in persecutions, in distresses for Christ's sake—"*
> II CORINTHIANS 12:10A NKJV

Paul expressed to the Corinthians that he now took pleasure in the reproaches, the necessities, and the persecutions he was experiencing as well as the distresses that arose in his life because of his ministry work. Why would Paul now rejoice in these seemingly terrible things when in II Corinthians 12:7 he seemed to be crying out for change? We know the answer to this question because Paul revealed the reason to the Corinthians. He told them:

> *"...for when I am weak, then am I strong."*
> II CORINTHIANS 12:10B NKJV

We could replace the word "for" with the word "because". The reason Paul could "take pleasure in infirmities, in reproaches, in necessities, in persecutions, in distresses," was "(because) when I am weak, then I am strong." It was "because" Paul had learned from Jesus how to be strong in His grace when he was weak in himself that he could "take pleasure" in his significant difficulties. We could render Paul's words this way:

> *"Because of the revelation I received from Jesus that I can be made strong in my inner man by the available provision of His*

strengthening grace, I now have a completely different perspective on my difficult circumstances. I can now take pleasure in my weaknesses, in mockings, in persecutions, in times when I don't have enough, and in any distress I experience for Christ's sake. I can approach all my difficulties with this new perspective because now I know that when I have depleted my own strength, I can receive the strengthening grace that is in Christ Jesus and be empowered by it!"

Paul could now rejoice in the circumstances because he had revelation of a New Covenant provision that he hadn't had before. Now he was "filled with the knowledge of (God's) will in all wisdom and spiritual understanding" concerning the available New Covenant provision of strengthening grace. He was now enlightened to the truth that in his time of weakness, he could be empowered by the strengthening grace of the Lord. He now knew that even when he was weak in his own strength, he could be empowered and made strong by the grace, the dunamis, that was in Christ Jesus!

The Revelation Paul received caused a Revolution in his thinking, in his perspective on tests and trials, and in his own experience! In fact, he told Timothy that at his first trial —no one stood with him, but that "the Lord stood with me and strengthened me."

Our purpose should be, "Lord, open my eyes like you opened Paul's eyes to the exceeding greatness of Your power toward me, a believer." (Ephesians 1:18-19)

Guy Duininck

Upon reading this post written by Guy Duininck, my spirit quickened, and I went to several translations to read II Corinthians 12. I had read it before over the years, but this time the words really got my attention. That night I was awakened by God for an extraordinary *wee-hour tutorial.* He placed me right in the middle of a role-play event.

A mob of people had gathered to pray for someone at the end of their rope. Life was too hard to go on. He had no strength to continue. The mob of believers standing around him was voicing all kinds of platitudes. "You can do it!" "You've got this!" "Never give up!" "Just trust God!" I was there observing all of this and listening to all the cliches, and the Holy Spirit rose up in me, and I began to pray with such power, unlike any other time I had ever prayed. The mob heard my voice loudly and fearlessly praying God's promises rising above their empty platitudes, and they began to nod and pray with the same faith and urgency. The man heard, believed and was strengthened by God's strength when he was sapped of his own and couldn't see a way out of his dilemma.

The role play showed me how to pray effectively and with power, even when I had often been one to offer platitudes as well. I finally understood that in my weakness, I *am* strong because what God has given me is His strength that renewed my strength. When we *surrender* to the reality of our own weakness and inability to make things better, we immediately become strong—strong in the Spirit. We appropriate God's power that He has linked up with His Spirit to our spirit. That's when everything turns around. This is the paradox of you can't, but you can.

During this tutorial, I remember telling God that this "when I am weak, then I am strong" line was crazy talk. It didn't make any sense to me. That's when He planted me right in the middle of the mob and gave me an opportunity to act it out. It all made sense at that point. I guess He showed me, didn't He? But our time together that night wasn't quite over. God led me to Romans:

> *But if God himself has taken up residence in your life, you can hardly be thinking more of yourself than of Him. Anyone, of course, who has not welcomed this invisible but clearly present God, the Spirit of Christ, won't know what we're talking about. But for you who welcome Him, in whom He dwells—even though you still experience all the limitations of sin—you yourself experience life on God's terms.*

> *It stands to reason, doesn't it, that if the alive-and-present God who raised Jesus from the dead moves into your life, He'll do the same thing in you that He did in Jesus, bringing you alive to Himself? When God lives and breathes in you (and He does, as surely as He did in Jesus), you are delivered from that dead life. With His Spirit living in you, your body will be as alive as Christ's!*
> ROMANS 8:9-11 MSG

In my weakness, I am made strong because of God's grace. He imbues me with His power to do *all* things. He also gives me the *power* and *influence* to encourage others to grab on to His strength and rise above their own physical/mental/emotional inadequacies to overcome their life's troubles. People will listen and respond to someone operating under the anointing and powerfully bringing the word of healing and deliverance to seemingly impossible situations. Pray like a crazy person and make the paradox "when I am weak, I am strong" a reality. I can't do it—but I can do it. How is that possible? Well—even in *my* weakness, I *can* do all things through Christ who strengthens me. We can then have the power to teach others that they have the same strength in their weaknesses to accomplish much too.

Here's a challenge for all readers: Read the entirety of II Corinthians 12 and Romans 8. It is a great encouragement and will build your faith exponentially.

TWO CENTS MORE

NOT A ROLL OF THE DICE

Your life does not get better by chance.
It gets better by change.
Stop wishing. Start doing.

A successful life depends on much more than a roll of the dice. It's purposeful action, wise planning, hard work, and the love and support of terrific friends. If you don't know where to start or what to do, reach out to get help from those who are skillfully trained. They can help devise a plan to make necessary changes. God has anointed people to come alongside those who struggle with life issues. Wishing and hoping—lamenting and moping—won't get it done.

Work hard so you can present yourself to God and receive His approval. Be a good worker, one who does not need to be ashamed and who correctly explains the word of truth.
II TIMOTHY 2:15 NLT

PERMISSION GRANTED

You're allowed to change your mind about the people and things
you want in your life. You're allowed to adjust your values and preferences
as you get older and wiser. You're allowed to evolve and be a different
person today than you were yesterday.
This is *your* life.

This happens all the time. We learn and change and grow over time. Hopefully, each chapter in life brings more maturity and understanding of our life's purpose. Becoming all we were created to be is the goal, and God presents new people and opportunities into the mix to help us get there. Personal responsibility calls for making wise choices that promote growth and well-developed maturity.

The righteous should choose his friends carefully,
for the way of the wicked leads them astray.
PROVERBS 12:26 NKJV

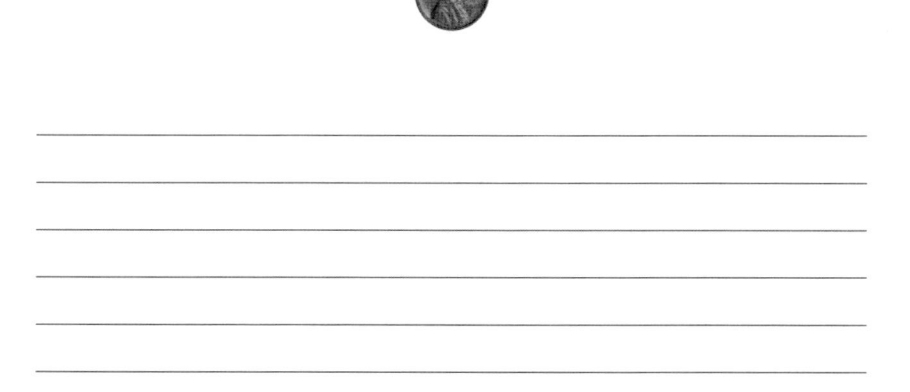

TWO CENTS MORE

ROCKING THE BOAT

If you avoid conflict to keep the peace, you start a war inside yourself.

There is a difference between being a peacekeeper and being a peacemaker. One wants to stop the boat from rocking, and one wants to let the boat rock until the cause is determined and solved.

Cheryl Richardson

A bigger conflict begins within and has internal ramifications. Always confront stuff, but be kind when you do. No healing or growth can happen when things are stuffed and buried. They have a way of developing a life of their own. Internal unrest is problematic on every level—spiritually, emotionally, and physically. Once that is handled, real peace will prevail.

Be anxious for nothing, but in everything by prayer and supplication, with thanksgiving, let your requests be made known to God; and the peace of God, which surpasses all understanding, will guard your hearts and minds through Christ Jesus.
PHILIPPIANS 4:6-7 NKJV

_____

_____

_____

_____

GET OFF THE FENCE

Instead of saying
"I'm human" as an excuse to walk in the flesh, try using
"I'm saved" as a reason to walk in the Spirit.

Get off the fence and stop making excuses. Using the "I'm Human" card as a license to do whatever you feel like doing without consequences is just plain stupid! You know better! And there *will* be consequences for that stupidity—you can count on it. Will you mess up? Of course, everybody does. Just stop making excuses for bad choices and grow up. *If* you are saved, you need to understand that grace is not cheap and should not be taken for granted. That grace cost Somebody His life just for you. Don't cheapen it by walking in the flesh. Come up higher and walk in the Spirit.

> *My counsel is this: Live freely, animated and motivated by God's Spirit. Then you won't feed the compulsions of selfishness. For there is a root of sinful self-interest in us that is at odds with a free spirit, just as the free spirit is incompatible with selfishness. These two ways of life are antithetical, so that you cannot live at times one way and at times another way according to how you feel on any given day. Why don't you choose to be led by the Spirit and so escape the erratic compulsions of a law-dominated existence?*
> GALATIANS 5:16-18 MSG

KEEP BLOOMING

Life might not be where you want it to be and
you might not have been what you could have been,
but it's not too late to become who you are.

Rather than focusing on what you wanted your life to be and lamenting that you fell short for whatever reasons, change your focus and get busy. No regrets. No wasting of precious time. Begin to do something moving forward. Stop looking in the rearview mirror. Grow fully into who you are right now—and who you are becoming. Life is fluid and ever-changing. Go with God's flow and become all you were created to be.

As you learn more and more how God works, you will learn how to do <u>your</u> work. We pray that you'll have the strength to stick it out over the long haul—not the grim strength of gritting your teeth but the glory-strength God gives. It is strength that endures the unendurable and spills over into joy, thanking the Father who makes us strong enough to take part in everything bright and beautiful that He has for us.
COLOSSIANS 1:10-12 MSG

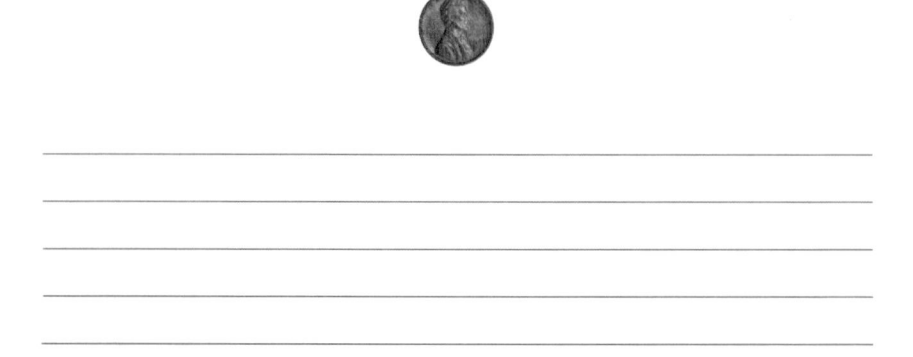

THE LADDER OF SUCCESS

*Our greatest fear should not be of failure,
but of succeeding at something that doesn't really matter.*

D. L. Moody

Failure is inevitable. Everybody fails at something sometime. Without occasional failures along the way, we would never pull ourselves up by our bootstraps and try again. According to Moody, the main thing is ensuring that we're putting our efforts into activities that matter. If we succeed at doing things well that have no purpose in the greater scheme of things, we are wasting our precious time. God has a little something to say about what matters. And then He will show us how to do it.

> *Don't waste your time on useless work; mere busywork, the barren pursuits of darkness. Expose these things for the sham they are. It's a scandal when people waste their lives on things they must do in the darkness where no one will see. Rip the cover off those frauds and see how attractive they look in the light of Christ.*
> EPHESIANS 5:11-13 MSG

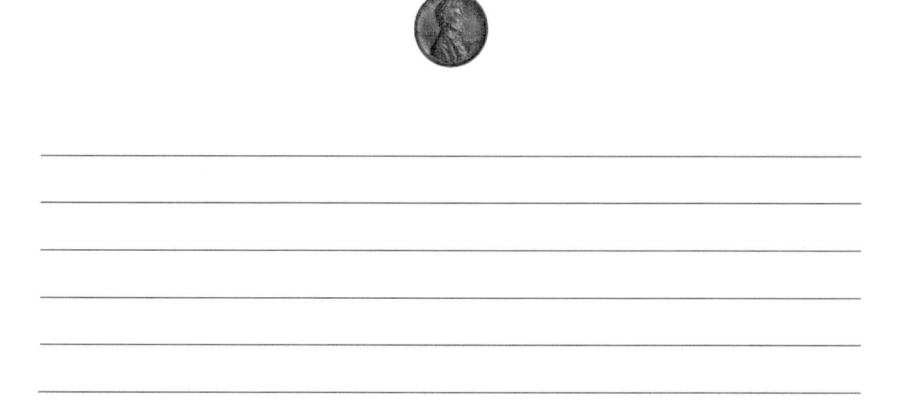

DON'T RESIST CHANGE

*One reason people resist change is that
they focus on what they have to give up,
instead of what they have to gain.*

TRUTH BOMB! So many people are settling on what they already see, know, and have experienced around them right now. It has become so familiar and normalized—"it is what it is." Some even admit it feels as though something is missing. And yet, to risk leaving the familiar behind and stepping into the unknown is scary. They have heard others tell them how good it can be, but they're not sure if they will ever deserve it or be able to have it that good. Maybe it's time for them to work on developing their trust muscle—and building their faith as well. The best is yet to come if they are willing to leave the toxic past behind, open the door, and walk into bigger and better possibilities. God's promises are real for whoever is willing to come, and His plan far surpasses anything we could ever imagine.

*Now we look inside, and what we see is that anyone united
with the Messiah gets a fresh start, is created new. The old life is
gone; a new life burgeons! Look at it! All this comes from the God
who settled the relationship between us and Him, and then
called us to settle our relationships with each other.*
II CORINTHIANS 5:17-19 MSG

YOUR ASSIGNMENT

When God has an assignment on your life,
you can't hang with everybody.

Pick your friends carefully and cultivate some safe people into your life. You may have to change your thinking and how you spend your time—especially with whom you spend it. If your associations with "friends" lead you away from your commitment to living a life that is pleasing to God, it's time to get a winning team of new friends—real ones. They come in all shapes and ages. They will enhance your life and encourage you to keep and complete the assignment that God has given you.

Escape quickly from the company of fools;
they're a waste of your time, a waste of your words.
PROVERBS 14:7 MSG

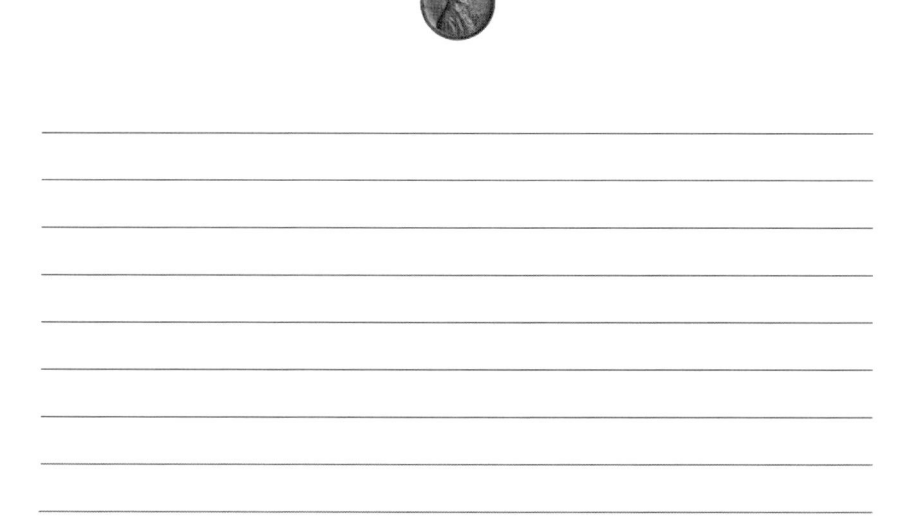

A DIFFERENT PERSPECTIVE

Sometimes what didn't work out for you
really worked out for you.

If this post relates to a relationship, it's possible that it may have been going on for quite some time. It's not unusual for relationships to hit snags and begin falling apart, especially if the people are not aware of the red flags or are unskilled in resolving the issues. It's also possible that the couple may have entered into a relationship that lacked God's blessing or wise and careful development of a safe connection. When it falls apart, there may be a time of mourning the loss—and legitimately so. The happily ever after went up in smoke. However, here's a thought: Maybe bemoaning the loss and the results that didn't materialize actually worked out for the best upon deeper investigation. Below is a good reminder:

> *So we are convinced that every detail of our lives is continually woven together for good, for we are his lovers who have been called to fulfill his designed purpose.*
> Romans 8:28 TPT

VICTIM MENTALITY

*Let me never fall into the vulgar mistake
of dreaming that I am persecuted
whenever I am contradicted.*

Ralph Waldo Emerson

This "persecution complex" smacks of a victim mentality. The ability and freedom to express differing viewpoints must be why offenses are running at an all-time high these days. However, there are some who are excessively intolerant of others and look at things in an entirely different way. That kind of resistance tends to feel pretty much like persecution. People don't like to be questioned or challenged by those who oppose their viewpoint but are simply seeking clarification. Having a different perspective might cause others to consider a different way of seeing things. It might even result in changing their mind entirely. Besides, wouldn't it be refreshing to be open to considering that *your* truth might not be *the* truth? Just because someone disagrees with you doesn't necessarily mean they're out to get you. Some are; most aren't. Chill for a minute! Talk about it like a mature adult. Everybody has a right to think and feel the way they do—so do you. Learn how to agree to disagree with others without starting World War III.

We are currently living in a confrontational culture. People are going toe-to-toe on nearly every issue in the political, spiritual, and emotional arenas. Ways of interpreting laws, the Constitution, and the Bible have caused much confusion and outright misinterpretations of what has been clearly noted and written down. Anyone courageous enough to freely express their beliefs—a guaranteed right—may very well come under a great deal of pushback, shaming, or worse. Make no mistake; this is persecution, and it's more than a feeling. As a result of these oppositional responses, it's perfectly understandable why many are simply choosing to hold their peace. Let's focus our energy on communication that will reap rewards as indicated in the Proverb below.

> *If you reason with an arrogant cynic, you'll get slapped in the face;*
> *confront bad behavior and get a kick in the shins. So don't waste*
> *your time on a scoffer; all you'll get for your pains is abuse.*
> *But if you correct those who care about life,*
> *that's different—they'll love you for it!*
> PROVERBS 9:7-8 MSG

DANGEROUS ANGER

*Anger is an acid that can do more harm to
the vessel in which it is stored than to
anything on which it is poured.*

Mark Twain

Anything allowed to sit in one place for any length of time is bound to get stagnant, incredibly toxic, and stink to high heaven. Pouring out venomous anger on others may take a toll on them, but they can wash it off and move on. Whatever is still reserved in the angry person's tank will continue to kill its keeper. Flush it out and fill the tank with life-giving ingredients.

*He who is slow to anger is better than the mighty,
and he who rules his spirit than he who takes a city.*
PROVERBS 16:32 NKJV

THE LOVE CONTAINER

The only meaningful thing we can offer one
another is love. Not advice, not questions about
our choices, not suggestions for the future, just love.

Glennon Doyle Melton

How do I strongly disagree with this post without sounding like I'm minimizing the power of love? Perhaps pointing out a different perspective will help. Love is smack dab in the middle of advice, questions, and suggestions. How can I say that? The Bible is loaded with verses that address all of this, and love is at the heart of it all. Proverbs, all by itself, is the book within The Book that teaches us everything we need to know about life. Love is the cornerstone, but it includes counsel, correction, and encouragement—all of which are very meaningful elements. Combine all of these, and we wind up with much more than "just love."

A refusal to correct is a refusal to love;
love your children by disciplining them.
PROVERBS 13:24 MSG

A MILLION REASONS

If you want to, you could find a million reasons
to hate life and be angry at the world
- or -
If you want to, you could find a million reasons
to love life and be happy.
Choose wisely.

What to do, what to do. Deuteronomy 30:19-20a in The Message says: *"I call heaven and earth to witness against you today. I place before you Life and Death, Blessing and Curse. Choose life so that you and your children will live. And love God, your God, listening obediently to Him, firmly embracing Him. Oh yes, He is life itself, a long life—"*

The choice is a slam dunk for me! The choice is mine, and I choose a million reasons to love life and be happy. I will fight through the negative events, and I *will* listen to my God and obediently embrace Him.

The commandments of the Lord are right, bringing joy to the heart.
The commandments of the Lord are clear, giving insight for living.
PSALM 19:8 NLT

_____
_____
_____
_____
_____

THIS IS LOVE

Love is not all you need.
You need mutual respect.
You need support.
You need trust.
You need boundaries.
You need people to be there when it matters.
You need space to grow and acceptance when you do.
You need people to show their love in a way you can understand.

Nedra Tawwah

Much can be said about the things we value and look to include in our lives. All the aspects mentioned in this post are what I'm looking for when welcoming friends into my circle. Trust, encouragement, support, and more are the attributes that matter. But, upon looking at the list, I realize that everything following the first line of this post is a definition of love. Real love is a package deal—the whole enchilada.

I have experienced times when challenges have appeared to be "above my pay grade." God was faithful and brought wonderful friends into my life when I needed them most. Recently I have been thinking about the people who have shown up for me during the tough times. I reminisce over these memories—seeing faces and the nuances of each chapter—some taking place even decades ago. You all helped me when I lacked the know-how and strength to do what was needed at the time. You walked by my side and encouraged me to keep on going and growing. So that's what I did. The love shown to me over the years has been priceless. If those of you reading this have been part of my life story, please accept my thanks and appreciation for the love you extended. We all get by with a little help—and love—from our friends.

Love suffers long and is kind; love does not envy; love does not parade itself, is not puffed up; does not behave rudely, does not seek its own, is not provoked, thinks no evil; does not rejoice in iniquity, but rejoices in the truth; bears all things, endures all things. Love never fails.
I Corinthians 13:4-8a nkjv

TWO CENTS MORE

WHO DOESN'T WANT IT?

Everybody wants loyalty, consistency, and somebody who won't quit. But everybody forgets that to get that person, you have to be that person.

I like to think that I am that kind of person! However, when the other person bails—as it is their right to do—I can and will let that person go. Not my choice, but theirs. I am not a boundary buster and will not force the issue.

Reciprocal action completes the healthy cycle. People unwilling to do their part short-circuit this process, and the seeds of entitlement begin to grow from the inside. The crop produced includes anger, hurt, disappointment, resentment, and much more. Learn how to become a safe person who attracts other safe people who understand give and take and welcome them into your healthy garden of treasured friends.

*You stick by people who stick with you,
you're straight with people who're straight with you.*
II SAMUEL 22:26 MSG

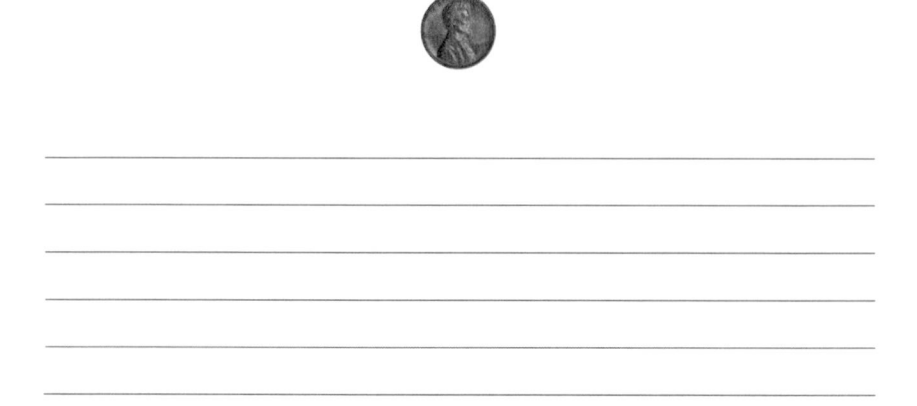

LIFE LESSONS

Seven things you learned in life:

1. Some people will never change.
2. You will be extremely grateful that some things didn't work out the way you once wanted them to.
3. You are growing—you are not the same person you were a year ago.
4. It is useless to stress change. Move on. Let go. Get over it.
5. A strong friendship doesn't need daily conversations. As long as the relationship lives in your heart, true friends will never part.
6. You have overcome challenges before. You have picked yourself up, dusted yourself off, and started again.
7. There is always, always, always something to be grateful for.

These seven things that we have learned in life seem so obvious when seeing them grouped in a neat little list. It's not likely that we would think about these all at once, though. I'd be willing to bet that those who have some years under their belt have probably even said a few of these—maybe all of them—at one time or another. It doesn't really matter. The point is that obvious lessons have been picked up along the way, and come to our remembrance when we need them.

Of the lessons listed above, the third stands out to me as it resonates most strongly within my spirit. Whether we are conscious of it or not, we are always growing. Looking back on my life, it is clear there are significant moments as well as inconsequential ones. But regardless of the scale of the moment, all these contribute to definite demarcation points affecting the trajectory of my life. Through it all, God has been there to direct my path, encouraging me to make needed changes. And though I haven't done everything right, God has been gracious and taught me what I needed to know to get back on track.

Am I different from how I was a year ago? That's hard for me to say, but I'll bet my friends would be able to better answer that question as I can barely remember what I had for yesterday's breakfast. Here's my hope and prayer—that I'm continually growing into the person God created me to be. I know God will help us get there—we are all His works in progress.

You will show me the path of life; in your presence is fullness of joy; at Your right hand are pleasures forevermore.
PSALM 16:11 NKJV

CHANGE YOUR FOCUS

Life can be difficult if all you see is everything that's wrong.
Start focusing on what's right, what's good, what's constructive.
No matter what you're facing, if you choose a positive mindset, you'll
emerge the winner. So if you want to feel better, you've got to think better.

Mufti Menk

Change your mind/thinking; change your life. The Bible has something to say about what Menk wrote, and I call this encouragement the "whatsoever" verse:

*Finally, brethren,
whatsoever things are true,
whatsoever things are honest,
whatsoever things are just,
whatsoever things are pure,
whatsoever things are lovely,
whatsoever things are of good report,
if there be any virtue and if there be any praise,
think on these things.*
PHILIPPIANS 4:8 KJV

Put aside negative, stinking thinking and focus on what God has to say about confronting the difficulties that you face in life from time to time.

_____
_____
_____

TWO CENTS MORE

START MOVING

Don't ask God to direct your steps
if you're not willing to move your feet.

How many times have we asked God to show us the way to go, what to do in any given situation, and then sat back, waiting for Him to do it? Often we already know, but we keep asking—longing for a different answer. Let's face it, when we enter into a relationship with the Lord, it's a partnership of reciprocity—a two-way street. He does His part; we must do ours.

> Your word is a lamp to my feet and a light
> to my path. I have sworn [an oath] and have confirmed
> it, that I will keep Your righteous ordinances [hearing,
> receiving, loving, and obeying them].
> PSALM 119:105-106 AMP

CHARACTER SIGNALS

When someone disrespects you,
beware the impulse to win their respect.
For disrespect is not a valuation of your worth,
but a signal of their character.

Brendon Burchard

This is true *if* you have done nothing to earn their disrespect. Why would you even want to earn or win their respect anyway? However, if you have character flaws that create difficulty for others to respect or trust you, it's time to get into self-reflection mode. Identify what areas need greater levels of principled maturity and get to it. Everybody has character signals that float to the surface when you actively look. Watch for them cropping up in your life and address them immediately, so your words will be seen as consistent and worthy of trust.

*Make a careful exploration of who you are
and the work you have been given, and then sink yourself into
that. Don't be impressed with yourself. Don't compare yourself with
others. Each of you must take responsibility for doing the
creative best you can with your own life.*
GALATIANS 6:4-5 MSG

SPOT THE DIFFERENCE

*The happiest people I know are evaluating
and improving themselves.
The unhappy people are usually evaluating
and judging others.*

Self-evaluation can be painful. A good, hard look in the mirror can reveal some not-so-pretty features. For some, it's easier to turn away and focus on the flaws of others. But all this does is prolong the inevitable need to apply correction in yourself. At this point, we must make changes. Know that no matter the depth of need, new levels of maturity are always possible with God's help. Figuring out how to apply God's instruction can bring new levels of satisfaction and confidence. The ultimate outcome is happiness which you recognize is possible only through a partnership with the Creator.

*Investigate my life, O God, and find out everything about me;
cross-examine and test me, get a clear picture of what I'm about;
see for yourself whether I've done anything wrong—
then guide me on the road to eternal life.*
PSALM 139:23-24 MSG

NEGATIVITY SUCKS

*While you cannot control someone's negative behavior,
you can control how long you participate in it.*

The longer I live, it becomes abundantly clear that life here is short—and getting shorter. When I recall events taking place earlier in my life, they feel as though they just happened—while others feel as though eons have passed. Closing in on eight decades of escapades and adventures of living the good life, the last thing I want to add to the mix is even a minuscule amount of negativity. What a waste of precious time! So pardon me if I choose to abstain and walk away from your negative behavior. I want to continue living in such a way that puts a smile on God's face and finish my race on a positive note.

*Don't be naïve. There are difficult times ahead.
As the end approaches, people are going to be self-absorbed, money-hungry, self-promoting, stuck-up, profane, contemptuous of parents, crude, treacherous, ruthless, bloated windbags, addicted to lust, and allergic to God. They'll make a show of religion, but behind the scenes they're animals. Stay clear of these people.*
II TIMOTHY 3:1-5 MSG

TAKE A WALK

Walk away from people who put you down.
Walk away from fights that will never be resolved.
Walk away from trying to please people who will never see your worth.
The more you walk away from things that poison
your soul, the healthier you will be.

Paulo Coelho

Walking *away* from toxic, negative, and dysfunctional people provides the time and opportunity to walk *toward* people who appreciate you and are nutritious for your soul. Peaceful encouragement from people who value who you are will bring greater fulfillment and enjoyment into your life.

Make no friendships with a man given to anger;
and with a wrathful man do not associate.
PROVERBS 22:24 AMP

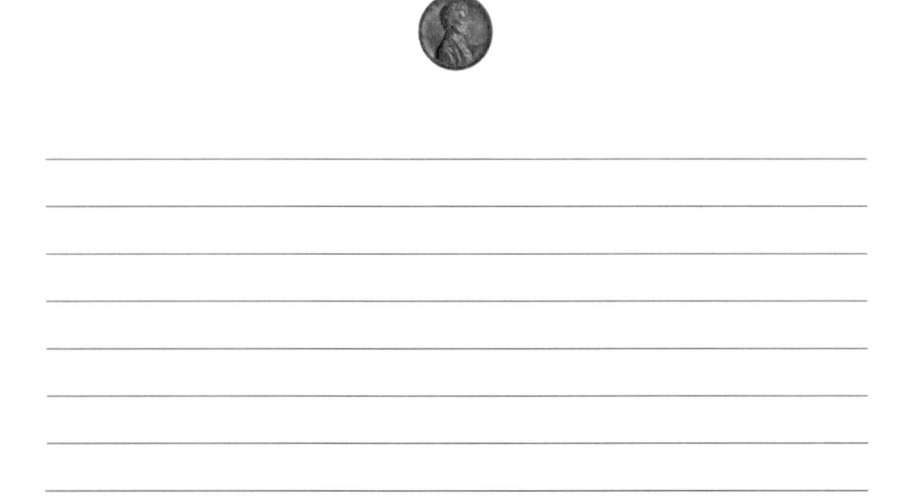

TRAUMA RESPONSES

Keeping quiet about your feelings in order to
keep the peace is a trauma response.

This might look like hyper-compliance because you have a history of being shut down when you've tried to speak up. Then you spend so much time trying to hold it in. So you start over-explaining and/or over-sharing to avoid rejection. And when that doesn't work, you might find yourself exploding due to the built-up resentment, anger, and frustration.

The lesson here?
When you keep quiet in order to keep the peace,
you start a war within yourself.

LovingMeAfterWe.com

This explains why so many relationships/friendships feel so one-sided. Past traumatic events result in a lack of vulnerability and openness with others. An emotional and psychological wall of protection is built and is largely impenetrable. Reciprocity is not possible until healing occurs, and sometimes the thought of the arduous work involved, along with the painful memories of the trauma, is too much to bear. Consequently, the relationship/friendship never quite reaches the desired goal of total commitment. Although terrible things may have occurred earlier in your life, there is hope for better days ahead. God provides an antidote for past traumas and is closer than you may realize. He is always with you and can heal your heart.

The Lord is close to the brokenhearted;
He rescues those whose spirits are crushed.
PSALM 34:18 NLT

TWO CENTS MORE

Don't be afraid, I've redeemed you. I've called your name.
You're mine. When you're in over your head, I'll be there with you.
When you're in rough waters, you will not go down.
When you're between a rock and a hard place,
it won't be a dead end.
Isaiah 43:1b-2 msg

TIME LIMITATIONS

One thing we know for sure is that we only have a limited number of days here on earth. So each day we can either find something to complain about *or* something to be grateful for. It's really up to us.

Doe Zantamata

If you think that your life sucks and that you can't come up with anything to be grateful for, maybe it's time to adjust your thinking and choose to live your life differently. Become thankful for everything, from the very big to the infinitely small. Then practice giving thanks every day. Look around and appreciate all the way down to the little things. Do this, and your life will change. If you decide to wallow in a "poor me puddle," take some time to really splash around in it to honestly contemplate just how that has been working for you. A much better plan is to take our eyes off the puddle and focus directly on God's promises because grateful hope becomes the more "promising" focal point when you do.

Thank [God] in everything
[no matter what the circumstances may be, be thankful and
give thanks], for this is the will of God for you [who are] in Christ
Jesus [the Revealer and Mediator of that will].
I Thessalonians 5:18 AMP

_____
_____
_____
_____

PUSH "PAUSE"

Experience doesn't make you wiser.
Evaluated experience makes you wiser.

Dr. John Townsend

It takes a thought to create an experience. How often have you just moved on from something without giving it another thought? It's time for a "Selah" moment. When you say, "This _____ always happens to me," you can count on it happening again. Your words are powerful and very often accomplish what you say. Words are the engine that brings movement and action, but thoughts are what spark the engine and start it chugging. When something begins going haywire, push "pause." Think about what's occurring and how you can make the necessary adjustments to improve the outcome. By consistently activating that "pause" to reflect and evaluate, greater wisdom will come.

*There's an opportune time to do things,
a right time for everything on the earth*
ECCLESIASTES 3:1 MSG

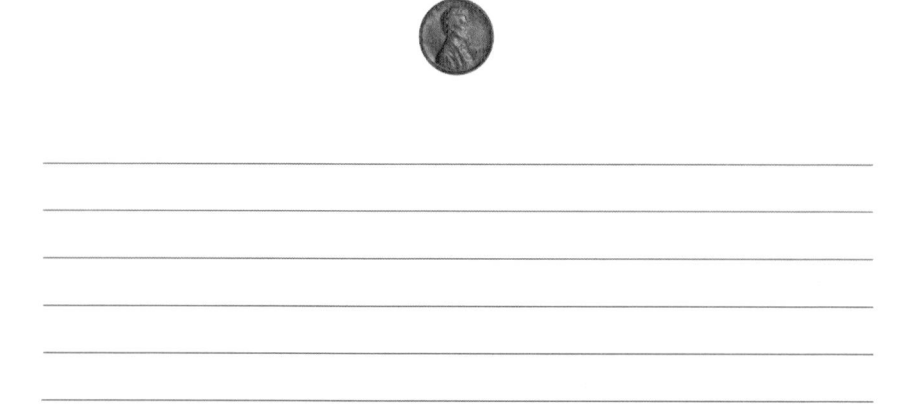

FLAT SQUIRRELS

Be decisive.
Right or wrong, make a decision.
The road of life is paved with flat squirrels
who could not make a decision.

The "maybes" don't work in life, especially for our big decisions. Maybe I will—maybe I won't. Maybe I can—maybe I can't. Do not be a "mugwump" with your "mug" on one side of the fence and your "wump" on the other. You cannot be a fence straddler forever. If you die on that fence of indecision, you might very well wind up a bit crotchety.

If you don't know what you're doing, pray to the Father.
He loves to help. You'll get His help, and won't be condescended
to when you ask for it. Ask boldly, believingly, without a second
thought. People who "worry their prayers" are like wind-whipped
waves. Don't think you're going to get anything from the Master
that way, adrift at sea, keeping all your options open.
JAMES 1:5-8 MSG

I CAN'T HEAR YOU

*It's hard to hear God's voice
when you've already decided
what you want Him to say.*

Sometimes we enter into conversations with others and have already written the script for what we want them to say in response to our agenda. It's so maddening when they go off this script and come out of left field with thoughts and opinions contrary to what we expect.

We do the same thing with God. We have already figured out the entire verbal exchange without even listening to Him. We tell Him what we want or think, and expect Him to say, "OK—you're right!" When He is able to break through our "sound barrier" and tell us what we need, it often goes in a totally different direction than what we wanted. Try this instead; listen to Him carefully and be quiet. Two ears; one mouth. Pay attention and accept what God has to say—it is always more beneficial to us than following the advice we *want* Him to say. The question really is— do you trust Him or not?

> *The plans and reflections of the heart belong to man
> but the [wise] answer of the tongue is from the Lord. All the
> ways of a man are clean and innocent in his own eyes [and he
> may see nothing wrong with his actions], but the Lord weighs and
> examines the motives and intents [of the heart and knows the
> truth]. Commit your works to the Lord [submit and trust
> them to Him], and your plans will succeed [if you
> respond to His will and guidance].*
> PROVERBS 16:1-3 AMP

*He who pays attention to the word [of God] will find good,
and blessed (happy, prosperous, to be admired) is he
who trusts [confidently] in the Lord.*
PROVERBS 16:20 AMP

WHEN ENOUGH IS ENOUGH

Just be smart enough to know when "enough is enough."
You can't complain about somebody crossing the line if you fail to set the boundaries. You can't complain about somebody wasting your time when you didn't require them to earn it. Sometimes you just have to let go. Not everything is meant to be a "forever" kind of thing. You have to be honest with yourself even if it hurts. You can't give people too many chances to make the same "mistakes."
Learn from it.
Grow from it.
Be done with it.

Rob Hill, Sr.

My daughter, Mara, says, "Forget about *enough is enough*. How about *enough is too much?*" She nailed it and is so right. When you cross the final line, it's over—done—*finis*. But it will never be over until you say, "No more." Take control and set your boundaries.

I have always felt it a calling to help others struggling to develop safe relationships and apply healthy boundaries. That's why I chose to lead groups addressing how to grow and mature in these areas. And though I've led many group topics over the years, I call my favorites the Trilogy: *Safe People* and *Boundaries* by Cloud and Townsend and *Changes That Heal* by Cloud. They all focus on inner healing from traumatic life events and handling the bumps of life in general.

So many people have difficulties navigating life with success, and the understanding and setting of boundaries is a key area of real impact. Each of the books in The Trilogy addresses how to have safe and life-affirming relationships using the central concepts from *Boundaries*. All three books are invaluable resources offering readers a chance to consider new perspectives and gain insights into how to clearly and confidently say, "enough is too much."

> *But now I write to you not to associate with anyone who bears the name of [Christian] brother if he is known to be guilty of immorality or greed, or is an idolater [whose soul is devoted to any object that usurps the place of God], or is a person with a foul tongue [railing, abusing, reviling, slandering], or is a drunkard or a swindler or a robber. [No] you must not so much as eat with such a person.*
> HEBREWS 5:11 AMP

REBUILD

In life, you will
fall out with people that you never thought you would,
get betrayed by people you trusted with all of your heart,
and get used by people you would do anything for.

That's life—stuff happens! Focusing on the betrayal, being used, and falling out with friends leads to bitterness, anger, and hurt feelings. So what are you going to do about it? How about focusing on the opportunity to learn from the disappointment of collapsed relationships and build new ones? Just be sure to build upon a rock-solid, firm foundation this time around.

[Let your] love be sincere (a real thing);
hate what is evil [loathe all ungodliness, turn in horror
from wickedness], but hold fast to that which is good. Love one
another with brotherly affection [as members of one family],
giving precedence and showing honor to one another.
ROMANS 12:9-10 AMP

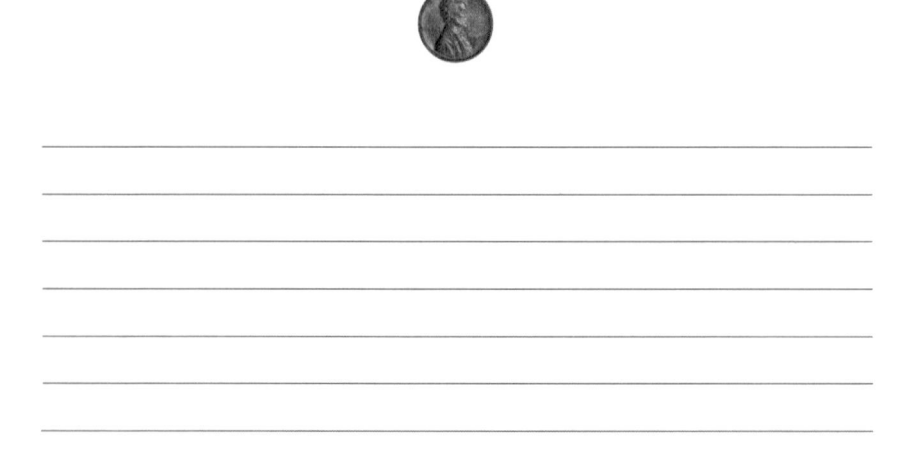

_____
_____
_____
_____
_____

"SHOULD" HAPPENS

The one word that projects shame and takes away freedom:
SHOULD
Don't "should" on people. It's not nice.

Rowgo

Many years ago, Jim Montagnes led a training on Choice Theory, based on studies that were researched by William Glasser. Also referred to as Reality Theory, I learned many concepts during this training, but the one concept that stuck with me was how the word "should" has been used on people. Not only is "shoulding" on others harmful to them, but "shoulding" on ourselves is to be equally avoided.

As time goes on and I continue to spend time with friends and family, I am more and more aware of the importance of my word choices and how I communicate my ideas and opinions with them. It's hard to take words back once they're spoken. Clarification is often needed to improve understanding, but remember that using the simple word "should" must be used judiciously when discussing intentions. This word can be perceived as judgmental and takes away a level of freedom from the recipient.

And when it comes to my self-talk, I've learned a better way to deal with my mistakes. Rather than verbally beating up on myself, I choose to say: "I realize I didn't make the best choice or do the right thing, so next time I'm faced with a similar challenge, I will make a different choice that I can feel better about." It sounds a bit cheesy, but it beats kicking myself and getting "should" all over me. Making a conscious choice to do better next time focuses on reaching solutions rather than casting blame.

TWO CENTS MORE

The steps of a [good] man are directed and established by the Lord when He delights in his way [and He busies Himself with his every step]. Though he falls, he shall not be utterly cast down, for the Lord grasps his hand in support and upholds him.
PSALM 37:23-24 AMP

CHOICE VERSUS PROCESS

> Forgiveness is not the same as healing. Sometimes people think, I don't need to talk about this event or this relationship, because I forgave that person. This is usually not true. It's more because they don't want to feel the depth of their hurt, sadness, and anger about the situation. A better perspective is that forgiveness is a choice and healing is a process. Begin the process of healing by forgiving.
>
> Dr. John Townsend

Forgiveness gets the ball rolling, but if there is ever a hope or desire for a restored relationship, talking about the situation that created the rift is required. "Sorry" and a quick "I forgive you" doesn't solve anything. Humility, vulnerability, and honesty will go a long way in healing the hurt and sadness, as well as alleviating the anger. If forgiveness is asked for and received, that's just the beginning. Talking about it will bring clarity to what happened and provides an opportunity to accept responsibility for the roles played in the event. Do this and heartfelt words of a commitment can be voiced to guard against the same thing happening again.

When people don't want to talk further about offenses, they are saying they're "over it" and want to move on. The error in this kind of thinking is that nothing is truly dealt with enough to bring a genuine resolution. It turns out to be a cowardly and immature way to deal with things. How can that be if an apology and forgiveness have taken place? Well—doing the obligatory short version leaves out the critical thinking part of the equation along with the opportunity to do some real problem solving as restoration of a broken relationship heals. Forgive? Yes, most assuredly—but that's just the beginning. Don't stop there. Now the healing part must begin. It's time to talk about it.

TWO CENTS MORE

Confess your sins to each other and pray for each other so that you may be healed. The earnest prayer of a righteous person has great power and produces wonderful results.
JAMES 5:16 NLT

INTENTIONALITY

A dream written down with a date becomes a goal.
A goal broken down into steps becomes a plan.
A plan backed by action makes your dreams come true.

This is how a dream comes to fruition. It's more than hoping and wishing. When I've heard people talk about their dreams, I ask, "How badly do you want it?" Sometimes they discount their longing and call it a pipedream, and it would never happen for them. Really? The Bible contains verses encouraging following dreams and asking God to help bring them to pass. However, some personal responsibility is required as well. God will not only make a way; He will show us how to get there. When He gives us marching orders, it is on us to do it. The Bible says to write down our plan. Once that is done, the rest requires our blood, sweat, and tears to bring it to fruition. Goals get met with a well-developed plan, great intentionality, and a lot of hard work, but that's also how great dreams come true.

Roll your works upon the Lord [commit and trust them wholly to Him; He will cause your thoughts, to become agreeable to His will, and] so shall your plans be established and succeed.
PROVERBS 16:3 AMP

FAILURE

Failure is nothing more than a chance to revise your strategy.

In the words of William Edward Hickson, "If a lesson you should heed, try, try again. If at first you don't succeed, try, try again." Persistence pays off in the end. If something is important and worth doing, keep at it. Consider that fresh and new perspectives will offer new strategies never considered before. That is where success gets its start.

> *But He said to me, My grace (My favor and loving-kindness and mercy) is enough for you [sufficient against any danger and enables you to bear the trouble manfully]: for My strength and power are made perfect (fulfilled and completed) and show themselves most effective in [your] weakness. Therefore, I will all the more gladly glory in my weaknesses and infirmities, that the strength and power of Christ (the Messiah) may rest (yes, may pitch a tent over and dwell) upon me! So for the sake of Christ, I am well pleased and take pleasure in infirmities, insults, hardships, persecutions, perplexities and distresses; for when I am weak [in human strength], then am I [truly] strong (able, powerful in divine strength).*
> II CORINTHIANS 12:9-10 AMP

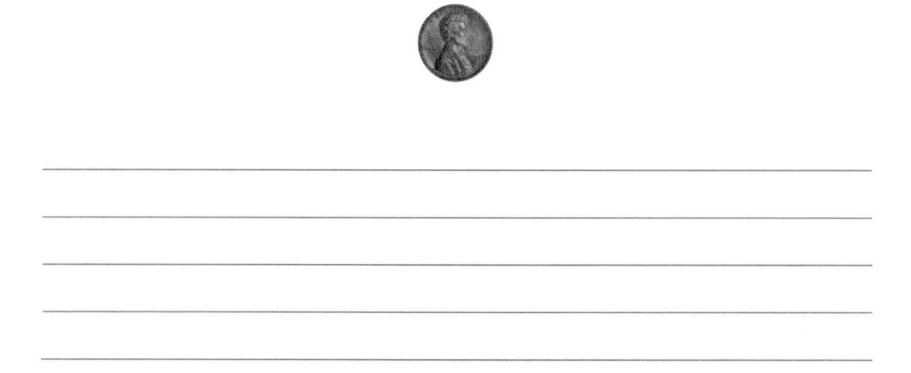

FLOOD EFFECTS

Every flood of trouble remakes the landscape of your soul—
making you bitter or better.

Ann Voskamp

What Ann is implying is that a choice must be made when problems arise. And we can absolutely count on having difficult situations in our lifetime. Some are predictable, some not so much. Often the situations that are so problematic are of our own making. We could have and should have known better, but we didn't do better. And, of course, issues outside our control blindside us at the worst times. Either way, we must choose how we react. There is no win or sense of satisfaction from a bitter, angry response. It just increases the deluge of negativity. The biggest win is when we look at whatever the "flood of trouble" represents and choose to learn from it and be in a better heartspace once it dissipates. "Better" really *is* better—it is well with my soul.

See to it that no one falls short of the grace of God and that no bitter root grows up to cause trouble and defile many.
HEBREWS 12:15 NIV

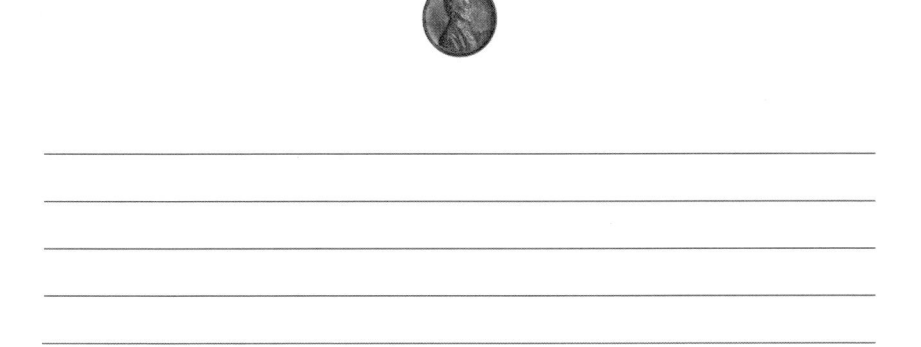

NOT A SPECTATOR SPORT

*The happiest people I know are
evaluating and improving themselves.
The unhappy people are usually
evaluating and judging others.*

There's always room for improvement, so there's always something to do. Each of us is a work in progress, but the operative word "work" implies effort. Some people would prefer to skip the hard work and focus on what's happening with others. They would much rather sit on the bench, be sideline coaches, and engage in spectator sports than get off the bench and get into the game. Working hard to evaluate and improve brings a sense of accomplishment. Who isn't happy with a win like that? On the other hand, there are no personal improvements or scores made while sitting on the sidelines critiquing the people who are actually participating and winning the game.

*Make a careful exploration of who you are and the
work you have been given, and then sink yourself into that.
Don't be impressed with yourself. Don't compare yourself with
others. Each of you must take responsibility for doing the
creative best you can with your own life.*
GALATIANS 6:4-5 MSG

GRIEF OVER GOOD DECISIONS

It's okay to be sad after making the right decision.

So many people have grieved the loss of a relationship that they hoped was their chance at living "happily ever after," but it turned out not to be. Having the courage to end a toxic relationship isn't easy, and grief over what could have been if things had been different is to be expected. It will take time, but Psalm 30:5b says: *"Weeping may last through the night, but joy comes with the morning."*

He heals the brokenhearted and binds up their wounds
[curing their pains and their sorrows].
Psalm 147:3 AMP

WASTELAND DWELLERS

If you feel like you've already wasted
a lot of your life, don't waste the rest of it
feeling bad about the part that you already wasted.
It is *never* too late to begin again.

Joyce Meyer

Get over the "shoulda, coulda, woulda" mentality, the pity parties, and the Blame Game—and do what my dad, the plumber, used to say: "It's time to pee or get off the pot." In other words, it's never too late to begin again—Michael Finnegan. Taking excessive time whining about days gone by wastes more time and avoids properly using the time we have left. This is a cycle that must break. Begin to live a life full of purpose and without regrets.

"Forget about what's happened; don't keep going over old history. Be alert, be present. I'm about to do something brand new. It's bursting out! Don't you see it? There it is! I'm making a road through the desert, rivers in the badlands."
ISAIAH 43:18-19 MSG

ANXIETY SUCKS

Anxiety makes you sit there and overthink every single thing. At times it makes you think people in your life are leaving you. You begin to feel abandoned and not worth anything because the most important person/people in your life don't want you. So you push away for fear of being hurt. You push them away so they can't discard you or leave you. When, in reality, nobody was ever leaving. Anxiety this bad makes you leave the ones you love. It sucks.

Right off the bat, something must be cleared up. Anxiety cannot *make you* do anything *unless* you let it. When the thoughts of all the things mentioned in this post become overwhelming, it's time to push "Pause" and take your control back. It's time to change up your thinking and renew your mind. Rather than pushing back and away from people that you *imagine* are going to leave or discard you, begin to lean into a new way of thinking. It will transform your life!

Anxiety is a fertile breeding ground for growing fear. The more seeds of anxiety are sown, the bigger the crop of fear will be. It's time to sow a whole bunch of faith seeds and harvest a huge crop of the kind of faith that will eliminate the fear that brings isolation. Anxiety, fear, and isolation are not God's plan for you.

> *Don't worry about anything; instead, pray about everything. Tell God what you need, and thank him for all he has done. Then you will experience God's peace, which exceeds anything we can understand, His peace will guard your hearts and minds as you live in Christ Jesus.*
> PHILIPPIANS 4:6-7 NLT

TWO CENTS MORE

Don't copy the behavior and customs of this world, but let God transform you into a new person by changing the way you think. Then you will learn to know God's will for you, which is good and pleasing and perfect.
ROMANS 12:2 NLT

I DECIDED TODAY WAS THE DAY

> I just woke up one day and decided I didn't want to feel
> like this anymore—or ever again.
> So I changed.
> I had lots of excuses for not being able to change,
> but at the end of the day, they were excuses.
> Being able to change starts with:
> Your decision to change.
>
> Steven Aitchison

A decision to change requires a thought and a resulting action. Thinking it and even saying it will not produce change. However, willingness to work on it to bring the desired change to pass will produce a quality life full of contentment and accomplishment. Changed thinking and an adjusted perspective will change a person's life trajectory.

Show me how you work, God; school me in your ways.
PSALM 25:3 MSG

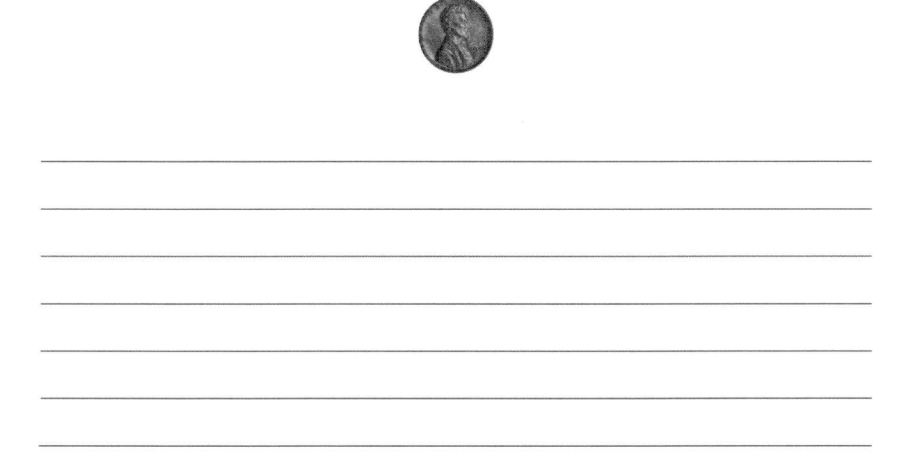

STUFF

The truth is that all the "STUFF" here on earth we work so hard to buy and accumulate does not mean a thing. At the end of the day— people will be cleaning out our "STUFF," going through our "STUFF," figuring out what to do with all our "STUFF"—this "STUFF" we've accumulated in our life. The only thing of *value* that remains are the *memories* and what we deposit into others. May we learn to spend less time accumulating "STUFF" and spend way more time making *memories*.

Over the past few years, I have been diligent about organizing my stuff and thinning out my accumulation of most of it. I have two adult kids who lead busy lives and have many responsibilities. The last thing I want to dump on them when I relocate to heaven is a boatload of stuff. On the other hand, much of my time is spent making wonderful memories with friends and family. In fact, as a people person, I find that taking time to meet up with people to make those memories is eating into the time I need to sort through my stuff. Balance is the key. I will continue to work hard on doing both.

Stockpile treasure in heaven, where it's safe from moth and rust and burglars. It's obvious, isn't it? The place where your treasure is, is the place you will most want to be, and end up being.
MATTHEW 6:20-21 MSG

STEP BY STEP

*God will not give you the next step
until you take the first one.*

How do we get from here to there? One step at a time. When we have a goal in mind, and we want to arrive at our desired destination, in all likelihood, we will have a plan on how to get there. Circumventing a well-thought-out plan and proceeding haphazardly is an ill-advised way to make any real progress.

God always has a brilliant plan and destination for all of us, but we sometimes get impatient and want everything to happen *right now!* Not so fast, Bucko! God wants us to get started one step at a time. When we do that, each successive step will be a no-brainer—but remember that trust and obedience are the key.

*The Lord directs the steps of the godly.
He delights in every detail of their lives.
Though they stumble, they will never fall,
for the Lord holds them by the hand.*
PSALM 37:23-24 NLT

PUZZLE PIECES

To be able to grow in spiritual understanding and to be able to put all the "pieces of the puzzle" in their right places, you must be able to hold more than one Truth at a time. When you cannot do that, then you will "force" Scripture interpretation and put Scriptures in places where they don't belong.

Guy Duininck

Yet another gold nugget from Guy Duininck! As Christians, we must learn to sense God's heart through prayer and confirm this through the instructions He's already provided. This means reading the Bible without cherry-picking passages to suit our purposes. Scripture balances and justifies Scripture, so read the *whole* thing and pray for greater understanding. As you do this, new opportunities to apply the Word of God will arise, requiring you to rely on your heavenly Father for encouragement and even more excellent guidance. It is not easy, but He has everything you need to live out His Word.

If any of you is deficient in wisdom, let him ask of the giving God [Who gives] to everyone liberally and ungrudgingly, without reproaching or faultfinding, and it will be given him.
JAMES 1:5 AMP

MORE THAN SCRATCHING THE ITCH

> Beneath every behavior there is a feeling.
> And beneath each feeling there is a need.
> And when we meet that need
> rather than focus on the behavior,
> we begin to deal with the cause,
> not the symptom.
>
> Ashleigh Warner

Bingo! Getting all the way down to the root is required. Scratching the itch on the surface doesn't address the problem or bring necessary healing and change. It takes time and very specialized attention to get to the root of the problem. Often it will take some outside help to gain insight and develop a treatment plan. There is hope for real and lasting healing and growth when that happens. There is also the possibility that resistance to doing the hard work will result in not addressing the symptom, and then nothing changes. It takes a real commitment to go deep enough to address the cause that sets everything into motion.

> *Then Jesus told this story:*
> *"A man planted a fig tree in his garden and came again and again to see if there was any fruit on it, but he was always disappointed. Finally he said to his gardener, 'I've waited three years, and there hasn't been a single fig! Cut it down. It's just taking up space in the garden.' The gardener answered, 'Sir, give it one more chance. Leave it another year, and I'll give it special attention and plenty of fertilizer. If we get figs next year, fine. If not, then you can cut it down.'"*
> LUKE 13:6-9 NLT

TWO CENTS MORE

*Let us not become weary doing good,
for at the proper time we will reap a harvest
if we do not give up.*
GALATIANS 6:9 NIV

SAY WHAT?

*You can't change the people around you,
but you can change the people around you.*

Perspective allows you to read this post and interpret it in two very different ways. There is no contradiction here at all; rather, each statement is true.

Relating to the first line of this post, trying to change the people around you is a boundary issue. You can make personal changes when you recognize a need to do things differently, but trying to force others to change to suit you is none of your business. That is called "boundary busting," so butt out.

The second line addresses a very different situation. When you feel like the association with certain people is no longer a wise activity, you are free to change this. There is an endless supply of people in the world, and according to many studies, almost all of them are craving to have more meaningful connections with others. There is a decent supply of people who would be your cup of tea. When you walk away from connections that no longer work well, you are free to select new people into your circle. Choose well.

*When you knock on a door, be courteous in your greeting.
If they welcome you, be gentle in your conversation. If they
don't welcome you, quietly withdraw. Don't make a scene.
Shrug your shoulders and be on your way.*
MATTHEW 10:13-14 MSG

*Don't compare yourself with others. Each of you must
take responsibility for doing the creative
best you can with your own life.*
GALATIANS 6:5 MSG

STICKS AND STONES

Researchers have shown that hurt feelings from
words affect the same area in the brain
—the cingulate gyrus—
as a broken bone or physical injury.

Don't tell me that words fail to pack a major wallop. Remember the old saying, "Sticks and stones may break my bones, but names will never hurt me?" What a crock! Words create deep wounds that don't appear in the form of physical bruises, cuts, and broken limbs. Medical attention can bring healing to physical injuries, but it cannot heal emotional or psychological damage. It is often difficult for people to even recognize that someone is in great internal pain and turmoil. Other times, suffering people will act out in ways that signal that these hurts were done to them in the past. They may also attract the same type of people that abused them before. If they understand the toxicity of that kind of connection, they may be able to do the hard work and find healing in the troubled area of the abuse dynamic. Ask God to reveal what He sees when you interact with others. You could also become a catalyst and healing agent to them.

Kind words heal and help; cutting words wound and maim.
PROVERBS 15:4 MSG

ZIP YOUR LIP

*There will always be someone who can't see your worth.
Don't let it be you!*

We do the most tremendous disservice to ourselves whenever our self-talk is contrary to what God has to say about us. He's crazy about us! If He had a refrigerator, our picture would be on it! We need to get a grip and zip our critical, self-abasing lip. If you must speak, speak the promises of God.

*I will praise You, for I am fearfully
and wonderfully made; marvelous are Your
works, and that my soul knows very well.*
PSALM 139:14 NKJV

KEEP SCROLLING

*You know you're getting old when your year of birth
is no longer immediately visible in drop-down
menus and you have to start scrolling down.*

Here's another way to look at it: As you drop down, you appreciate all the years you have lived to gain new wisdom and fresh perspectives, right the wrongs, and make priceless memories. Remember the special events and joyful times spent with family and friends. All those years are a treasure chest filled with invaluable life adventures. Embrace each new level and give thanks for the number of years of blessings you have received from God and others. And don't forget—you have had the opportunity of a lifetime to be a blessing to others as well. We can't save time in a bottle, but we can live our lives purposefully and make a difference—everything we do matters for eternity.

*But the godly will flourish like palm trees and grow strong
like the cedars of Lebanon. For they are transplanted to the Lord's
own house. They flourish in the courts of our God. Even in old age
they will still produce fruit; they will remain vital and green.*
PSALM 92:12-14 NLT

Wisdom belongs to the aged, and understanding to the old.
JOB 12:12 NLT

_____
_____
_____

CHANGE THE FORMULA

You're not stuck.
You're just committed to certain patterns of behavior because they helped you in the past. Now those behaviors have become more harmful than helpful. The reason why you can't move forward is because you keep applying an old formula to a new level in your life. Change the formula to get a different result.

Not only does this relate to habitual behaviors but also to the kind of people you continually allow into your life. It can become a Catch-22. People you choose to hang around may be involved in behaviors that take you far away from the person that you want to be. To "belong," you choose to do the things they are doing. You're stuck. On the other end of things, you may find yourself behaving in dysfunctionally toxic ways that draw people to you who would relish doing exactly what you're doing, perpetuating the downward spiral. Again—you're stuck. Both scenarios are detrimental to your growth and desired goals. It's time to change the formula. See how Paul did it in Acts 9.

Do not be misled. Bad company corrupts good character.
I Corinthians 15:33 NIV

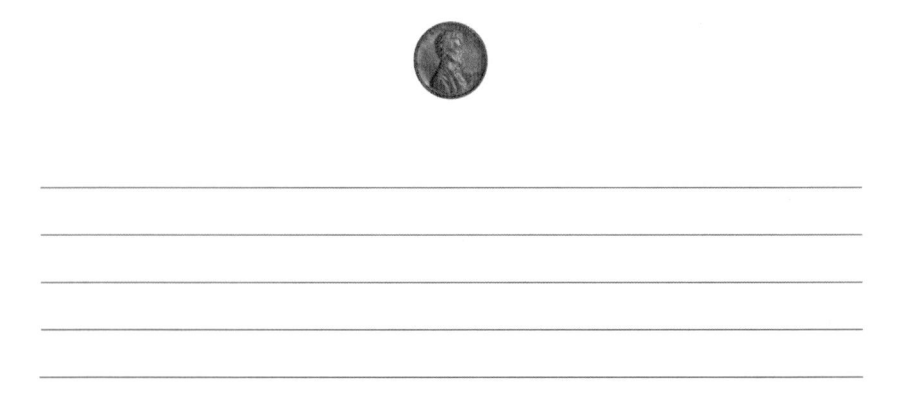

GROW UP

You are not responsible for the programming you picked up in childhood. However, as an adult, you are 100% responsible for fixing it. When you blame others, you give up your power to change.

David "Avocado" Wolfe

We all had issues when we were kids. Some had it much worse than others. If we managed to reach adulthood and have a bit of understanding about what went wrong, we can fix it. We might need some help, but we don't need to stay stuck in the errors of our past. Don't waste precious time playing the Victim Card. We must stop playing the Blame Game, whining about how things never seem to work out for us, and making excuses for bad choices because nobody ever taught us what we needed to do. As adults, we all have the freedom *and* the ability to learn, change, grow, and shine. If necessary, we can also seek the right people to walk with us and show us how it's done. It's on us to do it—no more excuses.

*Wise men and women are always learning,
always listening for fresh insights.*
PROVERBS 18:15 MSG

_____
_____
_____
_____

INDULGENCE OR TRANSFORMATION

Yes, Jesus hung out with prostitutes and drunkards and outcasts.
Here's the thing though—by the time Jesus was finished with these people,
they weren't prostitutes or drunkards or outcasts anymore.
Jesus came to transform people, not indulge them.
Christianity is about surrender, not comfort.
We are to align ourselves to His standard,
not the other way around.

Let's stop using this idea that Jesus hung out with everybody as an excuse to party on. When Jesus showed up, He didn't join in on what everybody was doing. He didn't appear to condone the shenanigans by giving everyone a high-five and behaving just like them. Jesus came to them right in the middle of what they were doing to show them a better way.

Even the religious people of the day tried to set Jesus up and challenge His authority and intentions. But He didn't back away from confrontation; He confronted. Jesus always addressed sin, called it what it was, and told them to change their choices and sin no more.

The religion scholars and Pharisees led in a woman, who had been caught in an act of adultery. They stood her in plain sight of everyone and said, "Teacher, this woman was caught red-handed in the act of adultery. Moses, in the Law, gives orders to stone such persons. What do you say?" They were trying to trap him into saying something incriminating so they could bring charges against him. Jesus bent down and wrote with his finger in the dirt. They kept at him, badgering him. He straightened up and said, "The sinless one among you, go first: Throw the stone."

Bending down again, he wrote some more in the dirt. Hearing that, they walked away, one after another, beginning with the oldest. The woman was left alone. Jesus stood up and spoke to her. "Woman, where are they? Does no one condemn you?" "No one, Master." "Neither do I," said Jesus. "Go on your way. From now on, don't sin."
JOHN 8:3-11 MSG

A LACK OF SEPARATENESS

I remember one woman, who came into therapy with extreme anger toward her family and all of their "expectations." I agreed with her that her family's expectations were wrong and that I understood her anger. She was very comforted that I agreed with her on that point. But when I suggested that they were not going to change and that she had to free herself from them by changing her attitudes toward them, she would get angry with me, saying, "You're just like them. You don't understand either." She felt if I did not agree with her victim stance, I didn't care.

I assured her that she had indeed been victimized growing up, but now she had to stop victimizing herself by freeing herself from her expectations of them. She couldn't understand that and said, "I don't have any expectations of them; they are the ones with the "shoulds".

"On the contrary," I said, "you're just like them. They say that you should be a certain way. And you say that they should be a certain way, or you will feel pressured. In other words, it's up to them to set you free so that you won't feel pressured. You're saying that they 'should not have shoulds,' and that it is the same thing that they are doing." I tried for a long time to help her see that until she took responsibility for internal "shoulds," she would never be free. She didn't expect those things from me. "I will always have to feel pressure by them until they let up." Since I wouldn't agree with her that it would be necessary for her family to change in order for her to get well, we hit a stalemate.

She felt that if I were on her side I would agree that her misery was their fault and not hers. I agreed with her that they had deeply injured her and were the source of much of their pain, but I asserted that they were not the ones continuing it in the present. She was an adult who could select new attitudes about life separate from theirs. But she felt that I was "being on their side" and that I was not understanding, so she quit coming to therapy.

I tried to help her comprehend that because I *was* on her side, I wanted her to take the power back that she had given them over her life. I wanted her to get free from their expectations, and the only way was to change herself. But she still believed that they had to change their attitudes first.

I saw her about three years later, and she was still stuck, still blaming. She was griping about how her family did this and that, totally neglecting her ability to change her attitudes about her need for them to be different. Since they were not different, neither was she. That is the essence of a lack of separateness.

Dr. Henry Cloud

This is where "should" raises its ugly head. Don't "should" on people—it's not nice. Dr. Cloud tried to explain to this lady with a victim mentality that what she continued to complain about was a boundary issue. If people would learn how to take care of everything that falls on their side of the property line, there would be no time left to be concerned with what's going on in all the other yards. The woman Dr. Cloud was trying to help had every opportunity to become free of her family's expectations of her. If she had been willing to change the way she thought everything needed to go, this story would have ended very differently. Even if her family had never changed, she could have experienced total freedom and moved on with her life. Instead, she chose to stay stuck and forever the victim.

> *From the fruit of his mouth a man is satisfied*
> *with good, and the work of a man's hand comes back*
> *to him. The way of a fool is right in his own eyes,*
> *but a wise man listens to advice.*
> PROVERBS 12:14 ESV

TWO CENTS MORE

*Fools are headstrong and do what they like;
wise people take advice.*
PROVERBS 12:15 MSG

2

MORE FOCUSED OUTWARD

A FAIR FARE

I arrived at the address and honked the horn. After waiting a few minutes, I honked again. Since this was going to be my last ride for my shift I thought about just driving away, but instead, I put the car in park and walked up to the door and knocked.

"Just a minute," answered a frail, elderly voice. I could hear something being dragged across the floor. After a long pause, the door opened. A small woman in her 90s stood before me. She was wearing a print dress and a pillbox hat with a veil pinned on it, like somebody out of a 40s movie.

By her side was a small nylon suitcase. The apartment looked as if no one had lived in it for years. All the furniture was covered with sheets. There were no clocks on the walls, no knickknacks, or utensils on the counters. In the corner was a cardboard box filled with photos and glassware. "Would you carry my bag out to the car?" she asked.

I took the suitcase to the cab, then returned to assist the woman. She took my arm, and we walked slowly toward the curb. She kept thanking me for my kindness. "It's nothing," I told her. "I just try to treat my passengers the way I would want my mother to be treated."

"Oh, you're such a good boy," she said. When we got in the cab, she gave me an address and then asked, "Could you drive through downtown?"

"It's not the shortest way," I answered quickly.

"Oh, I don't mind," she said. "I'm in no hurry. I'm on my way to a hospice." I looked in the rear-view mirror. Her eyes were glistening. "I don't have any family left," she continued in a soft voice. "The doctor says I don't have very long."

I quietly reached over and shut off the meter. "What route would you like me to take?" I asked.

For the next two hours, we drove through the city. She showed me the building where she once worked as an elevator operator. We drove through the neighborhood where she and her husband had lived when they were newlyweds. She had me pull up in front of a furniture warehouse that had once been a ballroom where she had gone dancing as a girl.

Sometimes she'd ask me to slow in front of a particular building or corner and would sit staring into the darkness, saying nothing. As the first hint of sun was creasing the horizon, she suddenly said, "I'm tired. Let's go now."

We drove in silence to the address she had given me. It was a low building, like a small convalescent home, with a driveway that passed under a portico. Two orderlies quickly came out to the cab as soon as we pulled up. They intentionally watched her every move. They must have been expecting her.

"How much do I owe you?" she asked, reaching into her purse.

"Nothing," I said.

"You have to make a living," she answered.

"There are other passengers," I responded.

Almost without thinking, I bent over and gave her a hug. She held onto me tightly. "You gave an old woman a little moment of joy," she whispered. "Thank you."

I squeezed her hand and then walked into the dim morning light. Behind me, a door shut. It was the sound of a closing of a life. I didn't pick up any more passengers that shift. I drove aimlessly, lost in thought. For the rest of that day, I could hardly talk. What if that woman had gotten an angry driver or one who was impatient to end his shift? What if I had refused to take the run or had honked once, then driven away?

On a quick review, I don't think that I have done anything more important in my life. We're conditioned to think that our lives revolve around great moments. But great moments often catch us unaware—beautifully wrapped in what others may consider a small one.

People may not remember exactly what you did or what you said—but—they will always remember how you made them feel.

Life may not be the party we hoped for, but while we are here, we might as well dance.

Unknown

We may grow old, but kindness *never* gets old. Major Godwinks can happen in the blink of an eye. There have been so many serendipitous moments in my life, but I cannot remember all of them—no matter how hard I try. There have been times that I have told myself that I need to write down something that just happened, but I usually just let that thought drift away and carry on with the next thing. Sometimes God is so kind—He is always kind, you know—that He brings those special little moments back to my remembrance. I love those priceless memories!

There is one thing that I do know for sure, though. I have *always* been aware when God has winked at me and gifted me with a memorable encounter with someone or something. I bask in the wonder of it all and have always been very thankful that He has chosen me to be a player in that particular moment in time.

Speaking of players, I was pleasantly surprised and blessed to reconnect with one of my nephews just recently. I hadn't been in contact with Brian, probably for about 45 years, except for one brief meeting at my parents' house in 1989. Family issues had resulted in an unfortunate estrangement. I had memories of Brian as a sweet, caring, thoughtful young lad, but then he was no longer a presence in my life. But here's how God can move to restore broken relationships. Brian and my sister, Deb, have been in regular contact lately, and their conversations have revealed that both Brian and I have published books. Using my sister as a conduit, I offered to send Brian my book, and he returned the favor by sending me his book of poetry.

You might be wondering why I'm even bothering to include this story in the post entitled *A Fair Fare*. The reason will become clear as I continue. Brian's book included a poem entitled *Sweet tea was more than enough*. When he was 14, he lived in South Carolina and made a bit of money mowing yards—$5 for small lawns; $7 for large. One couple had a large lawn, but the wife was being taken by her husband for cancer treatments. Brian would mow their lawn when the husband would take his wife for her treatments. Upon returning home, the husband would ask Brian how much he owed him. Brian always answered, "A glass of sweet tea will do." One day, after Brian had mowed, the man came home alone and didn't call out. He sat in his carport, holding his knees and weeping. Realizing what had happened, Brian knew enough just to sit and say nothing. The sweet tea was more than enough. His sensitivity was just like the driver who shut off the meter. Brian is still that kind, caring, and thoughtful lad I remembered, but now he is all grown up—and I'll bet he still has a huge empathy chip.

I want to encourage anyone who is reading this to stay on high alert for unexpected opportunities to show kindness to others. God orchestrates so many chances for us to become involved in special plans that He has laid out for those willing to rise to the challenge. He sees you through the eyes of love and gives you one of His winks. You'll know when it happens because you will get a little niggling from the Holy Spirit that something extraordinary is about to happen. If you put your busy schedule on hold for a while and respond to the invitation, some of the most rewarding and purposeful things will begin to happen in your life. God has a plan designed especially for you; get on the same page. Oh—and when something wonderful happens, do your future self a favor and *write it down!* When you recognize God is enjoying His time with you, those Godwinks can come fast and furiously. Life is an adventure when God prepares the itinerary!

> *Here is a simple rule of thumb for behavior:*
> *Ask yourself what you want people to do for you;*
> *then grab the initiative and do it for them!*
> LUKE 6:31 MSG

TWO CENTS MORE

AN ANTIQUE OF GREAT VALUE

The most valuable antique is an old friend.

Anything called an antique, by its definition, implies that it is something that has experienced some age. Unfortunately, some antiques have been left unattended and have fallen into disrepair—neglect rendering them discounted with a portion of their potential value lost. On the other hand, fine antiques that have been highly respected and received exceptional care are prized. The older they get, the more rare and valuable they become.

Likewise, friendships that stand the test of time require active care and encouragement to avoid being discounted over the long term. Remember that over time, friendships are the one element of our lives that give life a transcendently special meaning, even reaching into and impacting future generations. Take great care to foster authentic, long-lasting friendships, for they change lives and are as priceless as pure gold!

*Greater love has no one than this,
than to lay down one's life for his friends.*
JOHN 15:13 NKJV

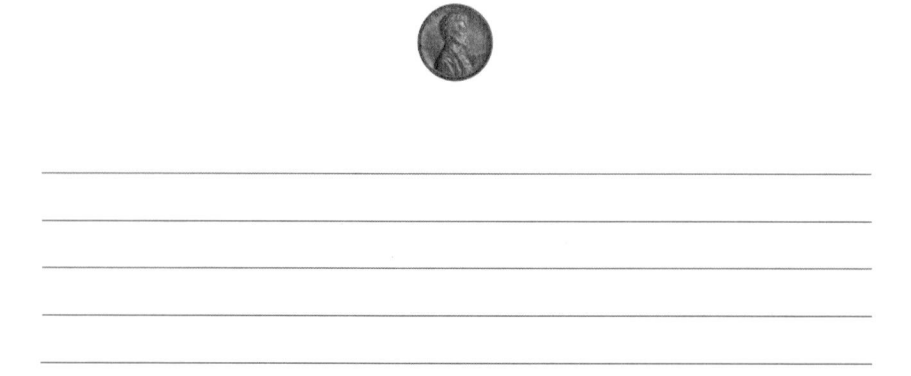

BAN THE BLAME GAME

Never blame another person for your personal choices—
you are still the one who must live out the consequences of your choices.

Caroline Myss

You may not like it, but that's the way it is. It's time to grow up and put the Blame Game away for good. Many things can be said about how others can influence your behaviors, words, and attitudes, but that will never be an excuse for why you decide to follow the crowd and please people to be accepted. In the end, you will always have to answer for your choices. One of the best ways to avoid making crucial, costly mistakes is to choose friends who will continually encourage you to do the right thing.

*Don't be misled: No one makes a fool of God.
What a person plants, he will harvest. The person who plants
selfishness, ignoring the needs of others—ignoring God!—harvests a
crop of weeds. All he'll have to show for his life is weeds! But the one
who plants in response to God, letting God's Spirit do the growth
work in him, harvests a crop of real life, eternal life.*
GALATIANS 6:7-8 MSG

MOMS FACING DIFFICULTIES

*Being a mother is learning about struggles
you didn't know you had and dealing
with fears you didn't know existed.*

Linda Wooten

Some moms face difficulties and struggles with their babies, and often feel ill-equipped to deal with the challenge. A combination of emotions, like anxiety, helplessness, and fear often rise up. The antidote for times like this is found in II Timothy:

> *For God did not give us a spirit of fear, but He has given us a spirit of power and of love and of a calm and well-balanced mind and discipline and self-control.*
> II TIMOTHY 1:7 MSG

When troubles arise, encouragement and help are available for moms who feel helpless and hopeless in tough situations. God is an ever-present help in times of need. Acknowledge the Giver of the gift of peace or whatever is needed at your moment, thank Him for it, open it, and use as directed. The Bible contains the directions. Read carefully and follow them step-by-step. They are the recipe for a successful and satisfying life for the babies—and the moms.

> *Whatever you do, work at it with all your heart, as working for the Lord, not for human masters, since you know that you will receive an inheritance from the Lord as a reward. It is the Lord Christ you are serving.*
> COLOSSIANS 3:23-24 NIV

MORE FOCUSED OUTWARD

This is my command—be strong and courageous! Do not be afraid or discouraged. For the Lord your God is with you wherever you go.
JOSHUA 1:9 NLT

And He said to me, "My grace is sufficient for you, for My strength is made perfect in weakness."
II CORINTHIANS 12:9A NKJV

TRUSTING HEARTS

*While someone begins to tell you the difficult parts of their story,
pull up a chair, lean in close and recognize they are offering you a gift.
A part of their journey. A piece of their heart.
So listen closely, avoid judgment, receive it with gratitude,
and treasure the rare gift you've been given.
The gift of a friend who trusts you with their heart.*

Becoming vulnerable and trusting someone with your whole heart can be risky and very scary. When life begins to feel a little off or when things begin to affect you in ways that bring sadness, fear, anger, uncertainties, and a whole host of indescribable emotions, you might feel an overwhelming need or desire to talk to somebody about what's going on. Finding a sounding board—anyone—to listen to your concerns may present a problem. Do you have someone that you feel you can trust enough to share some deep heart issues?

If you are willing to listen to someone's story without being critical and judgmental, count yourself blessed. God has given you the gift of empathy and a caring heart. Many don't have the patience to lean in and be on the receiving end of the stories and concerns of others. If you have anyone in your life who trusts you with their deepest heart issues, be thankful that God has placed you in their vicinity. If you do not, ask the Lord to be your sounding board and He'll provide the words and the friendships you need to flourish.

*Trust in the Lord with all your heart;
do not depend on your own understanding.
Seek his will in all you do, and he will
show you which path to take.*
PROVERBS 3:5-6 NLT

MORE FOCUSED OUTWARD

*Friends come and friends go, but a true friend
sticks by you like family.*
PROVERBS 18:24 MSG

WIRED FOR SAFETY

*Our brains are wired for connection,
but trauma rewires them for protection.
That's why healthy relationships are
difficult for wounded people.*

The Mind Journal

The simplicity of this defining statement explains a lot. The desire for safe connections exists in all of us, but we often cannot make them because we haven't been able to identify what absolute safety looks like. Trauma has produced an alternate circuitry, but our healing God understands the hearts and minds of His children and is quite capable to effect change and comfort us during the rewiring process.

*Is anyone crying for help? God is listening, ready to rescue you.
If your heart is broken, you'll find God right there;
if you're kicked in the gut, He'll help you catch your breath.*
PSALM 34:17-18 MSG

*For I know the thoughts and plans that I have for you,
says the Lord, thoughts and plans for welfare and peace and not
for evil, to give you hope in your final outcome.*
JEREMIAH 29:11 AMP

THE BEST REASON TO CHANGE

Dear Men:
Close your eyes. Imagine you have a daughter.
Imagine she is dating a guy just like you.
Did you smile? No? Then change.

It is essential to remember that every child that comes into the world has a man *and* a woman responsible for their birth, so let's flip this scenario. Turnabout is fair play:

Dear Women:
Close your eyes. Imagine you have a son.
Imagine he is dating a girl just like you.
Did you smile? No? Then change.

These are the type of questions I tend to talk about with my grandchildren. I am very aware that my kids heard my words of warning and instruction and watched my actions as they were growing up. Even as adults, they are watching to see if the words match up with the actions. Though I didn't do everything right, I am still aware of the importance of my conduct and how selecting strongly principled friends has a real impact on the next generation's choices.

Please hear my heart and get this message loud and clear. When it comes to our children's friends and future spouses, we must set good examples and help them hold to Godly principles during the selection process. Our Father God loves them fiercely and has provided them as His unique gift to the world. And their worth depends on what He says. With this statement, a good friend will always agree.

TWO CENTS MORE

*And above all things have fervent love for
one another, for love will cover a multitude of sins.*
I PETER 4:8 NKJV

THE LORD TOLD ME...

*If the Holy Spirit guides us,
He will do it according to the Scriptures
and never contrary to them.*

George Muller

This is a good one for the people who frequently like to say, *"The Lord told me _____ (fill in the blank)"*—as if this gives a credibility to whatever is said by making it sound spiritual and vetted by God. If the Bible cannot back up the statement, the Lord didn't tell you anything of the kind. You just said something you wanted to hear—and act upon. Don't forget, it is *thy* will be done, not *my* will be done. This reminds me of something Elisabeth Elliot said: "To pray, 'Thy will be done', I must be willing, if the answer requires it, that my will be undone."

> *There's nothing like the written Word of God for showing you the way to salvation through faith in Christ Jesus. Every part of Scripture is God-breathed and useful one way or another—showing us truth, exposing our rebellion, correcting our mistakes, training us to live God's way. Through the Word we are put together and shaped up for the tasks God has for us.*
> II Timothy 3:16-17 MSG

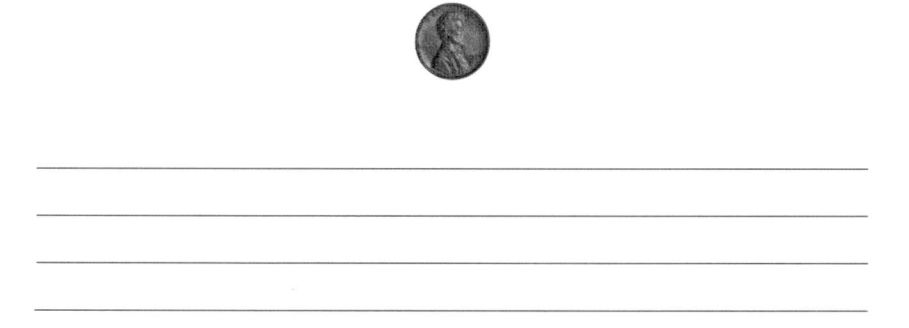

COMMUNICATION MODE

Communication Tip:
Your *tone* and the *way* you say something matters.

Communicating electronically, especially via text messages, is undermining the value of interactions. Errant or incomplete thoughts and misunderstandings can cause hurt feelings, anger, and relationship breakdowns. Believe it or not, even "Dear John" texting is sometimes used to end relationships in an unfortunate display of cowardice and disrespect. Even a phone call is way better than a letter or text. At least it allows for immediate verbal response for clarity and understanding.

Though it cannot be done in all cases, I recommend seeking out real face-to-face engagements, especially when discussing serious issues. Being in the same environment makes it possible to "read" what's going on. The actual words spoken, tone of voice, facial expressions, and body movements will always convey a greater depth of communication. When that happens, it is much harder to misunderstand the messages delivered. If we don't actively practice this level of openness and depth in our communication, we risk reducing our relationships to the meaninglessness of surface issues.

> *A bit in the mouth of a horse controls the whole horse.*
> *A small rudder on a huge ship in the hands of a skilled*
> *captain sets a course in the face of the strongest winds.*
> *A word out of your mouth may seem of no account,*
> *but it can accomplish nearly anything—or destroy it!*
> JAMES 3:3-5 MSG

*It only takes a spark, remember, to set off a forest fire.
A careless or wrongly placed word out of your mouth can do that.
By our speech we can ruin the world, turn harmony to chaos, throw
mud on a reputation, send the whole world up in smoke and go up
in smoke with it, smoke right from the pit of hell.*
JAMES 3:6 MSG

I CAN SEE CLEARLY NOW

Aging is like climbing a mountain.
The higher you get, the more tired you become,
but your view becomes much more extensive.

Ingmar Bergman

What's happening here is that older people have learned what to look for over time. The air becomes clearer and crisper and lacks objects distracting and blocking the view. As the years accumulate, physical limitations may begin to show up, with cataracts and glaucoma impacting the natural sight as our earth suit is wearing out. However, the soul realm develops an experienced clarity, and we can see things beyond the natural much better. Going higher is a beautiful way to look at life.

And so we are transfigured much like the Messiah,
our lives gradually becoming brighter and more beautiful
as God enters our lives and we become like Him.
II CORINTHIANS 3:18 MSG

PROBLEMATIC LOVE

There is no such thing as loving too much,
but giving or giving in excessively can be a problem.
Learn to make this distinction and behave accordingly.

Rowgo

We hear it all the time. God is love, and we are commanded to love one another. It doesn't matter whether we even like somebody. The command to love no matter what is a standard required by the Father, who loves us unconditionally. However, loving doesn't always include unfettered access to others. The Bible is clear when it spells out boundaries, which, by the way, originated with God. Sometimes the most loving thing we can do is to limit our giving or availability to others. If we don't learn to stop doing this, we will wind up enabling them to stay stuck and never grow to maturity. If we genuinely want to love well, we must teach those around us how to discover the things they must do for themselves and encourage them to trust God to provide for the things that only He can do.

*My son, do not despise the chastening of the Lord,
nor detest His correction; for whom the Lord loves He corrects,
just as a father the son in whom he delights.*
PROVERBS 3:11-12 NKJV

ROOT CANALS

You don't have to cheat to lose your girl or your wife.
You can lose her from a lack of communication, attention, and disrespect.
It's not all about what you *do*, sometimes it's about what you *don't do*.

This was written about romantic relationships and focuses on the need for the guy to better communicate with his lady. I'm all about relationships period—romantic, intimate ones and platonic friendships. So my "two cents" will be pretty generic and address all kinds of relationships.

Without a doubt, withdrawal and isolation create an emotional separation between people. Even in a marriage, an emotional divorce can begin forming even while living under the same roof. This is due to a growing feeling of emotional abandonment.

A broken connection results in a broken relationship. It takes two people working full tilt to bring healing and restoration. A spiritual and emotional root canal is the prescription needed to heal the affected and infected places. Damaged areas need to be cut off and removed.

I chose the "root canal" title because the lack of communication, attention, and respect are all root issues. A passageway or canal is required to navigate to the root of the problem. Getting to it may be painful and hurt like the dickens, but it won't be harmful. There is a significant difference. Only the action of dealing with it will bring about the much needed healing.

It might be difficult to undergo the treatment to achieve change, but if the relationship has value in other areas and can be salvaged, go for the gusto and do the hard work. Don't cheat yourself out of a chance to enjoy a healthy, fully committed relationship with someone you care for and value on many other levels.

Finally, fixing troubled relationships takes two people who recognize serious issues are threatening to sever their connection. There is an offender and an offended in this scenario. Sometimes the offenses go both ways. One must be willing to do whatever it takes to fix the problem; the other has to be willing to trust that the effort is legitimate and heartfelt. This boils down to a *trust issue*, and that takes insight, time, and a consistent change of behaviors and attitudes to bring about an honest and total restoration.

> *Understand [this], my beloved brethren. Let every man be quick to hear [a ready listener], slow to speak, slow to take offense and to get angry.*
> JAMES 1:19 AMP

TWO SIDES TO THE COIN

Sometimes you need to stop seeing the good in people and simply start seeing what they show you.

When investing time in developing relationships, evaluating others from multiple angles is prudent to ensure a reliable "fit". What people say and what people do can be worlds apart. To love all people is a command, but exercising discernment and wisdom is no less essential. There are some bad people in the world today who don't have your best interests at heart. You can still love them—*but from a distance—and far, far away!*

Become wise by walking with the wise;
hang out with fools and watch your life fall to pieces.
PROVERBS 13:19 MSG

DOUBLE STANDARDS

*It is vital to know the difference between
constructive criticism and destructive criticism.
Constructive criticism is when I criticize you.
Destructive criticism is when you criticize me.*

Tony Cooke

I get it now. This reminds me of an old saying: "What's good for the goose is good for the gander." Isn't it funny how we can twist words and meanings to come out in our favor while zapping others? Criticism is part of how we all operate in life. How we convey it is what makes it constructive or destructive. The rule of thumb is to always be kind and loving when delivering words of correction or reproof to others. And pray that when you're on the receiving end of these messages, kindness and love are extended to you as well.

*Now no chastening seems to be joyful for the present,
But painful; nevertheless, afterword it yields the peaceable
fruit of righteousness to those who have been trained by it.*
HEBREWS 12:11 NKJV

ON CRAVING FRIENDSHIPS

God created us to be in relationship with Him and each other.
Have you ever wondered why we need each other?
Why we crave relationships yet find it hard to build the kind we long for?

My craving for closer friendships surfaced as I sat across the table listening to the sounds of laughter and admiring the bond between two women I'd met at a lunch. What they had was uncommon. The way they loved each other, how well they knew each other, and how much they enjoyed each other reminded me of a Hallmark commercial.
But I wasn't watching television. This was real life.

And when I asked how long they'd know each other, they replied, "More than 60 years." More than 60 years? How had they met? What had they done to build a lifelong friendship? What moments and memories filled all those years and kept their hearts so closely knit together?
What's their secret?

Here's what I discovered:
- They were intentional about making their friendship last because it mattered to them.
- Things had to be planned and time together had to be given priority.
- They determined early on that they would be there for each other no matter what.

I thought about how different our generation is, how busy we are. How much more we rely on screen time more than face-to-face time. And a twinge of sadness came over me. Would there be anyone in my life I would have known for 40 or 50 years, much less 60 years, when I'm 70 or 80 years old? Besides my husband, which friend will be able to finish my sentences? Who will know me better than I know myself?

> From the beginning, God created us to be in relationship—with Him and each other. Designed in His image, our need for connection comes from God, who has always been in community: Father, Son, and Holy Spirit.
>
> Renee Swope

This is the most important thing to pursue as long as we live. According to studies, achieving solid relational connections will cause us to live longer. Having activities and interests in common initiates the ball rolling. When a real, honest, and vulnerable connection is made beyond the surface, a long-term friendship can develop on a deeper level.

I had a friend, Mary, whom I met on Saturdays for breakfast, and we went all the way back to elementary school over 65 years ago. Sadly, Mary passed away in September of 2021. I miss our Saturday mornings. Many friendships have come and gone over the years due to geographical distances and life changes, so the friendships I'm making for the long haul now are being cemented by being very intentional about staying closely in touch and meeting as often as possible. Some of my closer friends—Molly, Marsha, Jenn, Shelley, Norma, Barbara, my sister, Deb and more, though living miles away, technology makes it pretty easy to stay up-to-date.

My "local" connections start with my children, Russ and Mara. They are great friends who have been around for a lifetime. Some members of their families are bonus connections. I got a late start at getting intentional about building solid and lasting friendships, but over the past 30 or 40 years, I've been blessed with exceptional people in my life. God has graced me with two Glorias, Sherri, Lorrie, Suzie, and more. My cup runneth over! Thank God, I now understand how important friends are and how to bring honesty and vulnerability to the table so that the friendship looks a bit like a Hallmark commercial.

Update: My son used to be "local," but he and his family relocated to South Carolina in September of 2021. As you might imagine, I make as many trips down that way as I can to stay connected in my favorite face-to-face way.

> *...a real friend sticks closer than a brother.*
> PROVERBS 18:24B NLT

DEMANDS DON'T DO DIDDLY

*Our children learn life lessons from
us starting the moment they are born.
Our choices often become their choices, our
words their words, our actions their actions.
It is how we live, not how we demand they
live that has the most important impact
on who they will become.*

I'm quite sure some people would like to argue about how valid this post is, but it's easy to see in so many situations that words without corresponding actions have fallen on deaf ears and have proven pointless. Emphatic demands do not work, so save your breath. "You should this" and "you should that" must stop. Don't "should" on your children—it's not nice. Remember that they are always *watching* you but not always *listening* to you. When accompanied by matching behaviors, giving verbal instructions is much more powerful and honest. This behavior eliminates hypocrisy.

*Point your kids in the right direction—
when they're old they won't be lost.*
PROVERBS 22:6 MSG

EXIT STAGE LEFT

*When the wrong people leave your life,
the right things start happening.*

Personal choices of making wrong decisions and entering into toxic relationships have a way of short-circuiting successful living. This happens all the time. It takes some people considerable time to get a clue and get this through their thick noggins.

Perhaps it's time to dump some cast members of your life story and have them Exit Stage Left. It's time for them to leave. Bring in new cast members who will enhance your life story. They are safe people and know their trustworthy and enhancing part to play in your life. Have them Enter Stage Right—because they are the *right* ones to add to your ensemble. This new cast will make your story a hit!

*He who walks with wise men will be wise,
but the companion of fools will be destroyed.*
PROVERBS 13:20 NKJV

LET KINDNESS REIGN

> Not all things or people are toxic. There is no reason
> to start a war over someone's immaturity or imperfections
> that rub us the wrong way. That is the time for us to grow in
> patience and longsuffering, the ability to wait on
> people as they grow and mature.
>
> Dr. Henry Cloud

Everybody is imperfect, but there are some well beyond that. They are toxic. But be cautious, some have been misjudged as "toxic" when learning how to become who they were created to be. Take the time to learn how to extend *grace* and *patience*, lest you be labeled "toxic" for being a critical, judgmental person. Don't make the mistake of throwing people under the bus too quickly. Let kindness take precedence.

Always be humble and gentle. Be patient with each other,
making allowance for each other's faults because of your love.
Make every effort to keep yourselves united in the Spirit,
binding yourselves together with peace.
EPHESIANS 4:2-3 NLT

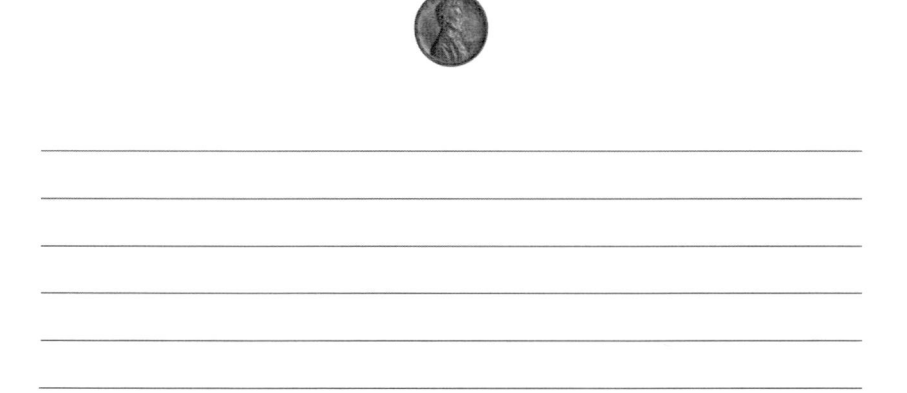

SEEDTIME

*You cannot force someone to comprehend
a message they are not ready to receive.
Still, you must never underestimate
the power of planting a seed.*

The month of May is traditionally the time to plant seeds for a garden where I live, but any time works for planting good message seeds. If the ground is not ready to receive the seeds or if the circumstances or weather are not conducive to bringing about growth, the seeds will not germinate. Don't let that deter you. Always plant those seeds. You may not be the one to tend them and see them through to harvest, but that's OK. Don't stop sowing!

*We each carried out our servant assignment. I planted the seed,
Apollos watered the plants, but God made you grow.
It's not the one who plants or the one who waters
who is at the center of this process but
God, who makes things grow.*
I Corinthians 3:6-7 MSG

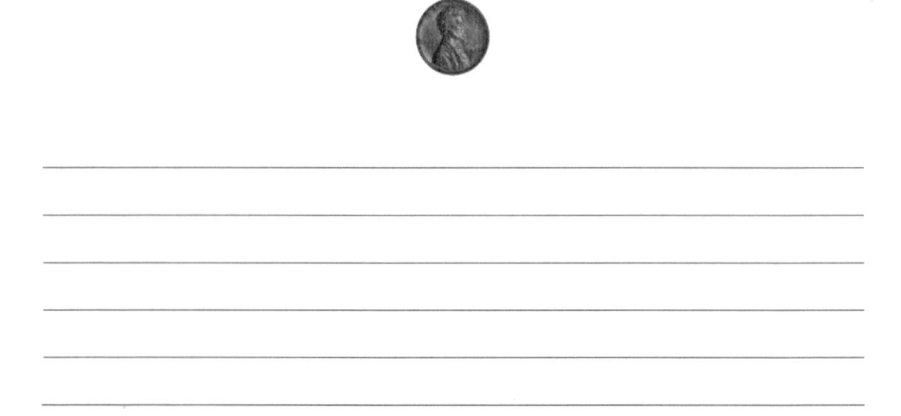

GO FOR RIGHTEOUS!

Y'all want a submissive woman but forget you have to be a righteous man. Being submissive does not mean to shut up and sit down when you say so. It means to trust you to lead, protect and provide. No woman is going to submit to a man who lies, acts controlling or cannot meet her emotional spiritual needs!

Geesh, ladies—fix your people picker. Hopefully, no woman will pick and settle for a controlling narcissist in the first place. If you wind up with someone like this, you are complicit in creating a toxic relationship. Both people in this scenario need to get a grip and learn what God's plan for their union must resemble.

When a husband has a great relationship with the Lord, he will also work on having a great relationship with his wife. The man submits to God and follows His instruction to love his wife unconditionally. When that happens, the wife *knows* she is loved and valued. Her response will be to submit to her husband and work in partnership with him to have the kind of relationship that puts a smile on God's face.

> *Seek the Kingdom of God above all else, and live righteously, and he will give you everything you need.*
> MATTHEW 6:33 NLT

> *Husbands, go all out in your love for your wives, exactly as Christ did for the church—a love marked by giving, not getting. Christ's love makes the church whole. His words evoke her beauty. Everything he does and says is designed to bring the best out of her, dressing her in dazzling white silk, radiant with holiness.*
> EPHESIANS 5:25-27 MSG

And that is how husbands ought to love their wives. They're really doing themselves a favor—since they're already "one" in marriage.
Ephesians 5:28 msg

GIVE AND TAKE

*I think it's important to realize that no matter
how good you are to people,
it won't make them good to you.*

Sometimes there is reciprocity, but sadly, not all the time. It would certainly be nice to see give and take in our connections with others, especially traits like kindness and goodness. If you're doing your part and it isn't returned, that's not a bad reflection on you—that's on them. You cannot force others to do the right thing, but you can spend time finding the kind of people who will. Maybe you need to tweak your people picker a little bit to get the "teeter-totter" effect activating. Concentrate on character issues as they are an absolute priority as life goes forward.

I have a grandson who is currently in college and majoring in a highly competitive field. During his first two years of college, he became well acquainted with a talented student who lacked safe people skills and exhibited a great deal of entitlement—likely due to his skill level. Revealing some toxic traits, this young man began to spread unmerited accusations of unethical behavior about my grandson. Of course, this made the environment uncomfortably stressful and nearly impossible to concentrate focused effort on the study. The chair of the department stepped in and addressed it, putting an end to the nonsense. By the third year, things settled down for the most part.

This ordeal gave my grandson a practical lesson in how to handle conflict with maturity. This has encouraged him to keep his nose to the grindstone and gain skills, and not forget tending to the most essential things—developing an excellent work ethic, working well with others, being an encourager, contributing to the common goals of accomplishment without sabotaging the work of others, and always seeking kindness. I believe employers will value exemplary character traits over and above mere talent and creativity. They are all important, to be sure. Still, if an employee cannot play well and be nice in the "sandbox," he will likely not last very long working where cooperation in a peaceful, positive environment is expected.

*And be kind to one another, tenderhearted,
forgiving one another, even as God in Christ forgave you.*
EPHESIANS 4:32 NKJV

*Here is a simple, rule-of-thumb guide for behavior. Ask yourself
what you want people to do for you, then grab the initiative and do it
for them. Add up God's Law and Prophets and this is what you get.*
MATTHEW 7:12 MSG

LITTLE ATLAS

A child's shoulders were not built to bear the
weight of their parent's choices.

Adults are responsible for making decisions about so many things, and often the choices made are very weighty and affect everyone who resides in their home—positively or negatively. Young children usually don't get a vote or have a say about those decisions—and rightfully so. After all, they *are* the children, and the parents are in charge. However, it becomes very problematic when the parents are foolish enough to make boneheaded choices that hurt their children. Trying to carry such heavy emotional baggage on their shoulders will stunt their emotional growth and possibly give them problems in the future. Don't do that to your children. Make the very best choices so they won't suffer from carrying a load they were never strong enough to bear.

Parents, don't come down too hard on your children,
or you'll crush their spirits.
COLOSSIANS 3:21 MSG

LET'S TALK

It's texting, emailing and messaging these days,
but nothing beats picking up the phone and talking to a friend.

Jim Hunt

I agree with this but prefer to take it one step further. Face-to-face, whenever it's possible, is absolutely the best! I make it a point to fill up my "dance card," so to speak, as much of the time as possible. As a bona fide people person, I crave human interaction more than just about anything. As my time winds down, nothing fills up my Love Tank faster than meeting with dear friends and family to talk about what's going on in our lives and hitting on subjects that matter.

*Therefore encourage and comfort one another and
build up one another, just as you are doing.*
I Thessalonians 5:11 AMP

WHAT'S THE DIFFERENCE?

*There's a difference between who we love,
who we settle for, and who we're meant for.*

Workingwomen.com

What's important is knowing the difference and being OK with it. Christians already know the difference. How? Because they know God's will for them from absorbing the Bible and having dedicated something this important to prayer. But too often, impatience short-circuits waiting for God's best, and choices are made to run headlong into situations that "feel good" at the time. Often, they won't "feel good" for long. To save lost time, heartache, and disappointment due to rash decisions, run potential relationships by God first. He has the final say any way you look at it, and your Father always knows best.

Can we settle for someone we're not meant to be with? Absolutely! But at some point, we become aware our choice fell short of God's best for us. Keep in mind that God is a miracle worker and can redeem the heart of anyone—but only if they are willing to follow His instructions.

*Don't become partners with those who reject God.
How can you make a partnership out of right and wrong?
That's not partnership; that's war.*
II CORINTHIANS 6:14 MSG

F-R-E-E-D-O-M!

Boundaries, of course, aren't the first thing that comes to mind for most people when they think about freedom. But they're essential if you want to avoid distractions and free yourself up to focus on the things you find most important.

Andy Andrews

Boundaries provide many benefits when consistently and adequately implemented. Safety is a big plus when boundaries are in place, but freedom is the highest benefit from my perspective. Once I have established what is important to me, I go after it. Many times, roadblocks pop up and try to deter me from reaching my chosen destination. But when I set up my boundaries and take charge of my own life without busting the boundaries of others, I can move forward freely and be about my own business. I endeavor to live in a way that pleases God, and because of that, He grants me the freedom to do so.

Therefore if the Son makes you free, you shall be free indeed.
JOHN 8:36 NKJV

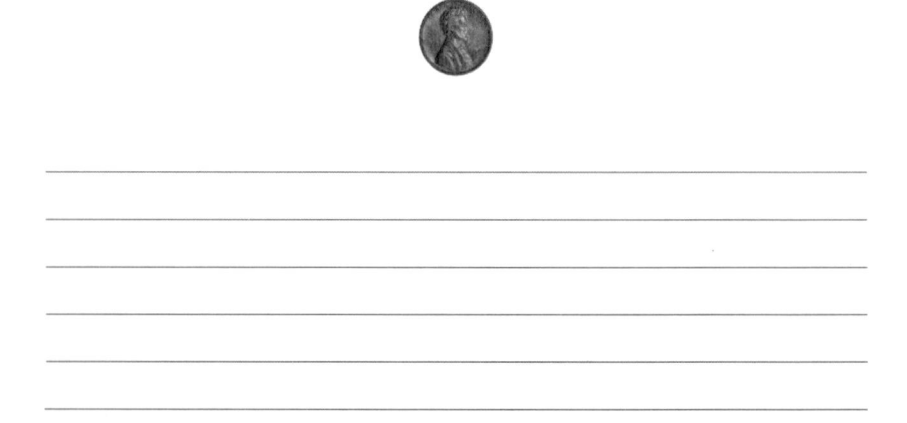

THE SPECTRUM OF FRUSTRATION

When you become frustrated with older people because of what they cannot do, think of how frustrated they must feel because they can no longer do it.

Yes—I am one of those "older people" now, and I am quite aware that I am not physically able to do many of the things that I once managed easily. For instance, I no longer pop up off the couch and move quickly anymore. I have become very purposeful even when I do that. I make sure my feet are solidly set on the floor before I start rocking to launch myself into a standing position. Once upright, I take a second or two before I begin to walk. Sometimes I'm standing there an extra moment as I try to remember why I got up in the first place. Being extra careful when I move about seems prudent because, living alone, I don't relish the idea of falling and not being able to get up. Speaking of getting up, sliding to the end of a booth to get up in a restaurant always has me hoping that nobody is looking. And any time I am putting forth the extra physical effort to do anything can bring about a little expulsion of other things too, but that disclosure is already TMI.

Thankfully, my mental acuity is still reasonably intact. Others who struggle with memory may be diagnosed with dementia or Alzheimer's and face unique challenges for themselves and those taking care of them. My sister spent years just showing up daily at a nursing home in her town and visiting with the residents facing all types of similar deficits. Many had very few visitors. Deb became their significant "family member" who was fully present for them to be whoever they were at the time. She listened to them, sang with them, and was a delightful presence in their lives. Known as the "Candy Lady," Deb carried bags of goodies on each visit—distributing their choice sweets with a smile. As far as I know, she didn't own any stock in any of the candy companies, but if she had any of these companies in her portfolio, she would be a wealthy woman today. Truth be told, she *is* rich beyond anything that money can buy. She is fulfilling God's assignment for her by spending priceless time with older adults who simply need to be in the presence of His grace and great patience.

Here is another perspective to consider: When you become frustrated with young children because of the things they cannot do, imagine how frustrated *they* are because they're not big enough or old enough to do those things yet. Love—*real love*—is patient and kind (I Corinthians 13:4). We must extend Grace at both ends of the spectrum.

> *With tender humility and quiet patience, always*
> *demonstrate gentleness and generous love toward one another,*
> *especially toward those who may try your patience.*
> EPHESIANS 4:2 TPT

MARA ALLIN

My daughter is watching me.
That's how important my decisions are.

My daughter, Mara, is fully grown and is still watching me. I'm sure I can tweak that a bit and say she is now keeping her eye on me to ensure I'm OK. The tables are turned, and she's never sure what I'll do next. Because retired people have more freedom to make their own schedules, the resulting unpredictability and spontaneity can become challenging for the family. Whatever the case may be, I'd better watch my step. Mara is keeping a very loving, caring, watchful eye on me. I believe I am past the earlier days of making foolish decisions, but I still want to conduct my life in such a way that will not cause her great concern or alarm.

*Let your light so shine before men,
that they may see your good works and
glorify your Father in heaven.*
MATTHEW 5:16 NKJV

UNCONDITIONAL CONDITIONS

Unconditional love does not
mean unconditional tolerance.

Unconditional love comes with vulnerability and straight-up honesty. That means some mindsets and behaviors that go sideways from acceptable standards must be confronted and challenged. Do not tolerate misbehaviors; this will alleviate and save loved ones from experiencing costly consequences. Confrontation out of love may create discomfort and maybe even anger and hurt feelings, but you must be able to say the hard things. *This* is what true unconditional love must do.

As iron sharpens iron, so a friend sharpens a friend.
PROVERBS 27:17 NLT

WATCH YOUR MOUTH!

*How you talk to your parents
says a lot about you—
I don't care how old you are.*

My parents have been gone a long time, and I still hold them in high regard. For some reason, honoring my parents was important to me. My dad was an elected official in our city and even served a term as mayor. I didn't ever want to do anything that would bring negative press, shame, or disappointment to my parents because of anything I did. And maybe, more than that, my desire to behave acceptably had something to do with one of the Ten Commandments. It's the only commandment that comes with a promise. It greatly concerns me when I hear how so many people talk to and about their parents these days. Young and old alike can be so disrespectful and unkind.

Perhaps another issue is a part of the problem. Parents must step up and stop tolerating how their kids talk to them. Earlier generations knew better than to openly and flagrantly disrespect their parents, no matter how they felt about them. They lived longer. What's that commandment with a promise say in Exodus 20? *Honor your father and mother, that your days may be long upon the land which the Lord your God is giving you.*

Parents: Put up a vital boundary and don't allow your kids to get away with blatant disrespect. Don't back down—this is how they will learn to treat others with respect.

TWO CENTS MORE

Children, do what your parents tell you.
This is only right. "Honor your father and mother"
is the first commandment that has a promise attached to it,
namely, "so you will live well and have a long life."
EPHESIANS 6:1-3 MSG

THE PROBLEM WITH HONESTY

More often than not, they do not have a problem with your honesty.
They have a problem with the fact that what you said
was not what they wanted to hear.

Madalyn Beck

When Beck refers to "They," this can be just about anybody in your life. If you are known to be an honest, trustworthy person, people who know you well may sometimes ask for some input and advice. And even though they may have given their permission for you to speak into their lives, there will be times that your "truth," your opinion, or your thoughts may not sit well with them. That's OK. Your words have been spoken and haven't gone unheard. Now let them chew on them and perhaps come to embrace and appreciate them. Different perspectives can bring change when delivered in love.

*Do not speak in the hearing of a fool,
for he will despise the wisdom of your words.*
PROVERBS 23:9 NKJV

A CARING HEART

*When you're mad at someone you love, be careful what you say—
because your mind gets angry, but your heart still cares.*

Words are powerful and can be so destructive. Be very careful when choosing the words you speak to people you love. Some might say that when they get angry, the words "just come flying out without thinking." Not true—thoughts produce words. When angry, it's time for a "Selah" moment. *Stop*—and calmly think about what you're thinking about, and engage your heart into the equation before blurting out hurtful words. And when you're angry, also be aware of *how* you speak to the people you love.

*Pleasant words are like a honeycomb,
sweetness to the soul and health to the bones.*
PROVERBS 16:24 NKJV

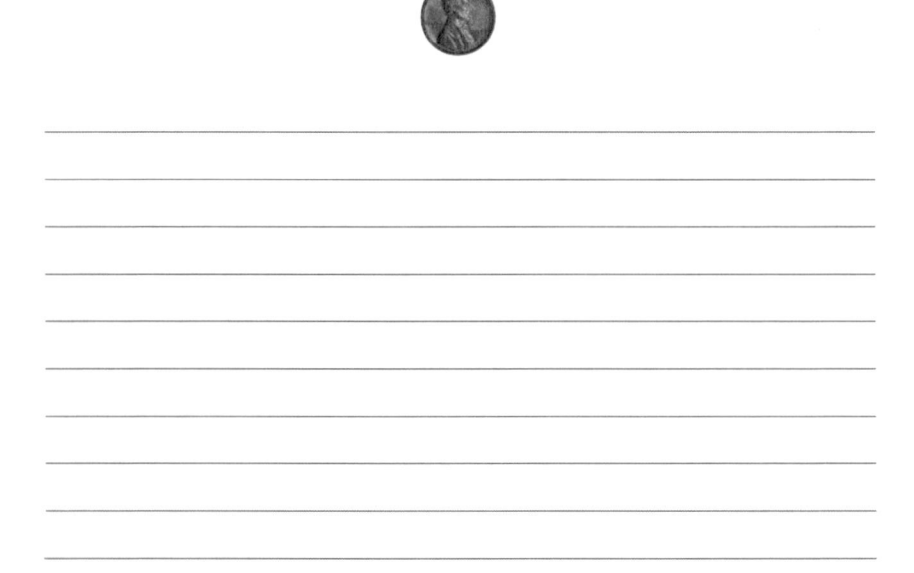

STERILIZE YOUR WORDS

Doctors sterilize their instruments before using them in a surgical procedure in order to not cause an infection and create a problem that didn't exist prior to the surgery.

Believers should "sterilize" their words by soaking them in kindness, love, and careful thought before they speak them in an attempt to "heal" or "help" others, lest they create hurts and offenses in others that didn't exist before they spoke.

Guy Duininck

This is an excellent post to ponder these days, especially considering the destructive, divisive content of so many viewpoints spoken by people with access to and control of the major programming available to the public. It's bad enough when individuals meet together and inflict harm on one another with hurtful, toxic, erroneous words. It becomes so much worse when a pandemic of thoughtless rhetoric spreads harmful, infectious ideology to thousands upon thousands of people.

We want to trust our doctors to administer safe, skilled, and sterile care for our physical well-being. We would also like to trust the people in the arenas of influence to take the same care and exercise great integrity when they open up their language kits and administer the tools we call "words."

Remember, there is One who monitors everything going on about us. God knows everything that we do, say, and think. Wouldn't it be nice to behave accordingly and let kindness and love take precedence over all the negativity? Just a thought.

*Let the words of my mouth and the meditation of my heart
be acceptable in Your sight, O Lord, my strength and my Redeemer.*
PSALM 19:14 NKJV

For out of the abundance of the heart the mouth speaks.
MATTHEW 12:34B NKJV

DOMINO EFFECT

Children need to learn to take responsibility for their
actions so they do not become adults believing
that nothing is ever their fault.

This can be a domino effect. Parents, take deliberate action to be exemplary role models, teaching your children how responsibility looks. The importance of this parenting level will show as your children take greater and greater ownership of their actions. That's how it's supposed to work. Let's cut out the "Don't do as I do; do as I say" nonsense.

Good friend, follow your father's good advice;
don't wander off from your mother's teachings.
Wrap yourself in them from head to foot;
wear them like a scarf around your neck.
Whenever you walk, they'll guide you
whenever you rest, they'll guard you;
when you wake up, they'll tell you what's next.
For sound advice is a beacon, good teaching is a
light, moral discipline is a life path.
PROVERBS 6:20-23 MSG

DREAM ON!

*You are never too old to set another goal
or dream a new dream.*

C.S. Lewis

I have found this to be very accurate! As my levels advance, I'm quite the dreamer. Now I have the time to do something about bringing my dreams to fruition. Who would've thunk I'd be writing a book (or two) at 78? Certainly not me! Of course, being a procrastinator of epic proportions might have contributed to how long it has taken me to accomplish these things. I had often thought about writing a book for years and never got around to it until now. However, now that I have, I feel like I'm in good company—Grandma Moses started painting when she was 78.

*And it shall come to pass in the last days, says God, that
I will pour out of My Spirit on all flesh; your sons and your
daughters shall prophesy, your young men shall see visions,
your old men shall dream dreams.*
ACTS 2:17 NKJV

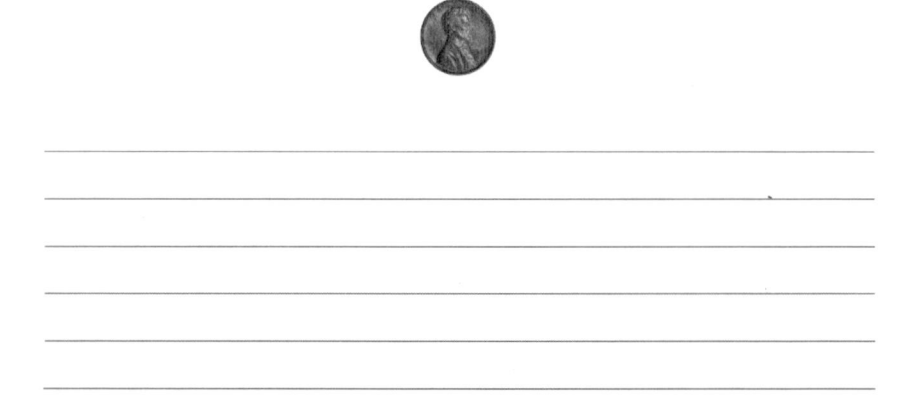

BREAK THE RULE... I DARE YOU

She's 98.
And the isolation and loneliness came over her in a river of tears at my visit. Not able to see her son or daughter for six weeks, she wants to die. Because at 98, the waiting is too much.
I offered to FaceTime her son. She cried more.
She wanted a real hug. I, in my PPE, said enough.
I bent over into her arms—she wrapped so tight around me.
I broke the rule.
I hugged her till she could breathe.
We both had a healing. I'd do it again. Love matters most.
The older folks in long-term care haven't been touched or hugged.
It's causing failure to thrive. Hugs are a necessary part of living.

A nurse

This showed up in May 2020, when the whole country was shutting down due to the Covid outbreak. After reiterating that studies about close relationships account for the longevity of life, my response at that time was the following: Lack of being permitted to connect with people will shorten lives. At my level, I am willing to risk getting out and living with my friends and family again. My health and quality of life are my responsibility. So, I'm deciding to connect with those having the same courage and mindset. I believe my life depends on it. Sometimes a hug can be so tight that I feel like I can't breathe. I loved how the nurse said, "I hugged her till she *could* breathe." That said it all.

Later on, in 2020, I survived a bout with Covid. My mindset remained steadfast; fear did not set in or rule me. Without human touch, failure to thrive can set in. Tangible love and human touch matter more than anything in these situations. Whether we live or die—and death is inevitable at some point—being able to connect and love one another matters most.

TWO CENTS MORE

*Therefore comfort each other and edify one
another, just as you also are doing.*
I THESSALONIANS 5:11 NKJV

PATIENCE

Being married won't heal you
and being single won't kill you.
Waiting on God is never a waste of time.

Better to wait on God to make the divine connection than being joined at the hip before—or even after—getting married. Do not make costly errors by moving quickly into relationships based on emotions and desperation. God has just the right somebody—have patience. Don't short-circuit the connection by going with your plan. That would be a big mistake and an enormous waste of precious time. When you emphasize your relationship with your heavenly Father, your heart will mature through a season of learning to love yourself, so you can best share love with your "someone."

*Wait on the Lord; be of good courage,
and He shall strengthen your heart; wait, I say, on the Lord!*
PSALM 27:14 NKJV

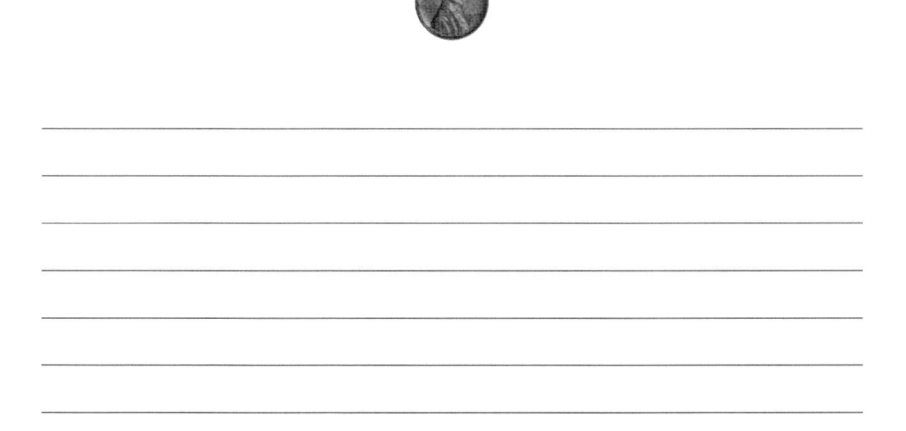

MAJOR TEST

The real test is being kind to unkind people.

My son, Russ, has a podcast called *The Ride*. He has done well over 200 episodes and has recorded them for multiple years on his morning work commute. The subjects are all over the place as they are unplanned and unscripted. Russ, in his wisdom, has trusted the Holy Spirit to speak words of encouragement, love, and correction through him. Each episode opens with music written and played by him as he begins with a hearty, "Good morning, fellow riders—this is your host, Rusty James, and this is *The Ride*!"

At the close of each episode, Rusty James—his moniker for The Ride—might change it up a bit, but he usually concludes with, "And remember to stay in the Word and pray for those who persecute you." When we feel like slapping our "enemies" upside the head, here's the tall order you'll find in Matthew:

> *But I say to you, love your enemies,*
> *bless those who curse you, do good to those who hate you,*
> *and pray for those who spitefully use you and persecute you.*
> MATTHEW 5:44 NKJV

Matthew 5 focuses on Jesus' teaching and preaching to His disciples. Starting with the Beatitudes—the "Be Attitudes"—and continuing to hit on a range of subjects, like murder and adultery in the heart, the sanctity of marriage, how He came to fulfill the law, going the second mile, and believers being salt and light. Jesus finishes off His conversation with them by addressing the "enemy" thing, reminding them that they had heard it said to love your neighbors and hate your enemies. He flipped that one upside down by giving that charge above. And didn't Jesus model that behavior and do just that all the way to the cross? If we say we follow Him, this is also a path we must tread.

> *"You're familiar with the old written law,
> 'Love your friend,' and its unwritten companion, 'Hate your enemy.'
> I'm challenging that. I'm telling you to love your enemies. Let them
> bring out the best in you, not the worst. When someone gives you a
> hard time, respond with the energies of prayer, for then you are
> working out of your true selves, your God-created selves.*
> *This is what God does.*
> *He gives His best—the sun to warm and the rain to nourish—
> to everyone, regardless: the good and bad, the nice and nasty.
> If all you do is love the lovable, do you expect a bonus? Anybody can
> do that. If you simply say hello to those who greet you, do you expect
> a medal? Any run-of-the-mill sinner does that. In a word, what I'm
> saying is, <u>grow up</u>. You're kingdom subjects. Now live like it. Live
> out your God-created identity. Live generously and graciously
> toward others, the way God lives toward you."*
> MATTHEW 5:43-48 MSG

REPETITION MATTERS

Me: No.

Kids: Hmmm. I feel like maybe you're not completely committed to that no. I'm gonna ask you 852 more times and see.

This is an excellent opportunity for parents to develop their "No" muscle—852 reps might just do it! Next time it might only be 834. Keep it up, and the number will quickly diminish to nothing. Sadly, too many parents are not persevering and are giving up the fight. They grow weary or distracted and say, "Whatever! Do what you want—you're gonna do it anyway!" C'mon, parents—who's supposed to be in charge? Do your kids a huge favor and help them understand that boundaries are imperative for their safety and, whether they believe it or not, for their actual freedom.

Just say "yes" and "no."
When you manipulate words to get your own way, you go wrong.
MATTHEW 5:37 MSG

TO BE OR TO DO

Are you a human being or a human doing?
High performing and successful people, especially leaders, often accidentally get lost in the "task" aspects of life: meetings, goals, objectives, phone calls, and more meetings. When you spend too much time in "task" and not enough in "connection," you run the risk of making decisions out of poor judgment, losing energy, making mistakes and being unfocused. All of these issues can be a direct result of not getting your relational tank filled.

Don't let 24 hours go by without some sort of meaningful conversation with someone you care about, even if it's only a few minutes. It will keep you working harder and better on what is important to you.

Dr. John Townsend

This is pure gold! I tend to be much more of a human being than a human doing. I love spending real time with people in person or even having a lively, meaningful conversation on the phone when time and distance don't allow the freedom to get together physically. Because of this preference, I often don't get much done, but I'm OK with that—usually. Whatever chores I neglect due to my desire to fill up on relational fuel will still be waiting to be done later, so I will eventually get around to the "doing" part. I'm just more focused on the most important thing—keeping the first thing first.

As they continued their travel, Jesus entered a village. A woman by the name of Martha welcomed Him and made Him feel quite at home. She had a sister, Mary, who sat before the Master, hanging on every word He said. But Martha was pulled away by all she had to do in the kitchen. Later, she stepped in, interrupting them. "Master, don't you care that my sister has abandoned the

TWO CENTS MORE

kitchen to me? Tell her to lend me a hand." The Master said, "Martha, dear Martha, you're fussing far too much and getting yourself worked up over nothing. One thing only is essential, and Mary has chosen it—it's the main course, and won't be taken from her."
LUKE 10:38-42 MSG

DO AS GOD DOES

Don't treat people the way they treat you.
Treat people the way God treats you.

Dave Willis

This is a toughie, but it's so essential and is way high on my list of priorities to work on and learn how to do. Some days are better than others depending on the circumstances and my state of mind, but I'm determined to keep on keeping on. That brings a smile to God's face, which makes me smile all the more!

Make a clean break with all cutting, backbiting, profane talk.
Be gentle with one another, sensitive. Forgive one another as quickly
and thoroughly as God in Christ forgave you.
EPHESIANS 4:31-32 MSG

PREDICTORS OF A LONG LIFE

A TED talk posted on Facebook addressed the factors
that could most be attributed to longevity of life.
Good nutrition, overcoming drug and alcohol
addictions, vaccines, exercise, fresh air,
and more contributed to length of
life, but the strongest and most
beneficial predictors for living
a long life had to do with...
relationships.

I LOVE THIS DATA! Many studies have come to the same conclusion. And the best part is that the Bible backs it up. Actually, it's the other way around. The Bible said it first, and all the studies that I've followed over the years agree with what God said in the first place. God continually calls us to have fellowship with one another. That is on His *high priorities* list. The other factors are important too, but the data seems to support the idea that the most significant predictors of long life correlate with aspects of the personal relationships we develop.

I have close connections with a few family members and friends who add high-octane fuel to my life and fill up my love tank. We talk at length about things that matter, and time stands still. Those are precious times of gaining insight and making significant growth. I believe they are my relational vitamins that aid my spiritual and emotional health.

The data also indicates that connecting with people in short spurts contributes to longevity too. I have *never* paid at the pump, no matter how bad the weather is. I prefer to chat with people who I've never met before. I might say something that will brighten their day, but it can also happen the other way around. I love going to my neighborhood cafe for breakfast so I can strike up a conversation with whoever is there. I make eye contact and say "Hello," "Please," and "Thank you" often, just in passing, to people I see. I'm a noticer! I crave human connection—it's in my DNA!

If I keep on doing what I always do, I might live forever. Wait—*I will!* It just won't always be here. The best is yet to come.

*Some friendships don't last for long,
but there is one loving friend who is joined to your heart.*
PROVERBS 18:24 TPT

PARENT ALERT

Begin early to instruct your children on the true values of life:
love for all of mankind,
kindness,
integrity,
trustworthiness,
truthfulness,
and devotion to God.

Dr. James Dobson

Do your children a tremendous favor and dutifully teach them about these character issues. Well beyond face-to-face instruction, model these things in the home and everywhere you go. Telling is good; showing is way more powerfully authentic. Do away with hypocrisy! The children are more likely to do what you do—not what you say. Lead by example.

*Direct your children onto the right path,
and when they are older, they will not leave it.*
PROVERBS 22:6 NLT

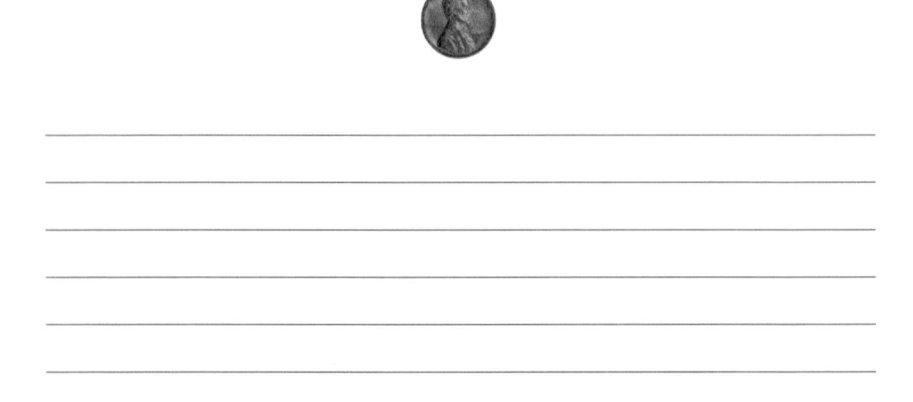

BORN TO JUDGE

It's not judging to have eyes.
It's not judging to know something.
You don't have to walk in someone else's shoes to see they are about to walk off a cliff. If you see someone about to walk off a cliff, yell and stop them. You can judge in service without a haughty or arrogant heart. You were born to judge just as you were born to think. Your whole life is a series of judgments and adjustments. Don't let people batter you from the bully-pulpit about judging to the point that you suppress your common sense. They are not holier than you because they call their judging "discernment." Don't listen to "non-judgers" who judge your judgments; it's hypocritical hogwash. We judge people constantly. We were born to judge. You can judge a behavior without condemning a soul. Someone's salvation is out of your jurisdiction, but once they have opened their mouth, the invitation to judge is irretractable. People often use the "judgment card" to hide when you are getting too close to the truth for comfort. Hang on to your judgment. Good judgment will keep you safe. Good judgment can and does save lives. Don't be afraid of your rightful power to judge others. Judging is one of your most powerful tools you have to protect those you care about, and yourself, from harm.

Bryant McGill

This is a critical perspective on the issue of judging. It makes way too much sense and will likely hit home too close for comfort for some folks. The very people who scream, "You can't judge me!" are the same people who feel convicted because we're hitting the nail on the head. The Book of Proverbs encourages confrontation, speaking the truth in love, and more. Drawing conclusions and making judgments turn out to be consistent vernacular. On top of that, we were born to judge!

TWO CENTS MORE

And we earnestly beseech you, brethren, admonish (warn and seriously advise) those who are out of line [the loafers, the disorderly, and the unruly]; encourage the timid and fainthearted, help and give your support to the weak souls, [and] be very patient with everybody [always keeping your temper].
I THESSALONIANS 5:14 AMP

OLD IS PRICELESS

It annoys me when people say,
"Even if you're old, you can be young at heart!"
Hiding inside this well-meaning phrase is a deep
cultural assumption that old is bad and young is good.
What's wrong with being old at heart, I'd like to know?
Wouldn't you like to be loved by people whose
hearts have practiced loving for a long time?

I am shouting a resounding *YES* in answer to the last question. The older people who have worked diligently on learning how to love deeply and well are much better at it than the younger generations. They know what works and doesn't work. It takes dedication and time to figure it out! That kind of love is priceless; you can take it to the bank and earn enormous dividends.

Wisdom is with aged men, and with length of days, understanding.
JOB 12:12 NKJV

FOREVER FRIENDS

There are friends in life—
and there are friends for life.

I have been blessed to have both kinds of friends. Sadly, I am missing my Saturday breakfast buddy/school friend. We were friends for 68 years, going all the way back to sixth grade. We enjoyed pajama parties and road trips to the lake when we weren't in school, but we also shared a boatload of the same classes throughout high school. Beyond those years, we continued to do things together. One of our constant weekly activities over the past 20 years was having breakfast together every Saturday. Our moms joined us when they were still alive. After they died, we continued to meet and break bread together.

Mary passed away in September of 2021 after a short illness. That was a devastating loss for me. Actually, over recent years, many of my long-time friends have died. As I near my eighth decade, I have come to terms with the fact that I will watch an increasing number of family and friends enter into eternity.

When any friendship of great depth involves a shared faith in God and a promise of eternal life with Him, it stands to reason that those relationships will go on forever—not just in this world, but in the forever world to come. Those friendships will never end; they just relocate. Friends *in* life—friends *for* life—*FOREVER FRIENDS!*

> *For we know that if our earthly house, this tent, is destroyed, we have a building from God, a house not made with hands, eternal in the heavens. For in this we groan, earnestly desiring to be clothed with our habitation which is from heaven...*
> II CORINTHIANS 5:1-2 NKJV

MORE FOCUSED OUTWARD

*We are confident, yes, well pleased rather
to be absent from the body and to be present with the Lord.*
II CORINTHIANS 5:8 NKJV

DON'T PUT UP WITH IT

Being called sensitive for reacting to disrespect
is manipulation at its finest.

This is a master manipulator:
"A person who controls or influences others
in a clever or unscrupulous way."

This is why we must love, accept, and trust ourselves,
so that we can stand up to unscrupulous behavior.

When we doubt our feelings and push them away, and then write
a story like, "Oh, they didn't treat me so bad, I must have done
something to provoke it" or you use toxic positivity and say,
"I shouldn't have reacted so negatively," we are giving in to the
manipulation and abandoning ourselves. It's okay to respond
"negatively". There is nothing wrong with you when this happens.

Of course, own your response in a situation, but make sure you
communicate that the other person *must* own their behavior too.
Otherwise, there can be no helpful resolution. Nothing will change,
And you deserve to be seen, heard, respected, and loved.

All of this is good and sounds like a masterful way to resolve problems, but just saying the other person *must* own their behavior doesn't make it happen. What will you do if the other person doesn't see anything wrong with their statements or actions? Here again is where boundaries need to be clearly understood. It is imperative to recognize manipulation. If you don't know when it's in full bloom, you may begin to believe that you're the one with the problem. You might even feel like you're a little crazy. There's a word for that—gaslighting. You begin to question your ability to understand what's going on, so you consent to the manipulator's explanation that you're mistaken and they have both the truth and the upper ground.

Get a grip and call manipulation what it is. The other person will most assuredly beg to differ with your assessment, and that's their right. That is the boundary issue. You cannot make them see things your way—even if you're right. Speak your piece and understand that sometimes others will not agree with you. You may decide to move along and find safer places to spend your time; that's OK. But being called sensitive when you push back against disrespect is a common way for a master manipulator to, well, manipulate. Stand up. Speak up. Disrespect is unacceptable—period!

> *Make a clean break with all cutting, backbiting, profane talk. Be gentle with one another, sensitive: Forgive one another as quickly and thoroughly as God in Christ Jesus forgave you.*
> EPHESIANS 4:31-32 MSG

PRETTY WORDS

True words are not always pretty;
pretty words are not always true.

Just the truth, ma'am! Speaking the truth in love (Ephesians 4:15) isn't always pretty, but it dramatically improves the odds of success when heeded. Healing, restoration, and growth will result from aligning with the Truth of God.

> *No prolonged infancies among us, please.*
> *We'll not tolerate babes in the woods, small children*
> *who are an easy mark for impostors. God wants us to grow*
> *up, to know the whole truth and tell it in love—like Christ in*
> *everything. We take our lead from Christ, who is the source*
> *of everything we do. He keeps us in step with each other.*
> *His very breath and blood flow through us, nourishing*
> *us so that we will grow up healthy in God, robust in love.*
> EPHESIANS 4:14-16 MSG

STAYING POWER

Employees stay when they are:

Paid well
Appreciated
Mentored
Valued
Challenged
On a mission
Promoted
Empowered
Involved
Trusted

Work climates matter. With a little play on words, it's a *whether* report that determines whether or not you'll stay. I've known many who have displayed a consistent work ethic and have exceeded the minimum requirements that so many others barely meet to get by.

The diligent workers, those more invested than simply seeking a paycheck, have said that the most disappointing thing is not being appreciated and valued for their effort. They are told that's their job and should do what's expected of them, while the slackers never seem to be reprimanded or face discipline. They expect the hard workers to pick up after them. Bosses and management, in general, must do a better job in their positions if they hope to have a better working relationship with their people in the trenches who are busting their butts to get the job done well. You might ask, "Why do they keep doing such a great job without any positive words from the higher-ups?" They do it because it's the right thing to do. It's called integrity!

I'm sure that the people doing jobs without appropriate positive reinforcement from their superiors are, in part, continuing to work due to a need to earn a living and pay their bills. However, their job satisfaction continues to erode, dropping their morale into the basement. How I wish people in the workplace would confidently find their voice and address the powers that be. Confronting concerns without fear of retaliation should be the norm. It might even help those in positions of authority to increase caring about how their workers feel, you know, to help them develop their empathy chip and change how they do business. A little give-and-take could go a long way.

For the Scripture says,
"You must not muzzle an ox to keep it
from eating as it treads out the grain."
And in another place, "Those who work deserve their pay."
I Timothy 5:18 NLT

SKEWED POINT OF VIEW

When a person expresses a point of view that you don't agree with,
but you don't prefer to discuss that point of view or argue with them,
you can simply respond with, "I will consider what you said."

This response is not contentious, and it also communicates respectfully that
you don't prefer to engage in a discussion or an argument at the time.

Guy Duininck

To some, this may look like the chicken's way out—especially if they were looking forward to an all-out argument of points of view that run counter and sideways from theirs. That's alright. Everyone has the right to decide whether or not they want to participate in an altercation that will, in all likelihood, solve nothing. Consider the cost. Engagement will likely increase ill will and fester in the bones.

Refuse to get involved in inane discussions;
they always end up in fights.
II TIMOTHY 2:23 MSG

TWO CENTS MORE

RELATIONSHIP GREEN FLAGS

Self-responsibility
Self-reflective
Supports your personal growth
Long-standing friendships
Practices self-care
Honors boundaries
Communicates openly
Healthy hobbies
Self-sufficiency
Spirituality
Vulnerability
Empathy

When you find someone who can tick off every one of these flags, act quickly. They would be a treasured friend to have in your corner. Do you know anybody like this? These are all very worthy goals to pursue. It would probably be helpful to reach out to my trusted friends and ask them for their assessment of how I'm doing in the relationship department. Who can you ask?

*The righteous should choose his friends carefully,
for the way of the wicked leads them astray.*
PROVERBS 12:26 NKJV

_____

_____

_____

SELF-DESTRUCTION

You cannot save everyone.
Some people are going to destroy themselves
no matter how much you try to help them.

Bryant McGill

Sad, but true. Can't really save anyone anyway. But Jesus can, and we can help to point the way. This has been God's plan all along. However, it is up to those struggling to see whether they want to rise to the challenge and get moving toward living a better and more fulfilling life.

*If you ignore criticism, you will end in poverty
and disgrace; if you accept correction, you will be honored.
It is pleasant to see dreams come true, but fools refuse to turn
from evil to attain them. Walk with the wise and become
wise; associate with fools and get in trouble.*
PROVERBS 13:18-20 NLT

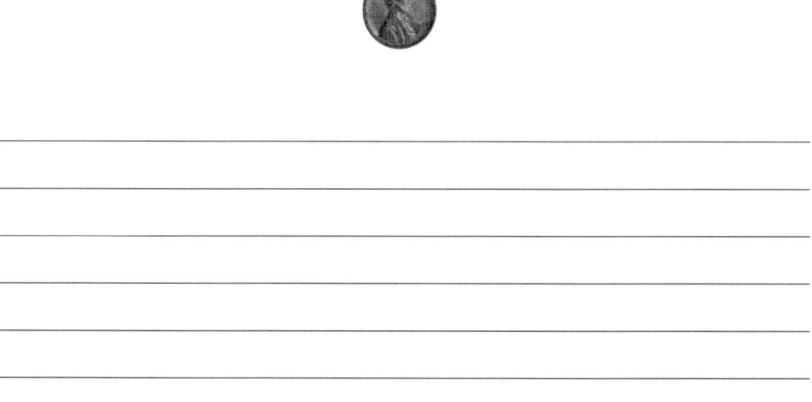

CONFRONTATION CONFLICTS

As friendships grow closer, conflict becomes more difficult to avoid. And this is often a good thing. Because the closer we get to each other's hearts, the more triggers rise into view. Because you can't fully know someone until you ignite each other's fire. You won't know if a connection has legs until it has been tested by conflict. And when it is, there is a choice to be made. Walk away in disgust or walk toward it in an effort to deepen the connection. Conflict isn't the adversary of connection. Fear of confrontation is.

Jeff Brown

Sadly, I have experienced this more than once in my lifetime. I'm usually a confronter, especially when I've had high hopes and a glimmer of promise suggesting that another person just might be in it for the long haul and desire a long, memorable, and safe friendship. Unfortunately, the "fight or flight" dynamic is way too prevalent, especially when two people are not skilled enough to fight for the relationship. It's easier to walk or run away, giving a potentially wonderful friendship no chance to develop into a priceless connection.

I don't think "walk away in disgust" is quite how I would describe a response to conflict. Unwillingness to talk about the issue is what I've experienced. The tendency has been for the person unwilling to talk about the problem to just go "ghost" and disappear. Later they may try to connect and act as if nothing ever happened. But nope, avoidant behavior doesn't cut it with me. A genuine connection requires reciprocity—an open and honest give-and-take. Eventually, the conflict must be addressed and resolved. Sweeping problems under the rug only results in lumpy rugs. Without a resolution, there is no chance of a real friendship.

*It takes a grinding wheel to sharpen a blade,
and so one person sharpens the character of another.*
PROVERBS 27:17 TPT

INTENTIONS DON'T COUNT

*The smallest act of kindness is worth
more than the greatest intention.*

Oscar Wilde

If I had a dime—scratch that—a quarter *(inflation)* for every time I've heard anyone say, *"I'm gonna _____"* and never followed through with the statement's corresponding action, I would be a wealthy woman today. On the other hand, even the smallest act of kindness doesn't go unnoticed; believe me, it is not easily forgotten. And quite often that kindness is so timely and significant that it gets shared with others. Simple acts of kindness are worth their weight in gold.

*And become useful and helpful and kind to one
another, tenderhearted (compassionate, understanding,
loving-hearted), forgiving one another [readily and freely],
as God in Christ forgave you.*
EPHESIANS 4:32 AMP

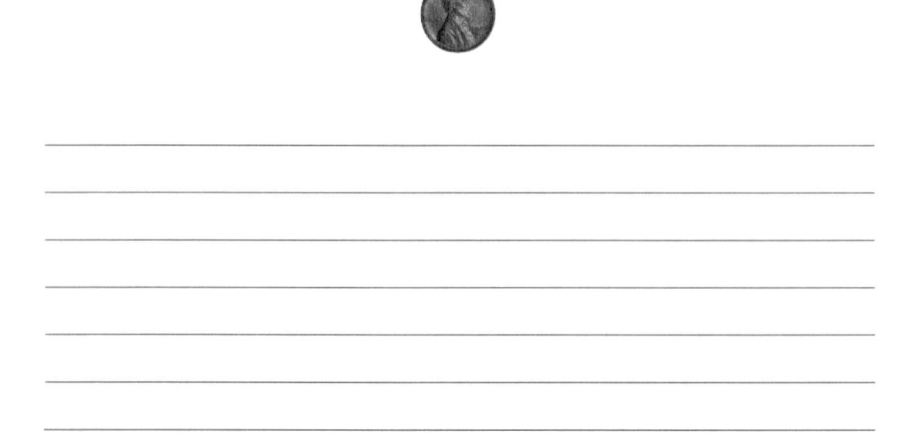

SAD BUT TRUE

Every child deserves a parent—
but not every parent deserves a child.

I'm seeing way too much going on related to the second half of this post. The real tragedy here is that the child isn't given a choice or a voice in this scenario. If you're not prepared, responsible, or mature enough to provide for all of a child's needs, don't be irresponsible by bringing a child into this world. And, for heaven's sake, don't get pregnant and terminate the child because you don't want to be bothered by having your fun life disrupted by caring for an unwanted child. There are plenty of ways available to protect against these "surprises." Children deserve so much more than that! Grow up first, then have children.

FYI—*In God's eyes, no child is ever an accident*! Don't ever say "Oops" and call your child an accident. That is psychological abuse. Your immature, self-serving behavior is responsible for your sweet, little life taking a turn that you weren't "expecting"—if you don't mind my saying it that way. Grow up first, then have children.

Behold, children are a heritage from the Lord.
The fruit of the womb is a reward.
PSALM 127:3 NKJV

Then our sons will be like plants nurtured in their youth,
our daughters like corner pillars carved to adorn a palace.
PSALM 144:12 NKJV

TWO CENTS MORE

*God-loyal people, living honest lives,
make it much easier for their children.*
PROVERBS 20:7 MSG

APPRECIATION

*Being told you are appreciated is one of the simplest
and most incredible things you can ever hear.*

My granddaughter, Hope, and I were talking about this. How hard is it to take a moment to appreciate and thank someone for going above and beyond in the workplace? The people who exhibit a great work ethic and stand in the gap for the "slackers" who often bail on their responsibilities or do a slipshod job are often taken for granted because they are always willing to get the job done. Maybe boundaries would come in handy here. A simple "No—I cannot" or "I will not"—would help bosses take notice of how their valuable employees have stepped up. This can apply to other situations as well. A simple "Thank you—I appreciate you" will go a long way.

*Whatever may be your task, work at it heartily (from the soul),
as [something done] for the Lord and not for men. Knowing [with
all certainty] that it is from the Lord [and not from men] that you will
receive the inheritance which is your [real] reward. [The One Whom]
you are actually serving [is] the Lord Christ (the Messiah).*
COLOSSIANS 3:23-24 AMP

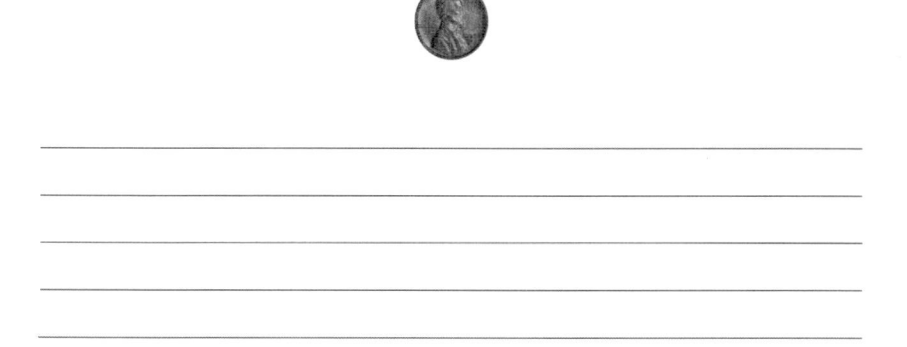

CHANGE

You can't *change* the people around you,
but
You can change the people *around you*.

This is so clever! Do you see how that works? At first glance, this post looks like a total contradiction, but it isn't at all. I emphasized a couple of key words to clarify the meaning. It's none of our business to try to change other people, even when we *know* a change must happen. But we can pick different people to hang around with when we realize *that* type of change is necessary. My friend, Jeri, tagged me and thought I would appreciate the slick message. I did! I love how the English language works and how it can add nuance to just about everything.

He who walks [as a companion] with wise men will be wise, but the companions of [conceited, dull-witted] fools [are fools themselves and] will experience harm.
PROVERBS 13:20 AMP

UPWARD MOBILITY

A true friend is someone who holds you to a higher standard.
A true friend is someone who makes you better by their presence.

Andy Andrews

The New King James version of Proverbs 27:17 says, *"As iron sharpens iron, So a man sharpens the countenance of his friend."* The Message states it differently, *"You use steel to sharpen steel, and one friend sharpens another."* Either way you look at it, true friends will make one another look better and work to be better. They really do hold one another to a higher standard. But, to make this work properly, it requires coming together and rubbing up against one another as in authentic, face-to-face interactions. It doesn't happen in an isolated vacuum. There may be times that true friends rub each other the wrong way, but that is how rough edges get knocked off, making things much better. True friends are present for one another and willing to be honest and vulnerable as they grow to higher levels.

As iron sharpens iron, so one man sharpens
[and influences] another [through discussion].
PROVERBS 27:17 AMP

WHO CAN I CALL?

*Those who help out a lot,
usually don't get helped out a lot.*

I have a very safe and loving tribe, so reciprocity is the norm. I am also aware that those who keep on giving often come up short when they have a legitimate need. My modus operandi is to keep doing what I have been called to do and trust that God has given me friends who will stand in the gap for me as needed.

I have worked diligently on being the type of safe friend described in Proverbs and Cloud and Townsend's *Safe People*. Over time, I have heard many refer to me as their "safe friend," which is a heartfelt compliment. However, as I look closely at these connections, the safety from their end has not really shown up in some cases. This saddens me, but it has helped me to tighten a smaller circle and identify the people who are genuinely in my corner no matter what. Knowing who we can count on when real needs arise is essential.

> *The godly give good advice to their friends;
> the wicked lead them astray.*
> PROVERBS 12:26 NLT

> *Don't befriend angry people or associate with hot-tempered people,
> or you will learn to be like them and endanger your soul.*
> PROVERBS 22:24-25 NLT

*Make sure you don't take things for granted and go
slack in working for the common good; share what you have
with others. God takes particular pleasure in acts of worship—
a different kind of "sacrifice"—that take place in kitchen
and workplace and on the streets.*
HEBREWS 13:16 MSG

WHO'S BEING DIFFICULT?

If someone tells you "you're being difficult,"
it may be because they're finding it difficult to manipulate you.

Arch Hades

What this post really means is that they've met their match. Pushback happens, and the manipulator's only recourse is to call you "difficult." They don't know how to argue or justify their control tactics. Use situations like this to exhibit extreme restraint. Don't be drawn into a competition when you know the truth you are standing for. It is not in your job description to give them satisfaction.

Fools have short fuses and explode all too quickly;
the prudent quietly shrug off insults.
PROVERBS 12:16 MSG

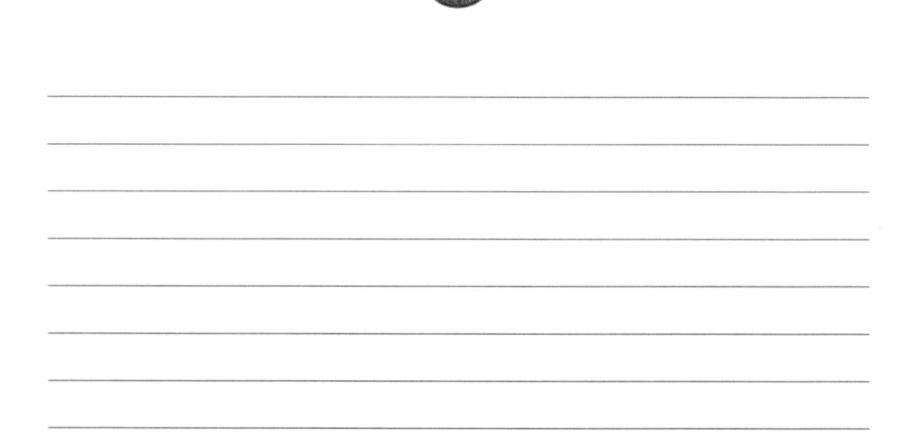

THE DIVIDING FACTOR

I no longer listen to what people say.
I watch what they do.
Behavior does not lie.

No kidding! Sometimes this can be called The Big Divide. Over the years, I have practiced watching how people conduct themselves. When I see those who spout many words without following through with the corresponding actions, I have learned that they are not likely to be dependable friends in my time of need. And at my age, I *need* people in my corner who will actually make good on what they say.

One thing I have always tried to do is say what I mean and mean what I say. The Bible speaks about this more than once, and the people who do this are people of integrity. If I tell someone I will do something, I do it—unless what I said I would do legitimately slips my mind. Yes, I suppose that does happen on occasion. But when I become aware of it, I address it. Too many times, others have told me what they're gonna do, but they simply don't deliver. Of course, they are free to do or not do whatever they choose, even after vehemently insisting they would follow-through. In cases like that, I reserve the right to cross them off my list of safe, dependable friends who will treat our relationship with reciprocity and teeter-totter trust.

The integrity of the honest keeps them on track;
the deviousness of crooks brings them to ruin.
PROVERBS 11:3 MSG

Honesty lives confident and carefree,
but Shifty is sure to be exposed.
PROVERBS 10:9 MSG

TWO CENTS MORE

"And don't say anything you don't mean. This counsel is embedded deep in our traditions. You only make things worse when you lay down a smoke screen of pious talk, saying, 'I'll pray for you,' and never doing it, or saying, 'God be with you,' and not meaning it. You don't make your words true by embellishing them with religious lace. In making your speech sound more religious, it becomes less true. Just say 'yes' and 'no.' When you manipulate words to get your own way, you go wrong.
MATTHEW 5:33-37 MSG

BLESSED

We may not have it all together,
but together we have it all.

I LOVE THIS! We are all works in progress. None of us have it all together yet. Hopefully, we will continue to learn and grow until we draw our last breath. *But,* while we are moving toward that end, let's remember to notice what's happening in our lives right now. As long as we have a circle of friends and family who love us unconditionally, we really do "have it all"—give thanks!

For it is God who works in you
both to will and to do for His good pleasure.
PHILIPPIANS 2:13 NKJV

_____
_____
_____
_____
_____
_____
_____
_____
_____
_____

TOXIC OXYGEN

Negative people need drama like it was oxygen.
Stay positive and take their breath away.

Sometimes it seems like negative people take up a lot of air space by filling it with endless accounts of high-drama. The more it can get ramped up, the better. At my age, I don't have time for that anymore. Getting the life sucked out of me—aka LIFE-O-SUCTION—by attention-seeking, dysfunctional people lost its appeal long ago. I prefer to hit it head-on and focus on solutions rather than problems. Being thankful and appreciating God's goodness in my life keeps my Joy Level high. If people choose to be negative, that's their right, but I won't be a member of their audience. My positive outlook will get air space and take their breath away. If they don't share the air, I'll take myself away.

> *Though the cherry trees don't blossom and the strawberries don't ripen, though the apples are worm-eaten and the wheat fields stunted, though the sheep pens are sheepless and the cattle barns empty, I'm singing joyful praise to God.*
> *I'm turning cart-wheels of joy to my Savior God.*
> *Counting on God's Rule to prevail, I take heart and gain strength. I run like a deer. I feel like I'm king of the mountain!*
> HABAKKUK 3:17-19 MSG

CHECK YOUR CREDENTIALS

If serving is beneath you, then leadership
is beyond you and not your calling.

The best Leader I know washed feet. Matthew 20:26-28 speaks of being a servant if you want to be great, and Jesus came to serve—not to be served. If you aspire to be a leader and refuse to have the heart of a servant, you won't be any good at it. Good leaders have willing followers. A bad leader turns around and sees no one there. Often, this type of "leader" must get behind his people and push and shove for them to do his bidding.

> *Within minutes they were bickering over who of them would end up the greatest. But Jesus intervened: "Kings like to throw their weight around and people in authority like to give themselves fancy titles. It's not going to be that way with you. Let the senior among you become like the junior; let the leader act the part of the servant."*
> LUKE 22:24-26 MSG

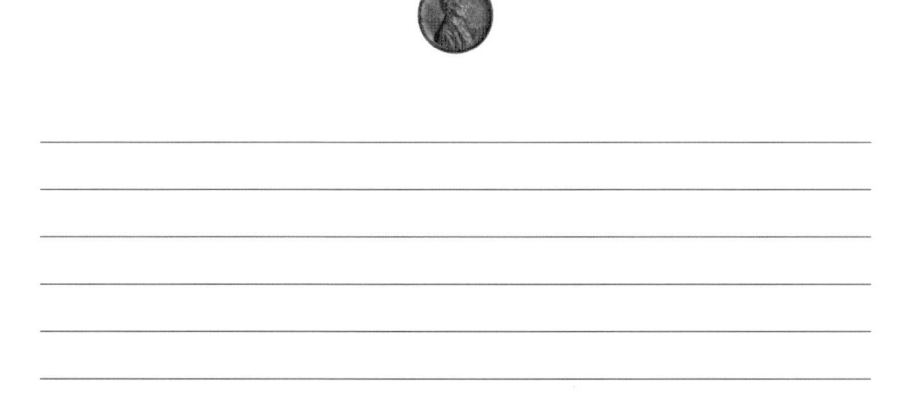

GIFT APPRECIATION

The people God put in your life are not there by accident. God put you with them on purpose. Don't take them for granted.

JCLU Forever

Over the years, I have met and spent varying amounts of time with many people. Some encounters were brief but significant; others lasted much longer—sometimes for years. So many have come and gone due to life changes, geographical relocations, and other factors. I call these people "crossroads friends." Due to modern technology, I have been able to reconnect with many of them via social media, which has been a total blessing.

God has been kind to me and brought some very safe people into my life. Many have seemed to show up quite by accident, but it's clearly evident that their presence in my life has a special purpose. I don't fully understand how or why I've been blessed with such favor, but I'm sure that it's all part of God's plan for my life. He knew I needed good people who would be there for the long haul, no matter what. My friends have added so much value to my life with their lovingkindness toward me. They have corrected me, laughed and cried with me, and helped me to grow into the person I am today. Most of all, they have encouraged me to keep God at the center of everything. Not all I've met have made that a priority. But, even with that, none of my connections have lacked significance. The lessons have been nonstop. As a die-hard people person, I am so thankful for all the people God has placed in my life.

You need to know, friends, that thanking God over and over for you is not only a pleasure; it's a must. We have to do it. Your faith is growing phenomenally; your love for each other is developing wonderfully. Why, it's only right that we give thanks.
II THESSALONIANS 1:3 MSG

SAFETY TOPS PEOPLE PLEASING

Teach girls to prioritize feeling safe
over being nice.

People pleasing can be a disaster if you're jumping through hoops trying to please the wrong people by shelving your values and integrity. Don't ignore character issues and risk losing yourself in the shuffle of "being liked" by the wrong people who turn out to be unsafe, toxic, and abusive.

The fear of man brings a snare,
but whoever trusts in the Lord shall be safe.
PROVERBS 29:25 NKJV

SPEAK UP

Life is difficult, unpredictable, and will hurt us with
disappointments and traumatic events. People will too!
This is the nature of life and with being a human being. So,
in an effort to "dodge responsibility" or maybe they truly
feel that what was said or done was okay and you're
the one with the problem, people will "act like
you hurt them" when they've hurt you.

Speak up with your truth with no
expectations of their understanding or
apologies. When you truly "get it" that this is how
some people are, it no longer matters. You feel no
need to change them or get them to see the truth.
You know the truth, so you keep on walking
your path, living your life with integrity,
and wish them well from afar.

Remember the words of Maya Angelou:
"When people show you who they are, believe them."

People who care make an effort, not an excuse.

Barb Schmidt

We all have a measure of traumatic life experiences and disappointments that contribute to our perceptions of our world. It should not be surprising that this can lead to conflicts when dealing with others as these different attitudes clash. All of it can get pretty messed up. When things go sideways, the tug of war begins. Whose fault is it when life gets messy? The Blame Game and accusations of wrongdoing can spiral out of control. Here's the vital thing to remember, though. Pray for insight and clarity about what's going on below the surface, no matter how it started or how heated the back-and-forth can get.

Whether the other person has done you wrong is beside the point. The question you must ask yourself is what you're going to do about it. You can ignore the whole thing, or you can have the courage to use your voice to express yourself. If you choose the latter option, speak calmly, without malice, explaining how you see what's happening. Allow them the same opportunity. You may not agree with one another, and you may indeed be the offended and hurt party. If that turns out to be the case, and they see nothing wrong with their behaviors, move along and live your life in a way that is pleasing to God. Don't stay stuck in hurtful places that continue to produce destructive traumas. God has better things for you, assuming you're interested in becoming all you were created to be.

Work hard so you can present yourself to God and receive His approval. Be a good worker, one who does not need to be ashamed and who correctly explains the word of truth.
II TIMOTHY 2:15 NLT

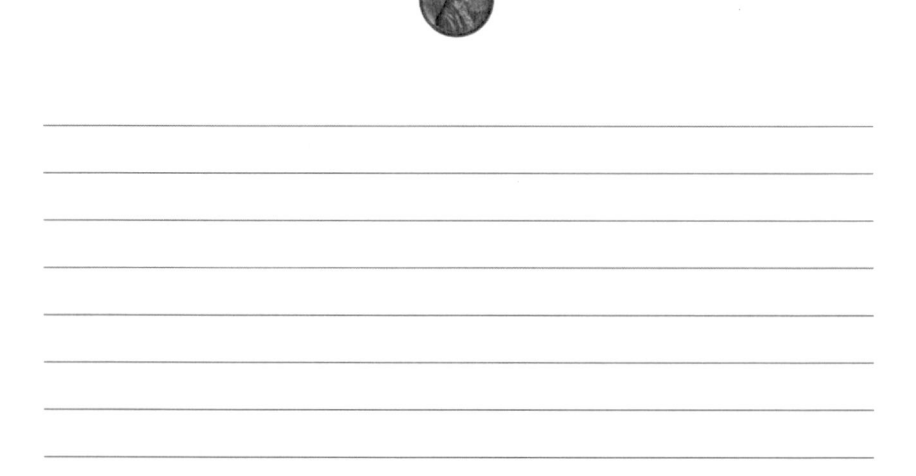

_____

_____

_____

_____

_____

_____

_____

EXCUSES KILL RELATIONSHIPS

Avoid anyone who has an excuse
every time you inform them that they've hurt you.
This means that they have no intentions of changing.

Kalen Dion

Basically, what they're saying is, "Get over it!" Well, it's not that easy to do when it keeps happening repeatedly. Maybe it's time to move on and slam the door shut on that chapter of your life. A relationship will not flourish when an empathy chip is missing. Remember these profound words from Benjamin Franklin: "Never ruin an apology with an excuse."

So then, each of us will give an account of ourselves to God.
ROMANS 14:12 NIV

A TIME FOR PAD AND PEN

When you're young, your grandparents try to tell you their history, and you don't care because it doesn't interest you at the time. Later on, you wish you had written down every word they said.

So here we are today. I didn't have much of a relationship with any of my grandparents, but times have changed. I have been involved with my grands and some great-grands at various times through the years. Whether or not they remember what I have shared with them remains to be seen. Much of what I've said is about who I am and what I consider the most important things in life. At any rate, I'm writing a lot of it down so that their memories are in black-and-white. If they hear my voice in their head, they might not remember exactly what was said or how I said it. But writing down my thoughts, beliefs, hopes, and dreams will make them less likely to be misinterpreted.

That precious memory triggers another: your honest faith— and what a rich faith it is, handed down from your grandmother Lois to your mother Eunice, and now to you!
II TIMOTHY 1:5 MSG

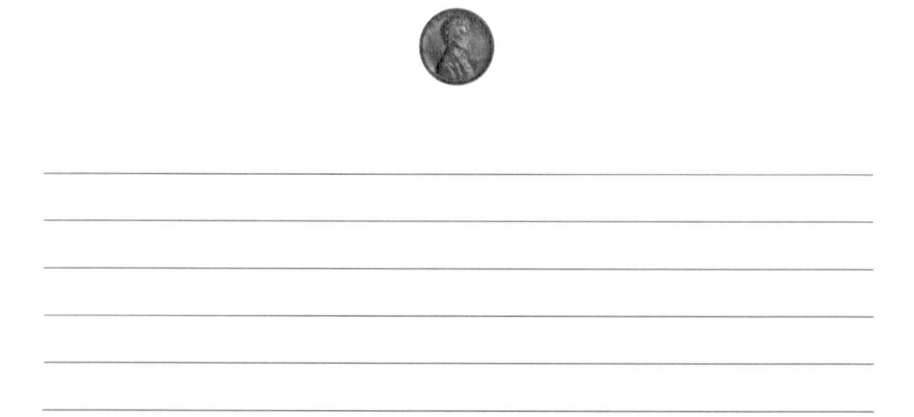

KNOCK IT OFF

Ungrateful people complain
about the one thing you haven't done for them
instead of being thankful for the
thousands of things you have done for them.

As I gave this post some thought, it occurred to me that sometimes the one complaint is all-encompassing. In a self-centered world, some just want things to *always* go their way. A sense of grandiose entitlement has replaced all thoughtful reason. What they want might be a different flavor for every day of the week, but they want what they want when they want it, with incessant complaints throughout. The bottom line is that you are not doing things the way they want them to be done, and you certainly aren't doing them fast enough. They are so honed in on what they're complaining about that they have no mind space to recall and be thankful for the things that *have* been done for them.

Personally, I would stop all interactions with people like this. Obviously, any efforts I might make to quell their complaints likely will not measure up at all. Life is too short to keep bashing my head against a wall built by ungrateful people.

Be cheerful no matter what;
pray all the time; thank God no matter what happens.
This is the way God wants you who belong to Christ Jesus to live.
I THESSALONIANS 5:16-18 MSG

TWO CENTS MORE

*Do everything without murmuring or
questioning [the providence of God], so that you
may prove yourselves to be blameless and guileless,
innocent and uncontaminated, children of God without
blemish in the midst of a [morally] crooked and [spiritually]
perverted generation, among whom you are seen as bright lights
[beacons shining out clearly] in the world [of darkness], holding
out and offering to everyone the word of life, so that in the
day of Christ I will have reason to rejoice greatly because
I did not run [my race] in vain nor labor without result.*
PHILIPPIANS 2:14-16 AMP

LOOK OUT FOR PRETENSE

People don't have to be perfect to be in our lives; in fact, perfect people don't exist. We can still enjoy healthy, great relationships if we choose the right people.
Unsafe people pretend that they have it all together; they'll apologize but won't change; they'll demand trust rather than earning it. At times, all of us manifest some "unsafe" behaviors. However, when we notice that a person is consistently unsafe, we need to be aware.

I write a lot about safe people and taking the time to develop meaningful, loving, and kind friendships. These are the connections that take time to grow in maturity and closeness. There is absolutely no person on the planet who is 100% perfect and safe, but there are people who can come close because they make their character development a matter of high priority. It's easy to differentiate a pretender from the real deal when you take the time to notice.

When I led groups that addressed relationships and how to grow, heal, and become the person God created them to be, one of my favorite books and group studies was *Safe People* by Cloud & Townsend. The information about becoming a safe person, as well as being able to identify safe people, was powerful and priceless. Picking up *Safe People* would be a significant investment and an excellent addition to your personal library.

A pretentious showy life is an empty life;
a plain and simple life is a full life.
PROVERBS 13:7 MSG

TWO CENTS MORE

Love from the center of who you are; don't fake it.
Run for dear life from evil; hold on for dear life to good.
Be good friends who love deeply; practice playing second fiddle.
ROMANS 12:9-10 MSG

MINI ME WOES

Oh boy, is it hard
trying to discipline
the you out of your child.

This would be funny if it didn't contain so much truth. The approaches we take as we parent, our attitudes, and our talk will be picked up by our children. Unfortunately, we tend to spend much time correcting and fighting to change our kids when the solution is to self-evaluate and reduce the corrosive influences partially responsible for creating the "monster" living under our roof.

> *Discipline your children while you still have the chance;*
> *indulging them destroys them.*
> PROVERBS 19:18 MSG

_____

_____

_____

_____

_____

_____

_____

_____

_____

MOTIVATED DEVIANTS

Narcissists do not pick losers. They target the best of the best.
The strongest. The smartest. The most capable.
The ones who surpass their own level.
So if you happen to have a narcissist in your life,
take a moment to think about the reality of that.
You're stronger than them. You're smarter than them.
You're a survivor. And they know it.
They NEED you, not the other way around.

NARCISSISM 101: Narcissists are motivated deviants who will do whatever it takes to latch on to someone who has everything that they lack. How sick is that? Here's the thing—the victim doesn't realize they've been targeted and groomed for their desired attributes because they are unaware they have any. They lack self-esteem and feel blessed to be "picked" by Mr./Ms. Wonderful until reality sets in. They *were* most definitely picked with an ulterior motive, but as time goes by, they begin to get picked apart. They get blamed for everything that goes wrong, and the self-esteem erosion continues. The victim starts to believe that *everything* is their fault.

It may take a village of people who know what they're doing to help convince someone subjected to this kind of abuse to walk away—no, better yet, run away. But once the victim learns that they really do have note-worthy attributes, even though beaten down and dormant for a season, they can begin resurrecting and capitalizing on them. As they begin walking tall, strong, and full of confidence, they can better find and trust the exact people who will value and celebrate them.

He who loves strife and is quarrelsome loves transgression and involves himself in guilt; he who raises high his gateway and is boastful and arrogant invites destruction.
PROVERBS 17:19 AMP

MAKE THEIR DAY

*You know you've grown
when you truly care about the impact
your words and deeds have on others.*

An empathy chip must be well-developed when interacting with others. Your impact on people with your words and actions can make or break their day. More importantly, how you feel about your interactions with others will indicate your maturity level and your heart toward them. Always be mindful of how other people are impacted by your presence in their life. It doesn't take long for others to know if you genuinely care about them. Take a good look inside yourself and ask, "Do I care for this person like Christ does?"

*Let me give you a new command: Love one another.
In the same way I loved you, you love one another.
This is how everyone will recognize that you are my disciples—
when they see the love you have for each other.*
JOHN 13:34-35 MSG

BLACK HOLES

Who gives you energy and who drains you?

Make sure you maximize the time with the former and minimize the latter. It's not all that simple because we are all "fixers". That is, you spend way too much time trying to repair, help or heal someone who has little interest in change and just likes to be with you because you are kind and a good listener. Basically, you are their antidepressant for a few hours, and then all the value is gone. Be intentional about being with people who, when you leave your conversation with them, you feel like "you" again: happier, challenged, more at peace.

Life is too short to invest in a lot of black holes.
You need the right people to keep you growing and healthy.

Dr. John Townsend

Avoid falling into the trap of LIFE-O-SUCTION. Seek out the kind of people who will fill up your love tank. Some of my friends are so kind and such good listeners, but sometimes their desire to help and just "be there" for others is fraught with frustration when it appears that nothing will ever change.

Life is too short to fritter away your precious time with people who are bound and determined to continue going down destructive paths. Of course, it *is* their right to do it, but you don't have to make the trip with them. You cannot change them and get them to think and behave differently, no matter how much time you spend with them and how hard you try. I realize you want a better life for them so badly that you can taste it, but what they choose to do with your wise counsel is totally on them.

To conclude, that means that the time will come when you've done enough and spent enough time with people who drain the life out of you, so—ya gotta know when to hold 'em, know when to fold 'em, know when to walk away, and know when to run. Focus on building a solid alliance with safe, loving people who will speak your language and be there for them for the long haul. Safe people will reciprocate.

Whoever loves instruction and correction loves knowledge,
but he who hates reproof is like a brute beast,
stupid and indiscriminating.
PROVERBS 12:1 AMP

PSEUDO-LOVE

The drugs never loved you,
and neither did the people giving them to you.

Real love is *never* destructive, but addictive drugs are—and they can kill. To someone whose thinking is all messed up, they might want to believe that their "associates," the dealers, really care about them. They may even say they love you, but, truth be told, they love your business, your money, and your dependence on them. As long as you crave what they have to offer, their "business" will flourish—but you won't. People who honestly love you will want the best for you—and drugs ain't it! Your dealers are providing you with lethal doses of life-stealers; this runs counter to love and is pure destruction.

The thief comes only in order to steal and kill and destroy.
I came that they may have and enjoy life, and have it in
abundance (to the full, till it overflows).
JOHN 10:10 AMP

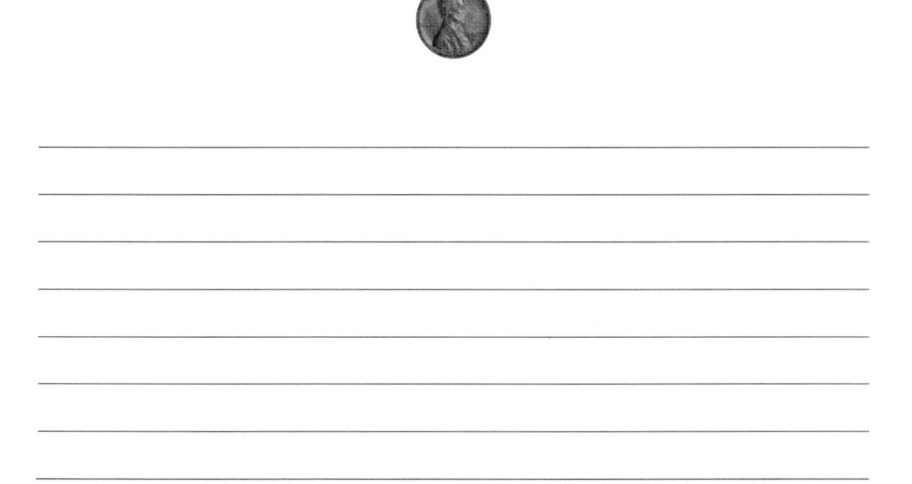

TEACHING OPPORTUNITIES

*Fathers, be your daughter's first love.
Open doors for her, pull her seat out, and talk to and treat her
with the utmost respect. Set expectations on how a man should
treat a lady and she will never settle for anything less.*

Hey fathers—how about bringing old-fashioned chivalry and manners back into practice? Even if you have never done these things for the mother of your children—or you've never done it period—it's time to start. If you have sons, show them how to treat their future girlfriends. Be their role model. Your daughters must see examples of how their future boyfriends should treat them. Anything less than good manners and respect won't fly. And, if your daughter has a brother, you can bet the farm that he will be eyeballing the guy who takes a shine to her. As fathers step up and focus on creating a safe and respectful atmosphere, they will significantly improve their children's relationship success. Show your children what a real man with manners looks like.

*Fathers, do not irritate and provoke your children to anger
[do not exasperate them to resentment]; but rear them
[tenderly] in the training and discipline and the
counsel and admonition of the Lord.*
EPHESIANS 6:4 AMP

_____
_____
_____

MAKE MEMORIES

In January of 2018, I was waiting for my granddaughter, Hope, to get out of class, and nostalgia hit. I remembered when my mom and I would wash the dishes together after dinner in the 1950s and 60s, long before dishwashers became commonplace. We sang a lot, and I learned to harmonize as I did my chores at the kitchen sink. As I sat reminiscing, two songs came to mind. I started humming and tapping my toe. I Googled both songs, and there they were! *Chickory Chick Chala Chala* and *The King of the Cannibal Islands.* They were crazy, fun kid songs. I loved having this special memory of Mom and me making music while doing a mundane chore.

Rowgo

Fast forward to January of 2022. As it happens, I have recently been thinking about the songs I'd like to share with my great-grands while I'm still here, and these two nonsensical songs made the list. Of course, there are bunches more. I don't want to forget *Jesus Loves Me, Jesus Loves the Little Children,* and many other Sunday School and scripture songs that are no longer taught or sung today.

Last week, my grandson, Steve, texted me that he sang *Bushel and a Peck* for his daughter Scarlet's bedtime song. As he sang, she kept saying, "Oma—Oma." That's her name for me. Now that warmed the cockles of my heart, because I'd only sung this song to her twice and my almost 2-year-old great-grand remembered who first sang it to her.

It still amazes me that my mom and I sang together over 70 years ago. I can't wait to make similar memories by adding more songs to the list with Scarlet and the rest of the great-grands. It might not seem like a big deal, but it really is. It certainly was to Scarlet! If I can fondly remember priceless times singing with my mom, maybe my precious littles will remember singing songs with their Oma. I know my kids and grandkids will not forget the many times we put our voices and instruments together to make beautiful music. The beat goes on—

> *Speak out to one another in psalms and hymns and spiritual songs, offering praise with voices [and instruments] and making melody with all your heart to the Lord.*
> EPHESIANS 5:19 AMP

> *I will sing to the Lord as long as I live.*
> *I will sing praise to my God while I have my being.*
> PSALM 104:33 NKJV

HOLD ONTO THE STRAW

You can't keep getting mad at people for sucking the life out of you if you keep on giving them the straw.

LIFE-O-SUCTION ALERT! What is it about boundaries that so many people don't understand? If they invite whatever their "straw" is, they bear a portion of the responsibility for being rendered incapacitated, sucked dry, smothered, and unable to breathe.

Don't be a complicit participant!

> *Make a careful exploration of who you are and the work you have been given, and then sink yourself into that. Don't be impressed with yourself. Don't compare yourself with others. Each of you must take responsibility for doing the creative best you can with your own life.*
> GALATIANS 6:4-5 MSG

TAKE YOUR VOICE ELSEWHERE

*Stay away from people who think you're arguing
every time you're trying to express yourself.*

There are people in the world who are bound and determined to be offended by just about everything, especially if it is in direct opposition to their viewpoint. Trying to have a civil discussion and talk about topics you feel are important may create a significant response. Sometimes it's just easier to go into a place of avoidance. Even if you say that you don't want to argue and create bad feelings, somebody is likely to say "but—" and proceed to pursue the subject. Sometimes the people accusing you of being argumentative instigate the disagreement in the first place. On the other hand, safe people appreciate hearing your point of view, even if they disagree with it. Nurture these relationships because these people care about you and are absolutely OK with you feeling safe enough to express yourself freely.

*Refuse to get involved in inane discussions;
they always end up in fights. God's servant must not be
argumentative, but a gentle listener and a teacher who keeps cool,
working firmly but patiently with those who refuse to obey.*
II Timothy 2:23-24 MSG

OFFENSES GALORE

Truth does not mind being questioned.
A lie does not like being challenged.

Does this explain why so many people are walking around highly offended by others? Asking questions and requiring clarification about anything is a sign of an inquiring mind wanting to learn, mature, and expand in knowledge and wisdom. If anyone is less than truthful and feeling vulnerable, questions will feel like an inquisition or an all-out attack. This is likely to provoke anger and a fair amount of pushback. When that happens, it's easy to tell that the questions have hit a nerve—but stand confidently on truth, because lies must be confronted and challenged.

For the time is coming when [people] will not tolerate (endure) sound and wholesome instruction, but, having ears itching [for something pleasing and gratifying], they will gather to themselves one teacher after another to a considerable number, chosen to satisfy their own liking and to foster the errors they hold. And will turn aside from hearing the truth and wander off into myths and man-made fictions.
II Timothy 4:3-4 AMP

_____
_____
_____
_____

TWO CENTS MORE

RUNNING STOP SIGNS

It can be one of the most difficult things in the world to set a boundary with someone in your inner circle who is breaking your heart with their choices. But if you want to protect your relationship with that person, you must be powerful enough to hold up your commitment to pursue the standard of respect in your interactions.

Danny Silk

On the subject of boundaries, God has set them from the very beginning, and as His kids, we would be wise to follow His lead. We are told to stand firm—yes means yes, and no means no. Being double-minded points to instability. It is tough to confront the choices of loved ones, but unconditional love dictates how important it is to hold fast to God's standards.

> *Just say "yes" and "no."*
> *When you manipulate words to get your own way, you go wrong.*
> MATTHEW 5:37 MSG

I have noticed more and more lately how boundaries set by parents are slip-sliding away. They make emphatic statements to their kids that something is going to or not going to happen if _____ *(fill in the blank)*. The kids push the set limits or boundaries, and the parent goes into reset mode rather than following through with what they said originally.

God's boundaries are forever unchanging—He means what He says. So when parents try to teach kids that they can count on God and that He is Truth and doesn't lie, the kids look back at how their parents have been their earthly example of "truth" to them. When their parents have told them something, they could count on it—right? It depends on how consistently the boundaries are managed. Don't say it and set it unless you're prepared to follow through and do it. If the kids can't count on their parents to be truthful with them, how then will they trust that their heavenly Father can be counted on to always speak the truth and deliver on what He says He will do?

> *The instructions of the Lord are perfect, reviving the soul.*
> *The decrees of the Lord are trustworthy, making wise the simple.*
> *The commandments of the Lord are right, bringing joy to the heart.*
> *The commands of the Lord are clear, giving insight for living.*
> PSALM 19:7-8 NLT

It is time to follow through by setting reasonable boundaries and standing firm. Be a person of character who can be trusted to say what you mean and mean what you say. This applies to *all* people—not just parents and kids.

My "two cents" on Danny Silk's post wandered into the parent/child arena because I have observed significant boundary violations in these relationships. However, I can quickly go back to Danny's emphasis and address the heartbreaking aspects that occur when people very close to us make devastating and damaging choices. Once again, boundaries are essential to develop and enforce to maintain a life of integrity—even when it involves the people in our inner circle.

Setting boundaries with close friends and family is not always going to be understood or accepted, but that's their problem—not ours. Living a life to honor God, His commands, and His purposes for us will not always be popular or welcomed with open arms, but His way will always trump mortal thinking. To acquiesce to erroneous choices made by loved ones will only enable them to continue down the same destructive path.

> *And we are instructed to turn from godless living and sinful pleasures. We should live in the evil world with wisdom, righteousness, and devotion to God.*
> TITUS 2:12 NLT

Putting up a STOP sign might just help them understand that they need to make a U-turn, and look for a better, healthier, and safer destination. However, there is no guarantee that they will choose to do anything other than run that STOP sign and continue down the same destructive road. If they make that choice, we don't have to be passengers along for that ride. When we have set our boundaries, and they have been ignored, we need to hop off.

> *The land you have given me is a pleasant land.*
> *What a wonderful inheritance! I will bless the Lord who guides me;*
> *even at night my heart instructs me. I know the Lord is always with*
> *me. I will not be shaken, for he is right beside me. No wonder my*
> *heart is glad, and I rejoice. My body rests in safety.*
> PSALM 16:6-9 NLT

A TOXIC EQUATION

*If you tell a child that an abusive parent
"really does love them,"
then how are you going to tell a teenager
that abuse is not love?*

Paula Goodwin

Defend Survivors.org

THIS IS THE $64,000 QUESTION! If a child has grown up being told that their abusive parent "really does love them," how in the world will they ever learn what real love looks like? They may even develop conflicting versions of what real love looks like based on the training they received in the "safety" of their home. Some might say that the parents did the best they could because they were abused as children and their parents told them they were loved. Really? Imagine how the parents felt as youngsters. It cannot have been a pleasant upbringing, and I'll bet they said they would never be abusive to their kids. And yet, very often, history repeats itself with the parents living what they've learned. They may get mad and say they can't help it, even blaming their kids for "making them" say and do abusive things to them. Often, the parents are sorry for what they did, but the abuse continues. Learned behaviors from the past could be a reason for the abuse, but it's never an excuse.

Eventually, the kids grow up and enter into their own relationships, raising the next generation. Hopefully, they will get help to heal from the wounds—external, but especially internal—that they suffered at the hands of their "loving" parents. Real love does not intentionally inflict pain of any kind upon others—physical, emotional, or psychological. Abusive dating, parenting, and marital practices are *NOT OK—EVER!* All relationships must be safe and loving. Abuse in any form is NOT love!

*Love is patient and kind.
Love is not jealous or boastful or proud or rude.
It does not demand its own way. It is not irritable, and
it keeps no record of being wronged. It does not rejoice
about injustice but rejoices whenever the truth wins out.
Love never gives up, never loses faith, is always hopeful,
and endures through every circumstance.*
I Corinthians 13:4-7 NLT

LOOK FOR THE MAIN MESSAGES

Six Little Stories

Once all villagers decided to pray for rain.
On the day of prayer, all the people gathered,
but only one boy came with an umbrella. That is faith.

When you throw babies in the air,
they laugh because they know you will catch them. That is trust.

Every night we go to bed without any assurance of being
alive the next morning, but we still set alarms to wake up. That is hope.

We plan big things for tomorrow
in spite of zero knowledge of the future. That is confidence.

We see the world suffering,
but still, we get married and have children. That is love.

On an old man's shirt had a sentence written on it:
"I am not 80 years old; I am sweet 16 with 64 years of experience."
That is attitude.

Wow! Just about all of us have done some of these things, but we probably haven't readily come up with a single word that our actions have demonstrated. We tend to live our lives on automatic without giving a thought about the faith, trust, hope, confidence, love, and attitudes that we activate by our very actions.

I love these meaningful little stories—they remind me to take a moment to think about what is driving me to do what I do. Everything I do has a purpose under heaven.

TWO CENTS MORE

*Steep your life in God-reality, God-initiative,
God-provisions. Don't worry about missing out.
You'll find all your everyday human concerns will be met.*
MATTHEW 6:33 MSG

SAFETY NETS

*Rescuing someone who continues to make
poor choices is not called love. It's called enabling.
Stop enabling and refuse to be a safety net, so that they can grow up.*

You might "mean well," but it doesn't help. There will likely come a time when you realize your good intentions and help have worn you out while the person you have repeatedly rescued is stuck and not getting any better. They might have also developed a sense of entitlement and expected you to jump to their rescue when trouble came—as it always seemed to return. Unfortunately, you became a willing enabler and complicit in the problem. By bailing them out of their trouble time after time, you've robbed them of any initiative to learn how to take care of themselves. Once you've had enough and say "No more," they may become angry or even decry that not helping them isn't very loving. Although this may be a valid opinion from their perspective, it is still the best thing you can do for them—and yourself. Setting healthy boundaries causes you to "stay in your own yard," and they will be allowed to learn how to grow up and take care of their "side of the fence."

> *Let me give you some good advice; I'm looking you in the eye and giving it to you straight: "Don't be ornery like a horse or mule that needs bit and bridle to stay on track."*
> PSALM 32:8-9 MSG

> *Stay calm; mind your own business; do your own job. You've heard all this from us before, but a reminder never hurts. We want you living in a way that will command the respect of outsiders, not lying around sponging off your friends.*
> II THESSALONIANS 4:11-12 MSG

TWO CENTS MORE

A man of great anger will bear the penalty [for his quick temper and lack of self-control]; for if you rescue him [and do not let him learn from the consequences of his action], you will only have to rescue him over and over again.
PROVERBS 19:19 AMP

FUNNY—NOT FUNNY

I just discovered my age group! I am a Seenager (senior teenager).

I have everything that I wanted as a teenager, only 55-60 years later. I don't have to go to school or work. I get an allowance every month. I have my own pad. I don't have a curfew. I have a driver's license and my own car.

I have ID that gets me into bars and the wine store. I like the wine store best. The people I hang around with are not scared of getting pregnant, they aren't scared of anything, they have been blessed to live this long, why be scared? And I don't have acne. Life is Good!

Also, you will feel much more intelligent after reading this, if you are a Seenager. Brains of older people are slow because they know so much. People do not decline mentally with age; it just takes them longer to recall facts because they have more information in their brains. Scientists believe this also makes you hard of hearing as it puts pressure on your inner ear.

Also, older people often go to another room to get something and when they get there, they stand there wondering what they came for. It is NOT a memory problem; it is nature's way of making older people do more exercise.

SO THERE!

What could I possibly say about this? Well—you know me—there are a few things. My "pad" heats up when I plug it in. Acne makes a visit every now and then. It was nice to have that "hearing problem" cleared up. Wine is not at the top of my shopping list. And finally, unfortunately, many of the seenagers I have met are fearful about many things—especially the upcoming unknowns. I want to encourage you to live without fear and know what your future looks like by spending time with the One who can actually see it.

TWO CENTS MORE

*Show respect to the aged; honor the presence of an elder;
fear your God, I am God.*
LEVITICUS 19:32 MSG

SET THE BAR HIGH

*A woman should never invest in a relationship
she wouldn't want for her daughter, nor allow any man
to treat her in a way she would scold her son for.*

Quotes 'n Thoughts

As a noticer of many things, I have observed too many women of all ages willing to sell themselves short and settle for much less than they would *ever* wish on their own kids—even on days that the kids are so "bad" that they're almost ready to give them away. If parents really want the best for their kids, and by and large, they do, why don't they want and value the same thing for themselves?

What moms choose to do and how they do it is setting an example for their kids to follow. Don't be surprised when the example their role models have lived in front of them becomes how they choose to live their lives. Moms may have said "Don't do as I do; do as I say," many times, but kids are savvy and will hear and recognize double messages; they are more likely to repeat the behaviors they have observed rather than heeding the message they have heard. Break the cycle! Your kids deserve better—and so do you!

> *Summing it all up, friends, I'd say you'll do best by filling your minds and meditating on things true, noble, reputable, authentic, compelling, gracious—the best, not the worst; the beautiful, not the ugly; things to praise, not things to curse. Put into practice what you learned from me, what you heard and saw and realized. Do that, and God, who makes everything work together, will work you into his most excellent harmonies.*
> PHILIPPIANS 4:8-9 MSG

TWO CENTS MORE

*Here is a simple, rule-of-thumb guide for behavior:
Ask yourself what you want people to do for you,
then grab the initiative and do it for them.
Add up God's Law and Prophets
and this is what you get.*
MATTHEW 7:12 MSG

MY FAVORITE HOME

What's your favorite place?
I don't have a favorite place.
I have my favorite people.
And whenever I'm with my favorite people,
it becomes my favorite place.

Niyaz Ahemad

Home is where the heart is—or so I've heard. If somebody asked me which home I lived in over my lifetime was my favorite, I would identify the home where I currently reside. "This one!" Wherever I am at any given time is my favorite place. It doesn't matter if it's a grand estate, a tiny house, a travel trailer, or an apartment. Being around my favorite people tends to be where I get the most enjoyment out of life, and my love tank gets filled to overflowing. Wherever I live, I will always make a concentrated effort to welcome friends who bring their special brand of love and goodness with them. They warm the cockles of my heart. So *my* home—my *favorite* home—will always be where my *heart* is. My heart is filled with my favorite people.

The place where your treasure is, is the place you will
most want to be, and end up being.
MATTHEW 6:21 MSG

CONNECTING IN PERSON

> When people have a healthy and honest friendship, Facebook is a great way to stay in touch because it is so convenient and efficient. The other side is true as well. If a relationship is struggling, it's hard to fix it over digital connections. Anything negative or confrontational seems much worse when you read it. I tell people to not confront each other digitally at all, as it is easy for the responder to feel attacked or judged. Facebook is a way to connect, but face-to-face has not yet been matched in relationships. It's important to connect with friends in person.
>
> Dr. John Townsend

Preach it, Dr. Townsend—my sentiments exactly! I enjoy Facebook for many reasons: keeping in touch with distant friends, staying connected to friends who I don't see often enough, putting some quirky humor and grammar pet peeves out there, sharing my heart, and hopefully, encouraging my friends as God prompts me to do so. However, nothing will ever take the place of face-to-face connections—which, by the way, is God's best plan.

Airing dirty laundry, anger, bitterness, perceived wrongs, attention-seeking drama, and unforgiving rants on Facebook says much about the writer's character. There is enough negativity in the world already. Rather than airing perceived wrongs done to you for all the world to see, it's time to grow up and actively work to resolve issues face-to-face. Remember, most readers aren't invested in these grievances anyway and wonder why someone would expose their problems and angst so indiscriminately. Engaging in this behavior undercuts your ability to be seen as a reliable, mature, and safe person for others. It's your choice. But please, keep it between yourself and the one stirring up so much emotional drama in your life. The rest of us are already dealing with our own stuff. Our plates are full. *Enough already!*

Let's adhere to what Thumper always said—"If you can't say nuffin nice, don't say nuffin at all." Let's build one another up and work to develop authentic relationships face-to-face whenever possible. Facebook and other social media sites have their positives, but they have allowed people to avoid direct connections and stay relatively isolated. God is relational, with Christ setting the example of how we relate to one another—honestly, directly, lovingly, and yes, in person. When we do it His way, we will reap the benefits of meaningful and deep friendships.

> *Be gracious in your speech. The goal is to bring out the best in others in a conversation, not put them down, not cut them out.*
> COLOSSIANS 4:6 MSG

BIRDS OF A FEATHER

*The fastest way to change yourself is to hang out with
people who are already the way you want to be.*

Reid Hoffman

This is a great way to start, but change doesn't happen by osmosis. It takes recognition and ownership of things that need to change, responsible action, and honest-to-goodness hard work. But, for sure, hang out with the people who will encourage you and show you how it's done. They're the best role models and cheerleaders who will help you reach your goals.

If you surround yourself with those who bring you closer to God, you will gain nourishment from spiritual soul food. Focus on a steady, healthy diet of emotional, psychological, and spiritual nutrition that will feed, build, grow, and satisfy your craving for "soul" food. Doing otherwise is counterproductive and holds little promise for a bright future. The ultimate goal is to become who you were created to be. Develop safe, mature friends who have learned a thing or two and are already walking on that stable path and become travel buddies.

*Pattern yourselves after me [follow my example],
as I imitate and follow Christ (the Messiah).*
I CORINTHIANS 11:1 AMP

READY OR NOT...

You can't make somebody be ready for what you are ready for,
and you are not obligated to wait around for them to make up their mind.

Chris Sain Jr.

Waiting for someone else to come alongside you may result in a missed opportunity for growth and blessings—especially if the other person doesn't feel the need or has no intention to mature and grow with you. This would indicate a lack of commitment to building an authentic and healthy relationship. It may have looked promising early on, but over time it may have pointed out an unsafe trait or two in the connection. Maybe a switch was flipped out of the blue without warning. Perhaps the other person realized they weren't up for the challenge to match your growth, and they got scared and bailed. Either way, keep doing what you know in your heart is the right thing. The safe people who are ready, willing, and able to pursue their own growth will appreciate your desire to move on and will join you on your journey.

*No prolonged infancies among us, please.
We'll not tolerate babes in the woods, small children who are easy
prey for predators. God wants us to grow up, to know the whole truth
and tell it in love—like Christ in everything.*
EPHESIANS 4:14-15 MSG

_____
_____
_____

AVOID TOXIC EMPATHY

*Empathy that comforts people in their dysfunction
instead of calling them out of it is not Christlike.
Empathy not rooted in honesty can cripple a person,
rather than help a person. If you can't speak the truth to
someone, sometimes it's best not to speak at all.*

Empathy—real, legitimate empathy—requires being truthful. Otherwise, it's just manipulation and the disingenuous controlling of the emotions of others. Telling the unadulterated truth as lovingly as possible can be difficult, but it is the kindest thing you can do in the long run. The book of Proverbs encourages this principled behavior in several passages. To be truthful with others, even when it's hard, is the epitome of unconditional love.

I understand why people just go silent and do not speak about things that should be confronted. It's a preference to avoid anger, pushback, and hurt feelings. Sometimes it feels easier to say, "Fine—whatever!" However, I'm getting more fearless about this because I'm too old to miss opportunities to speak up. This is especially true when my silence could contribute to someone missing out on becoming the person God created them to be. I *will* speak up as lovingly as possible because I don't want to leave anything unsaid before I'm out of here. Because I love you, I will say some things that may ruffle your feathers and challenge you to consider changing a toxic mindset to allow growth. I'm not often going to choose silence when the truth has the potential to break down prison doors never meant to hold us.

And you will know the truth, and the truth will set you free.
JOHN 8:32 NLT

*...Then we will no longer be immature like children.
We won't be tossed and blown about by every wind of new teaching.
We will not be influenced when people try to trick us with lies so
clever they sound like the truth. Instead, we will speak
the truth in love, growing in every way more and more
like Christ, who is the head of his body, the church.*
EPHESIANS 4:14-15 NLT

HOME SCHOOLING FOR REAL

Children hear everything you say.
And they mimic everything you do.
Give them a good example.

Sometimes parents get frustrated and angry about what their kids say and do, but maybe this post explains why. They learn to live what they experience in life. So, if you're the grownup in the home, *be one!* Set the tone. When your kids are young, you're setting the example of how to speak and act more than anyone else because they're spending the lion's share of their time with you. Children are highly influenced by their surroundings, and studies have shown that a significant percentage of what they will learn about life occurs in their first five years. This isn't related to book knowledge—math, history, science, etc.—but rather to character issues such as trust, compassion, honesty, loyalty, genuine love, and safety. Parents often underestimate the impact they have on their younger children. *Everything* they do matters. The trajectory of a child's life highly depends upon the lessons spoken and exhibited in the home.

Train up a child in the way he should go [and in keeping with his individual gift or bent], and when he is old he will not depart from it.
PROVERBS 22:6 AMP

MUM'S NOTE

Good morning Sugar,

I have taken your PS3 controllers hostage—
- Clean your room—to *my* standard, not yours.
- Make your bed—properly! If you see lumps, strip it back and start again.
- Put your dirty clothes *in* the washing basket. *Not* next to it or on top of it!
- Put your clean clothes away where they belong! *Not* where you feel like shoving them.
- Have a shower and *wash your hair!*
- Hang your wet towel on the towel rack neatly to dry. (It won't ever dry properly in a heap on your bedroom floor)

And in return, I will tell you the location of your controllers.

Love, Mum

To all frustrated moms: This is a teachable moment that could last a lifetime if pursued consistently. Setting clear boundaries and expectations with rewards or consequences will help to eradicate a sense of entitlement in your kids. Take control of the controllers. Ask yourself—who is in control? The parent or the child?

Too often, a parent has repeatedly told their kids to do something, only to have their statements ignored. Often, parents wind up disgusted, throwing their hands up in the air, huffing and puffing, "Never mind—I'll do it myself!" We've all done it at one time or another, haven't we? Well, there you go! The training for a sense of entitlement has begun. This must stop!

It's time to deliberately assess what's happening and take immediate action. Parents, own how you might have contributed to the problem and address the way you deal with these dysfunctional household scenarios. Whether it feels like it at first or not, changing the "dance" of how things are handled in the home will slowly show promise. The kids begin learning to take responsibility for their own lives, and when turned loose in the world, they will have the tools to take proper care of themselves with maturity. Clear expectations and consistent boundaries help to float their relationship boats for a lifetime.

> *Make a careful exploration of who you are and the work you have been given, and then sink yourself into that. Don't be impressed with yourself. Don't compare yourself with others. Each of you must take responsibility for doing the creative best you can with your own life. Be very sure now, you who have been trained to a self-sufficient maturity, that you enter into a generous common life with those who have trained you, sharing all the good things that you have and experience.*
> GALATIANS 6:4-6 MSG

LIVE LIFE WITH GUSTO

Dear Ones -

This is a line my 73 year-old mother said to me the other day, while she was issuing a gentle warning not to fall into the trap of letting your life get smaller as you get older.

She was talking about how frustrating she finds it that—somewhere around the age of 50 or 60—she watched as so many of her peers stopped making goals and long-term plans for adventure and exploration in their lives. Instead, they began shutting down and making their lives smaller and their minds smaller too. She got so weary of listening to them making self-deprecating jokes about how old they were, how much their bodies hurt, and how bad their hearing and eyesight was getting. She felt they had surrendered to age far, far, far too soon. My mom said, "Nothing is more frustrating to me than listening to people who are still vital saying, 'Well, at our age, you have to be careful.'"

No. She begs to differ. As you get older, there is no more time to be careful, and no more *reason* to be careful—at least as my mom sees it. Instead, this is the time to seize as much life and joy and adventure and learning and novelty as you possibly can. As my mom said, "I hate seeing people slide themselves into the grave far before their time. Death will come when it comes—but it's crazy to sit around waiting for it. If you're not dead yet, you're not done yet."

My mom thinks that everyone should have a five-year plan for their lives, and also a ten-year plan, and a twenty-year plan—and that every few years you have to revisit your plans to see if your goals and aspirations have changed—and that you should never stop making these plans, even as you age. (Especially as you age!) She has shared with me the travel she wants to do in the next 20 years, the work she wants to finish, the projects she wants to begin, the cultures she wants to explore, the people she wants to enjoy, and her fitness goals. It's inspiring.

I have heard people speak of their lives as if they were finished at 30, done at 40, washed up at 50, too late to start over at 60, no more chances at 70. But are you still here? Then you aren't done yet. Don't make your life smaller as the years pass. If it's time to start over, then it's time to start over. If you aren't where you planned to be, then it's time to make a new plan.

Today I ask you all to share the most inspiring stories you know (from your own life or the lives of others) about people who refused to be done yet, because they aren't done yet.

Rise up, everyone, and keep rising. We are still here. There is much to be done and enjoyed. Let's go. *Onward!*

LG

I feel more alive at Level 78 than I have in my entire life! It has taken on more meaning now than ever before. There is more excitement and relevance as I continue learning and growing. I am more passionate about the things that matter to me, and as each day passes, I feel the urgency to connect, share, and encourage others to live life with gusto and become all they were created to be.

Grandma Moses started painting when she was 78, so I feel like I'm in pretty good company since publishing the first book of this series. I told my kids I didn't want to leave anything significant unsaid, so I've been tying up loose ends and writing them all down. My greatest desires and fervent prayers are that the priceless connections I have made with my family and friends will continue after our earth suits wear out and we relocate to heaven.

Live life like you mean it—appreciate the gift and continue to find your purpose. We all have an assignment to complete while we are still here. You might ask, "What *is* that assignment?" For starters, while you are still breathing, Psalm 150:6 says, *"Let everything that has breath praise the Lord. Praise the Lord!"* The Bible has countless instructions to help along the way. Continue to live your life to the fullest. Follow God's guidance and reap the benefits here and for all eternity. Selah!

> *Therefore you shall be careful to do as the Lord your God has commanded you; you shall not turn aside to the right or to the left. You shall walk in all the ways which the Lord your God has commanded you, that you may live and that it may be well with you, and that you may prolong your days in the land which you shall possess.*
> DEUTERONOMY 5:32-33 NKJV

3

MORE FOCUSED UPWARD

READ THE INSTRUCTIONS

I've heard Christians called "Bible thumpers," "Jesus freaks," and much worse over the years. These characterizations are usually spoken disdainfully or in mocking tones.

Rowgo

Whenever I purchase something that requires some assembly or instructions for operation, I tend to read the directions and follow them before screwing it up altogether. My parents taught me that I didn't know everything and that I needed to be well-informed and read the directions before launching out on doing anything I knew nothing about.

I am not ashamed to admit that I often go to the Instruction Manual to find out if I am getting the most out of what was purchased for me. Here's the kicker—I didn't even have to buy it. It was a gift of mercy and grace purchased for me by Someone who loved me very much. I guess that's how I feel as a Christian when it comes to living the life designed by the Manufacturer for me to live. All I must do is refer to the instructions when I realize that my life is being short-circuited and compromised by how I operate it and the choices I make that go contrary to the instructions.

I still don't have all the answers, but I know much more today than I knew 50 years ago. When I'm stumped, I also know Who has all the answers—so I ask Him to help me out. And He never leaves me hanging!

I will continue to consult the Bible daily for greater wisdom and understanding so that I can continue to grow and become more and more of the person I was created to be. You will hear no apologies from me on this issue. My desire in this life is to follow God's directions to the best of my ability, so when this life is over, He will say, *"Well done, good and faithful servant."* (Matthew 25:21)

The world has plenty of descriptors for believers, as do we within the family of God. But whatever your descriptor—whatever floats your boat— just make sure that what you're trusting in isn't full of holes.

I am a student of the Instruction Manual and a follower of Jesus. I am not without flaws, and I sometimes make unwise choices, but every day I try to become more like Him. All that being said, is He my Father and am I His kid? The answer is a resounding and unequivocal *yes!*

As to whether I see myself as a Bible thumper or Jesus freak? Indeed, I'll embrace those as well.

> *There has never been the slightest doubt in my mind that the God who started this great work in you would keep it and bring it to a flourishing finish on the very day Christ Jesus appears.*
> PHILIPPIANS 1:6 MSG

COINCIDENCE?

What is the shortest chapter in the Bible? Psalm 117
What is the longest chapter in the Bible? Psalm 119
Which chapter is in the center of the Bible? Psalm 118
Fact: There are 594 chapters before Psalm 118
Fact: There are 594 chapters after Psalm 118
594 + 594 = 1188
What is the center verse in the Bible? Psalm 118:8
Does this verse say something significant about God's perfect will for us?
The next time someone says they would like to find God's perfect will
for their life and they want to be at the center of His will,
just send them to the center of His Word:

It is better to trust in the Lord than to put confidence in man.
PSALM 118:8 NKJV

Coincidence? I think not! God has *always* been very intentional in how He does things and can be found smack dab in the middle of everything we face. We just haven't always noticed that or acknowledged Him. I think it's about time! What do you think?

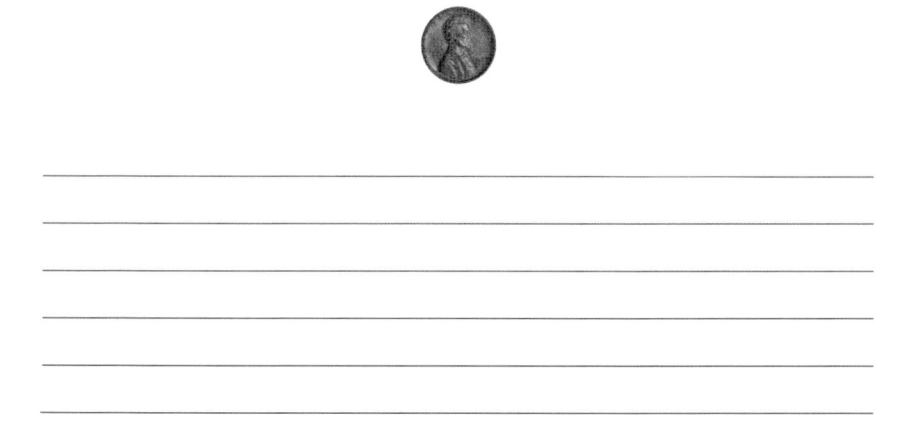

THE BIG BLACK SPOT

So this week, I cut down a tree in our front yard and while drilling holes in it preparing to kill the stump/roots, I got to the middle where this big black spot was and as I began to drill into it, I realized quickly it was completely rotten in that 5-inch spot.

The tree is close to 20 years old and looked perfectly healthy, but after slicing it down only to realize what was ugly within it would have eventually killed it over time. I begin to wonder when did this happen. Was it the ice storm several years ago? But whatever it was, something traumatic happened that changed the tree's inside for sure, yet still it kept on looking like it was healthy and growing on the outside.

I sensed the Holy Spirit speaking to me. If you were sliced open, exposing your core, what would be seen that wasn't healthy and possibly rotten? How often do we appear to be healthy on the outside, but have something ugly spreading and rotting out our insides? It's so easy for something in one season to affect our long-term spiritual health.

Don't let the offense, rejection, or pain of yesterday define your destiny. We should all ask Jesus to examine our hearts, like David, to have heart surgery regularly for real, pure spiritual maturity. Create a right spirit within us all, so we may abound in all the good things Jesus has in store.

Rick Sparks

We live through various seasons throughout our lifetime, and sometimes things happen that have a significant effect on us that will show up as we move forward. Traumas that are not addressed tend to create behaviors and mindsets that can be very detrimental in navigating our lives. Getting to the root of the damage that has been done and examining the extent of how it has affected everything is very important. Seeking others who are skilled in Christ-centered assistance is highly appropriate. This dignified and focused approach can properly treat the pain resulting from past offenses and attacks. The Holy Spirit, our comforter, provides an extravagant peace even as the discovery and healing of past hurts take place. The result will bring healthy growth and a fruitfulness that remains.

> *Create in me a clean heart, O God,*
> *And renew a steadfast spirit within me.*
> PSALM 51:10 NKJV

DELAYING GRATIFICATION

Learning to delay pleasure is a sign of maturity.
Adults devise a plan and follow it.
Children do what feels good.

Delaying momentary gratification and holding out for God's best is the best feeling in the world. Besides, taking the time to work on developing patience is a beneficial activity to pursue. If we need a role model to study and get a clue about real patience, we won't have to look very far. God is the Poster Father of Patience. How many times have we put Him on hold to wait for us?

I waited patiently for the Lord;
and He inclined to me, and heard my cry.
PSALM 40:1 NKJV

UNCERTAINTY

*The way we deal with uncertainty lets us know
whether Jesus is ahead of us leading or
behind us just carrying our stuff.*

Who's in charge? That would be a great question to ask immediately when uncertainty raises its ugly head. I'm getting much better at answering that question straightaway these days. Relegating Jesus to the role of porter and carrying all my cases of stuff is just plain nonsense. And the thought of tipping Him when He delivers my baggage to my chosen destination is ludicrous and just plain laughable—as if Jesus needs tips on or for anything. Nope, I've finally learned that the best way to go when I don't know which way to go is to trust that Jesus *always* knows the way. Where He leads me, I will follow.

*My sheep hear My voice, and I know them,
and they follow Me.*
JOHN 10:27 NKJV

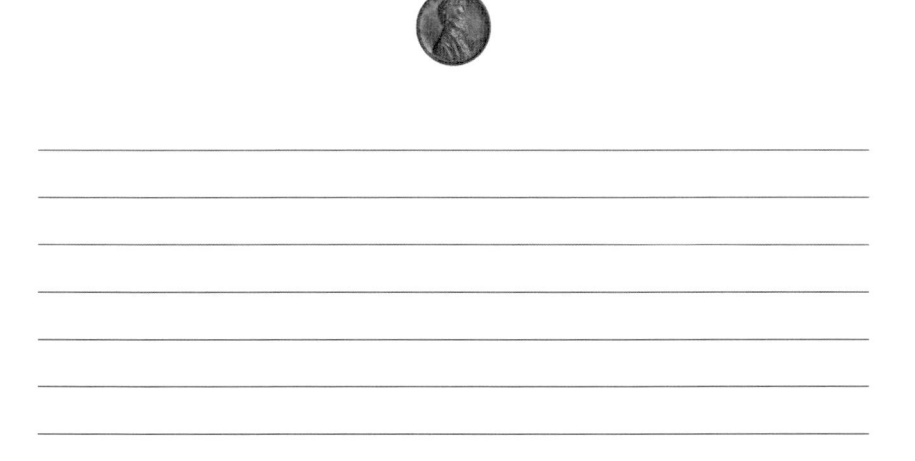

BE AWARE

*We're already in the presence of God.
What's absent is awareness.*

The "Omnis" is what God is. He is Omniscient; He knows *everything.* He is the only "know-it-all" that I know. God is Omnipotent; He is *all-powerful.* He is stronger than principalities and powers in high places and strong enough to handle whatever troubles we will face in this life. And we may not "feel" it or be aware of it at times, but God is Omnipresent. He is always *here.* He is an ever-present help to us when we call upon Him.

> *God is our refuge and strength, a very present help in trouble.*
> PSALM 46:1 NKJV

In this very troublesome time of political and spiritual unrest, some people refer to this time in history as the Woke Generation. With all the confusion running rampant everywhere, it's hard to tell just how "woke" people really are. Varying opinions and "facts" have created great divisions. "Woke Generation" or not, perhaps it is high time for all of us to *wake up* to the presence of God! He *is* here, He doesn't miss a thing, and His justice will prevail. Make no mistake—this is not a half-truth that can be easily picked apart by the fact-checkers. We must be aware of and live according to God's unchanging truth.

> *Depart from evil, and do good; and dwell forevermore.*
> *For the Lord loves justice, and does not forsake His saints; they are*
> *preserved forever, but the descendants of the wicked shall be cut off.*
> *The righteous shall inherit the land, and dwell in it forever.*
> *The mouth of the righteous speaks wisdom,*
> *And his tongue talks of justice.*
> PSALM 37:27-30 NKJV

Is there any place I can go to avoid your Spirit? To be out of your sight? If I climb to the sky, you're there! If I go underground, you're there! If I flew on morning's wings to the far western horizon, you'd find me in a minute—you're already there waiting!
PSALM 139:7-10 MSG

TWO CENTS MORE

EVIL WEAPONRY

Satan's greatest weapon is man's
ignorance of God's Word.

A.W. Tozer

It's one thing when people who don't profess allegiance to the Lord are ignorant about the words of Scripture, but what I *really* struggle with are believers consulting the culture for direction before seeking God. Tozer went to the Word to easily identify the timeless nature of Satan's greatest weapon—and he died many decades ago! Fast forward to the present day. I know many of my friends dive deeply into the Word for their marching orders and encouragement and need to be closely connected to the One who put everything we need to know in it. I encourage you to do likewise.

My mom was my role model for living out her commitment to the Lord. She had several Bibles that were all marked up and held together with rubber bands. She enjoyed a healthy diet of spiritual food every day. Even when confronting a sickness in her aged body, she spent a night actively stomping about her room. When I woke and heard the commotion, I asked what she was doing, and she replied, "I am putting the devil under my feet!" Now *that* spoke volumes to me. Even in a state of delirium, the Word of God was so deeply ingrained in her spirit that she rose to her feet to wage battle against Satan. She knew that she had the power to do that because her time spent in the Word taught her how to effectively use the Scripture to make the attacks of the enemy come to naught.

During World War II, my mom's brother, Herman, was a POW in a German camp. Uncle Herman wrote about it in a piece he called *My Longest Day*—but it actually lasted much longer than a day. While he was a prisoner, he and some of his friends would gather to have private "church services" when the time was allowed. My uncle had committed many Scriptures to memory from his days in a Christian school and around the family table. God was highly revered and talked about often in the Zichterman household. It was definitely a House of Prayer.

Whenever I visited my mom's sister, Helen, and her husband, Jim, their Bible was open without fail on their dining room table where they had devotions and prayer every morning. After Aunt Helen went to be with Jesus, Uncle Jim continued to read the Bible and pray daily. I am so thankful for my mom's family and the legacy of faith they left for me.

Both of my children are very familiar with God's Word, and I pray that the generations to follow will pick up on the practice. They are going to need it big time. We are in the middle of End Times, and it ain't gonna get easier. Satan would love for all people—especially Christians—to be Word illiterates. The power in the Word of God has already defeated Satan, but it is up to us to get after it and unleash it in *our* life to remove any doubt as to whose words we revere more highly.

> *Put on the full armor of God, so that you can take your stand against the devil's schemes. For our struggle is not against flesh and blood, but against the rulers, against the authorities, against the powers of this dark world and against the spiritual forces of evil in the heavenly realms. Therefore put on the full armor of God, so that when the day of evil comes, you may be able to stand your ground, and after you have done everything, to stand. Stand firm then, with the belt of truth buckled around your waist, with the breastplate of righteousness in place, and with your feet fitted with the readiness that comes from the gospel of peace.*
> EPHESIANS 6:11-15 NIV

TWO CENTS MORE

The Book of the Law shall not depart from your mouth, but you shall meditate in it day and night, that you may observe to do according to all that is written in it. For then you will make your way prosperous, and then you will have good success.
JOSHUA 1:8 NKJV

WHO AM I... REALLY?

I still am who He says I am!

Christine Caine

When I used to lead groups that focused on inner healing and learning how to live fulfilling and quality lives, I would encourage everyone to embrace what God had to say about them. Often that challenge would be met with a question. How am I supposed to know what God says about who I am? Well, God's Word is loaded with verses about how much He loves us and how He sees us. One significantly powerful statement in the Bible about who I am is quite simple—I am *"...the righteousness of God"* (II Corinthians 5:21). I'll take it! That's who I am. There are so many affirming verses that tell us who we are and how God sees His kids. Arguing with Him is an exercise in futility. Even when we don't think, feel, or believe it to be true, Father always knows best. And He is especially fond of us!

> *For He made Him who knew no sin to be sin for us,*
> *that we might become the righteousness of God in Him.*
> II Corinthians 5:21 NKJV

TRUTH BE TOLD

Strange isn't it?
You know yourself better than anyone else,
yet you crumble at the words of someone
who hasn't even lived a second of your life.
Focus on your own voice; it's the only one that matters.

This is a "Truth Be Told" kind of post. The truth is that people who don't even know us form opinions about us thanks to social media and the lightning-fast word of mouth. They really don't know anything about us—except for what we choose to show them. And in some cases, that can really be something.

As for knowing ourselves? Well—that depends. How often have we heard people wonder about who they are, how they think about things, and what they should do in certain situations? I mean—really! In desperate times, we're stumped too.

Let's get to the truth of the matter. God knows us inside and out, and He has a great deal to say about us—and He is spot on every time! He created us; what He has to say is all that matters in the long run. Let's face it—we aren't always kind to ourselves with our self-talk. We say things that are not very accepting or loving and define ourselves by our own words because we think we "know how we are."

It's time to let God be the One to have the final say. We can now recognize that others haven't known us accurately, and they have fed us their opinions and judgments long enough. Perhaps in our ignorance, we have done the same. When we alter course and choose to speak over our lives as God does, we'll start seeing our behaviors align accordingly, and our voice will carry a much greater consistency and authority.

*Oh yes, you shaped me first inside, then out; you formed me in
my mother's womb. I thank you, High God—you're breathtaking!
Body and soul, I am marvelously made! I worship in adoration—
what a creation! You know me inside and out, you know every bone
in my body; you know exactly how I was made, bit by bit, how I was
sculpted from nothing into something. Like an open book,
you watched me grow from conception to birth; all the
stages of my life were spread out before you, the days
of my life all prepared before I'd even lived one day.*
PSALM 139:13-16 MSG

GET TO THE ROOT

When the Holy Spirit prays the will of God through you,
He goes right to the exact root of the problem.
You and I might only realize the symptom.
He deals with the cause.

Gloria Copeland

This is so good! True healing doesn't occur when only dealing with symptoms. The Holy Spirit is our Helper and will reveal what is going on and how to pray effectively to address more than symptoms. We need to get human thoughts and solutions out of the way and let the Holy Spirit pray perfect prayers through us. The Holy Spirit knows what's going on and can pray perfect prayers through us—even when we don't have a clue how to pray. Getting to the heart of the problem is a root issue. Healthy roots produce good fruit—and it will be fruit that lasts.

Likewise the Spirit also helps in our weaknesses.
For we do not know what we should pray for as we ought, but the
Spirit Himself makes intercession for us with groanings which cannot
be uttered. Now He who searches the hearts knows what the mind of
the Spirit is, because He makes intercession for the saints
according to the will of God.
ROMANS 8:26-27 NKJV

ROCK-SOLID FAITH

Having rock-solid faith doesn't mean we will never have questions. In fact, there will always be things we can't figure out, won't understand, and may never know the answer to. There are so many things I don't understand, and I have to make a daily decision to give those things to God. For you and I, the real question is—will we trust God even when we cannot trace Him? When we don't understand the why, the how, or how long, that's when we remember and take comfort that God is in control. There is no other person, belief system, religion, philosophy, or cause that can do what only He can do. He is faithful to honor all His promises. May we be faithful to believe Him and trust Him daily.

It takes faith—
to keep *following* Jesus
to *wonder* and not *wander*
to *trust* when you don't *understand*
to live on *purpose* and stay on *mission*
to navigate the *injustice* and *suffering* in our world
to *get up* and *keep going* when you face a setback
to hold on to the truth that *God is good* when life is not.

Christine Caine

It takes faith "to wonder and not wander," and it reminds me of the lyrics of the song, *I Wonder As I Wander*. We do that, don't we? We're always trying to figure stuff out. We go through our lifetime trying to find our purpose and understand why things happen the way they do. There seems to be an elevated level of suffering, unrest, anger, and injustice today. It appears that much is falling apart, with hopelessness on the rise.

But rest assured, my friends, "My hope is built on nothing less than Jesus' blood and righteousness." Some of you may have grown up in the church back in the day when hymns were sung, and you might be starting to tap your toe and hum this familiar old favorite. The next line you may recall is, "I dare not trust the sweetest frame, but wholly trust on Jesus' name." It's a great song, and the message of encouragement to keep the faith is embodied in that hymn. Google it for the rest of the lyrics. It will restore some hope, adjust your focus, and point you in the right direction. Here is the chorus and final line: "On Christ the solid rock I stand—all other ground is sinking sand." This song contains many foundational and timeless truths that are still being declared today.

Life may present some real challenges that appear to be insurmountable, but God is still on His Throne; He knows what's going on, and He's got the whole world in His hands. Did another song just pop into your head? Never give up, follow the Lord, immerse yourself in His Word, and have faith that He is an ever-present help whenever you need Him. Go ahead and wonder and ask your questions, but be sure to quiet down enough to hear His answers and reassurances. God isn't going anywhere—He will *never* leave or forsake you.

> *Trust in the Lord with your whole heart, and lean not on your own understanding; in all your ways acknowledge Him, and He shall direct your paths.*
> PROVERBS 3:5-6 NKJV

NEVER ALONE

*Because of the Gospel, I wake up every day
knowing that if I die today, I'll be with Jesus.
If not, He'll be with me.*

WIN-WIN! How can it get any better than that? Blessed assurance, Jesus is mine. Living out the rest of my life after walking with the Lord for over fifty years, the peace I experience every day gets the joy bubbling like an artesian well. I don't have to pump it up—it's just there. So many of my friends have lived their dream here on earth while serving the Lord and been able to relocate to heaven to spend eternity with the One they served. I'm not necessarily in a hurry to join them, but I must admit that sometimes I feel a little homesick for what's to come. I'm 100% confident that the Word of God is faithful. While I continue to finish my assignment here, I am assured that Jesus continues to walk with me, talk with me, and tell me I am His own—every single day.

> *We live with a joyful confidence, yet at the same time we take delight in the thought of leaving our bodies behind to be at home with the Lord. So whether we live or die we make it our life's passion to live our lives pleasing to him.*
> II CORINTHIANS 5:8-9 TPT

I CAN ONLY IMAGINE

Mercy Me recorded the song, I Can Only Imagine, back in 2001. It was written by Bart Millard. It was later made into a movie by the same title. This song has been shared several times on Facebook over the years. I finally decided to comment.

My son, Russ, sang *I Can Only Imagine* at my mom's celebration of life in June of 2005. Every time I hear the song, I weep—because I can only imagine what my mom and so many other dear ones are doing right now in heaven. I often think about what it will be like when I join them.

My daughter Mara, and a dear friend, Wendy, also sang songs that were hand-picked by my mom—*Amazing Grace, We Shall Behold Him,* and more—that would make it clear to everyone in attendance how much she loved the Lord and looked forward to spending eternity with Him. Some days I can hardly wait to join her; other days, I realize that God still has an assignment for me to finish here. Either way, I am in awe of my heavenly Father and His steadfast, unconditional love for me.

How about you? Can you relate?

> *He will wipe every tear from their eyes, and there will be no more death or sorrow or crying or pain. All these things are gone forever. And the one sitting on the throne said, "Look, I am making everything new!" And then he said to me, "Write this down, for what I tell you is trustworthy and true."*
> REVELATION 21:4-5 NLT

*And he also said, "It is finished! I am the Alpha and the Omega—
the Beginning and the End. To all who are thirsty I will give freely
from the springs of the water of life. All who are victorious will
inherit all these blessings, and I will be their God,
and they will be my children.*
REVELATION 21:6-7 NLT

BE STILL AND KNOW

It's not that God is silent.
It's that our distractions are sometimes too loud.

This has a lot to do with focus. Here is a good reminder for Christians to follow from Colossians 3 in The Message, "*Since then, you have been raised with Christ, set your hearts on things above, where Christ is, seated at the right hand of God. Also, set your minds on things above, not on earthly things.*"

God speaks to us in a still, small voice. Elijah experienced that in I Kings 19 when he tried to run from Jezebel and find safety. Elijah was running every which way but loose, but he couldn't find God in the wind, an earthquake, or a fire. All of them were major distractions, for sure, but he heard God speak to him in a still, small voice. God wasn't silent, but He got Elijah's attention when He spoke softly.

If you want to get someone's attention, speak softly—they will lean in. That's how my kindergarten teacher, Miss Thompson, got the attention of a room full of rambunctious five-year-old students. She quietly struck a chord on the piano, and we all scurried to "the rug" in the center of the room to hear what would happen next. It was kinda like an EF Hutton moment.

Quiet yourself and listen for the still, small voice of the Holy Spirit, which people sometimes refer to as your conscience or a gut feeling. Hush up—focus—and listen. That still, small voice is powerful and effective.

Then He said, "Go out, and stand on the mountain before the Lord." And behold, the Lord passed by, and a great and strong wind tore into the mountains and broke the rocks in pieces before the Lord, but the Lord was not in the wind; and after the wind an earthquake, but the Lord was not in the earthquake; and after the earthquake a fire, but the Lord was not in the fire; and after the fire a still small voice.
I KINGS 19:11-12 NKJV

RADICAL LIVING

*If you're obeying the Bible,
you look radical to the lukewarm.*

Lukewarm Christians seem to be growing exponentially in numbers these days. Making the Bible fit their agenda and mindset is dangerous, dishonest, and hypocritical. As they interact with Christians trusting in the Word of God, holding to its line, and living in ways that please God, this principled behavior seems to offend them big time. They want these on-fire Christians to lighten up and go with the flow. Times have changed, don't ya know? No wonder people in the world call Christians hypocrites, as they are seen as living their lives only to suit themselves. Let's not be guilty of this and live as Christians in name only, but rather, purposefully show the principles of Christ in our deeds and lifestyle.

*You shall love the Lord your God with all your heart,
with all your soul, and with all your strength.*
DEUTERONOMY 6:5 NKJV

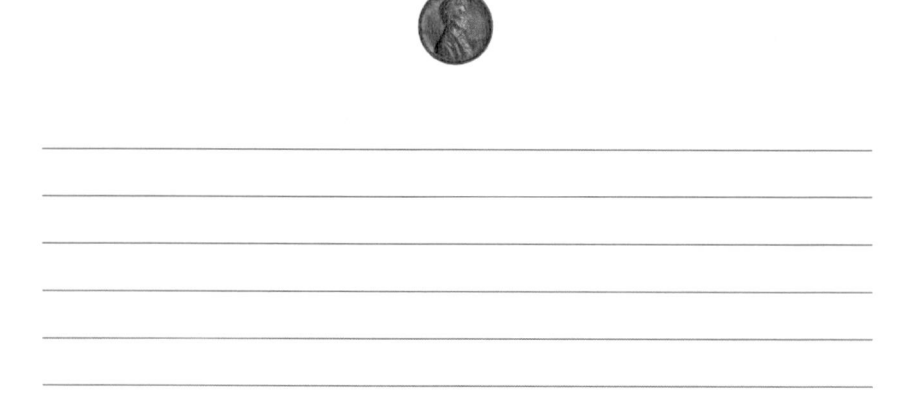

WHAT REALLY MATTERS

Living a joyful and positive life is an inside out proposition. Getting the interior renewed and redesigned and full of great character traits is the best way to show people how to see God working out His plan in your life. What's truly on the inside will start bubbling and manifest itself to those with whom you spend time. Don't think for a minute that that doesn't matter. Great relationships are born out of making the right and genuine connections. The best way to start is by making a genuine, heartfelt connection to God first. He is the absolute best One who can put everything else together. Perspective brings focus and value to every situation and relationship. You can count on Him to make it happen.

Rowgo

Life can be such a puzzle so much of the time. We have lost track of what the finished product is supposed to look like. We all hold the pieces to our own puzzle in our hands, but sometimes we don't know where to put them or where they fit. That's why asking God where to place them is so cool. He already sees the big picture because He created it for each of us from the beginning of time. As we work out our life puzzle with His assistance, the excitement of seeing the picture coming together brings great joy and satisfaction.

...remember the former things of old; for I am God, and there is no other; I am God, and there is none like me, declaring the end from the beginning and from ancient times things not yet done, saying, 'My counsel shall stand, and I will accomplish all my purpose,'
ISAIAH 46:9-10 ESV

TWO CENTS MORE

Therefore, if anyone is in Christ, he is a new creation; old things have passed away; behold, all things have become new.
II Corinthians 5:17 NKJV

CHRIST-LIKE INTERNET CONTROL

*Let every image looked upon be pleasing to You,
for I am grafted into the line of the King,
called and authorized as Your holy representative
to a world in desperate need of integrity.*

*Let every word spoken and every idea texted,
posted and published be given to lift up my brothers
and sisters, as this is fitting for those You have
chosen as true witnesses of the crown.*

Rusty James Rowgo

A long overdue PSA: If only people would take this message to heart, it could change everything. Our thoughts would straighten out, and our minds could be renewed, according to Romans 12:1-2. Our words and actions would align. Integrity would become the new normal, and Facebook would take on a new identity. When will we ever learn?

Many of us have learned this but are unwilling to do it. We still sit in the driver's seat as we steer our lives off the straight and narrow. In essence, we have been "educated" beyond our level of obedience. And that's a dangerous place to be. It's time to straighten everything out, allow God to *be God,* and make His Word our infallible GPS. And there would never be a need to recalculate our route again.

> *Therefore, I urge you, brothers and sisters, in view of God's mercy, to offer your bodies as a living sacrifice, holy and pleasing to God— this is your true and proper worship. Do not conform to the pattern of this world, but be transformed by the renewing of your mind. Then you will be able to test and approve what God's will is— his good, pleasing and perfect will.*
> ROMANS 12:1-2 NIV

TWO CENTS MORE

*And whatever you do in word or deed, do all in the name
of the Lord Jesus, giving thanks to God the Father through Him.*
COLOSSIANS 3:17 NKJV

CONVERSATIONS THAT MATTER

Girl: "What are your goals in life?"
Guy: "To hear 'Well done, good and faithful servant.'"

Oh, how I wish young people would have meaningful conversations like this rather than the meaningless, empty, nonsensical drivel I have observed through the years. This introductory conversation could easily lead to topics much deeper than the typical blather. As the girl heard the guy's response, I could guess she might have asked him to explain what that would look like. What does that mean? How would he live his life to hear that affirmation? What was he hoping to do and accomplish in life? Then the guy could begin to ask the girl the same questions, just to see if they're on the same page. If they are, it will make sense to investigate further. This young couple might be ready to embark on a conversational adventure leading toward a life-changing destination. Make a point in your conversations to "lean in" to the eternally meaningful and witness the change in depth of your relationships' quality, character, and integrity.

> *His lord said to him, "Well done, good and faithful servant; you have been faithful over a few things, I will make you ruler over many things. Enter into the joy of your lord."*
> MATTHEW 25:23 NKJV

COMPLACENCY

Complacency is a feeling of calm satisfaction with your own abilities or situation. Complacency is one of man's greatest weaknesses. It has a way of slowly taking over our minds, making us so comfortable, we are actually stuck! God has so much more in store for your future, and I know for a fact, you won't find it in your comfort zone.

Creflo Dollar

I have often said that life is an adventure. If it really is an adventure, it seems to me that it would be nothing like a so-so existence. Complacency smacks of blah! No risks, no incentives to achieve great things, and no excitement. Just getting by—almost without a pulse. I think of Eeyore, Winnie the Pooh's woebegone friend. Nothing really mattered to him. He was "content" to live a dull gray life—just ho-hum. In fact, Eeyore was continually focused on negativity and how nothing would ever turn out right. Depression was his reality. How sad! God has so much more to offer. Yes, there will be ups and downs, but at least life in the realm of God's influence is sure to bring adventures, challenges, achievements, and a truly vibrant—color.

And whatever you do, do it heartily, as to the Lord and not to men.
COLOSSIANS 3:23 NKJV

CUT TO THE CHASE

*When you just can't seem to fix any of it,
it may be God's way of telling you to surrender all of it to Him.*

If you decide to cut to the chase, start right here at the very beginning by surrendering to God as your first action item. Calling on Him as a last resort is a terrible way to go and a foolish waste of time.

When faced with a troublesome situation, we tend to fuss and try to solve the problem. I cannot begin to tell you how many times I've done this. Sometimes the solutions have come quite easily, and I'm pleased as punch. Other times I have run into problems above my pay grade and reached out to others for help. I reason that God has put people in my life who can assist me when I cannot figure things out.

I realize that, in a sense, I'm actually asking God to help all along. Either I need His direction to know how to do it myself, or I'm asking Him to send me someone who can help. The key is acknowledging His presence and surrendering to His love and expertise to meet my needs right where I am.

*Whatever I am, wherever I am, I can make it through anything
in the One who makes me who I am.*
PHILIPPIANS 4:13 MSG

COUNT THE COST

*What it costs you to obey God,
disobeying Him will cost you more.*

This post is definitely a true statement. I've done both—many times—throughout my life. Because I truly love the Lord and want to please Him with joyful obedience, I feel terrible when I don't do it.

The actual cost of disobeying God has exposed me to some very real consequences. Entering into unsafe relationships and getting involved in unsavory and dangerous activities contrary to God's plan for me have all ended badly. I knew better at the time, even when I was in the thick of it, but that didn't stop me—until I came to my senses. Sometimes it took me more time to "straighten out and fly right," but at least I learned that it's never too late to turn around and get back on the right track. God is full of grace and mercy and is always ready to welcome me back into the fold when I mess up.

My forgiveness was purchased for me at the cross and I received it when I asked Jesus to be my Lord and Savior. I haven't arrived yet, and I can say that my times of disobedience have diminished greatly. When I have chosen to do things my way rather than God's way, I have learned to count the cost, recognizing beyond a shadow of a doubt that it simply isn't worth it.

Even with my earthly parents, who loved and cared for me, there was something deeply planted in my innermost being. It was the desire to please them and not do anything that would bring them shame or disappointment. The same is true when I think about my relationship with God. He is a good Father who wants the best for me, but He is also a God with rules and boundaries. He blesses my obedience when I do things His way, even when I prefer to do things my way due to my sin nature. The "cost" is minuscule when I "do" life His way compared to what happens when I'm a willful, disobedient child. When I know better, it's *always* beneficial to do better. Besides, I love to see my Father smile and give me one of His famous Godwinks.

> *He who has My commandments and keeps them,*
> *it is he who loves Me. And he who loves Me will be loved by My*
> *Father, and I will love him and manifest Myself to him.*
> JOHN 14:21 NKJV

YAY OR NAY

When God wants to bless you,
He puts a person in your life.
When the enemy wants to destroy you,
he also puts a person in your life.
Wisdom is knowing who sent who.

Discernment comes in handy! Carl, my brother from another mother, commented: "When people want to bless and curse themselves, they also bring people into their lives!" I agree with him. We have a tendency to take things into our own hands. Sometimes it works out well and can be a blessing; other times it can be disastrous. Maybe we would do well to check our decisions out with God *before* we act on them. He will let us know whether or not we're spot on. People will be put in our lives, but it's up to us to determine how their presence will affect us—and take whatever action is necessary to maintain stability.

> *The thief does not come except to steal and to kill and to destroy. I have come that they may have life, and they may have it more abundantly.*
> JOHN 10:10 NKJV

IT IS WELL WITH MY SOUL

I ran across this hymn with lyrics written by Horatio Spafford

Spafford's wife and four daughters were sailing home to him in 1873 on the SS Ville de Havre. Unfortunately, it was rammed by a British vessel. The four daughters drowned, but Spafford's wife survived. As he was on his way to pick up his wife, the captain of the ship he was on let him know that they were passing over the site of where his daughters lost their lives. It was at that time that the grieving father went onto the deck of the ship and penned his declaration:

When peace like a river attendeth my way
When sorrows like sea billows roll
Whatever my lot, Thou hast taught me to say
It is well, it is well with my soul.

Though Satan should buffet, though trials should come
Let this blest assurance control
That Christ has regarded my helpless estate
And has shed His own blood for my soul.

My sin, oh the bliss of this glorious thought
My sin, not in part, but the whole
Is nailed to the cross, and I bear it no more
Praise the Lord, praise the Lord, O my soul!

And Lord haste the day when my faith shall be sight
The clouds be rolled back as a scroll
The trump shall resound, and the Lord shall descend
Even so, it is well with my soul.

TWO CENTS MORE

It is well (it is well)
With my soul (with my soul)
It is well, it is well with my soul

Music affects me like nothing else. Music with a powerful message, especially like this song based on a specific event, literally gives me chills and unspeakable anticipation and joy.

The day is coming for everyone who is breathing and living their best life today when we will draw our last breath and transition from this life to the next. For some of us, it will be sooner than for others. Whatever the case may be for me, I'm ready—and it is well with my soul.

> *God is our refuge and strength, a very present help in trouble. Therefore we will not fear, even though the earth be removed, and though the mountains be carried into the midst of the sea; though its waters roar and be troubled, though the mountains shake with its swelling. Selah*
> PSALM 46:1-3 NKJV

PICK YOUR LENS

*Either Scripture will be the lens
through which you view the world,
or the world will be the lens
through which you view Scripture.
Ultimately, one or the other will be your authority.*

Dustin Benge

No contest here. How the world has viewed Scripture lacks an understanding of its powerfully divine nature. This has resulted in confusion and even complete rejection for many. This is our enemy's intent but simply asking God to reveal Himself through His Word is the first step to eroding this cultural veiling of its inherent power.

The Bible is unwavering, and its truth has stood the test of time, even declaring the wisdom contained as recognizable only through the Spirit of God. This is key as these words are living and breathing life. This is not merely a "good book"—it's *the Book*, our Survival Guide, fully capable of directing us through this life here and preparing us for our future home.

> *And don't for a minute let this Book of The Revelation be out of mind. Ponder and meditate on it day and night, making sure you practice everything written in it. Then you'll get where you're going; then you'll succeed. Haven't I commanded you? Strength! Courage! Don't be timid; don't get discouraged. God, your God, is with you every step you take.*
> JOSHUA 1:8-9 MSG

TWO CENTS MORE

The person without the Spirit does not accept the things that come from the Spirit of God but considers them foolishness, and cannot understand them because they are discerned only through the Spirit.
1 CORINTHIANS 2:14 NIV

NO COMFORT ZONE

*If you want a religion to make you feel really comfortable,
I certainly don't recommend Christianity.*

C.S. Lewis

I'm not a fan of religion at all. Truth be told, I *hate* religion! I prefer to build a genuine relationship—an intimate friendship, if you will, with the One who created me. There is a big difference between religion and authentic Christianity. Many days it feels like I'm in a war zone, walking out my life as a Christian. Too often, religion can fall into a "feel good" state, making up coping mechanisms for whatever we face. But, seeking and settling into a comfort zone is contrary to the challenge of a decision to follow Jesus. Christianity is not for sissies! Jesus invites us to take up His cross and follow Him (Luke 9:23). That involves suffering. We are also told to put on the whole armor of God (Ephesians 6:13-17). Why? Because the devil is like a lion seeking whom he may devour (I Peter 5:8). Jesus faced all-out attacks and conflicts as He walked out His life; we will too. But, like Him, we shall overcome.

> *These things I have spoken to you, that in Me
> you may have peace. In the world you will have tribulation;
> but be of good cheer, I have overcome the world.*
> JOHN 16:33 NKJV

FOR SUCH A TIME AS THIS

Don't feel sorry for or fear for your kids because the
world they are going to grow up in is not what it used to be.
God created them and called them for the exact moment in time
that they're in. This life wasn't a coincidence or an accident.

Raise them up to know the power they walk in as children of God.
Train them up in the authority of His Word.
Teach them to walk in faith knowing that God is in control.
Empower them to know they can change the world.

Don't teach them to be fearful and disheartened by the state
of the world, but hopeful that they can do something about it.
Every person in all of history has been placed in the time
that they were in because of God's sovereign plan.

He knew Daniel could handle the lion's den.
He knew David could handle Goliath.
He knew Esther could handle Haman.
He knew Peter could handle persecution.
He knows that your child can handle whatever challenges
they face in their life. He created them specifically for it!

Don't be scared for your children but be honored that God chose *you* to
parent the generation that is facing the biggest challenges of our lifetime.
Rise to the challenge. Raise Daniels, Davids, Esthers, and Peters!

God isn't scratching His head wondering what He's going to do with
this mess of a world. He has an army He's raising up to drive back the
darkness and make Him known all over the earth.

Don't let your fear steal the greatness God placed in them.

> I know it's hard to imagine them as anything besides our sweet little babies, and we just want to protect them from anything that could ever be hard on them, but they were born for such a time as this.
>
> Alex Cravens

Amanda, a former student of mine, commented that she had never thought this way about what Cravens wrote. My response was that a different perspective can correct our lens and vision. Coming at it from a spiritual perspective dramatically changes how we view what's happening in the world. We need to learn how to see things through God's eyes—and it ain't over 'til the trumpet sounds.

Amanda was precisely right when she said that the best protection or armor we could give our kids is to know God and His Word. No kidding! Our responsibility at this time is to train our kids in the way they truly need to go. Parents cannot sit idly by and wait for their kids to decide whether God exists and has anything of value to say. They need to know there *is* a God, and they ain't Him. Kids need to get off the throne, stop ruling their own lives, and let God be God. His Word contains everything they need to live a fearless, successful life, so they must know it and follow the instructions. Parents, you are to live out the example.

Think about it, educators have a curriculum and are given the task of teaching their students what each school district feels they need to know, and they use textbooks and other resources to accomplish that goal. Children have an understood responsibility to learn as they grow to become dependable adults contributing to society. Well, the Bible is the *ultimate textbook!* We need to get our game-face on and not neglect the most important thing—our kids' spiritual survival and well-being depend on it.

TWO CENTS MORE

Be strong. Take courage. Don't be intimidated. Don't give them a second thought because God, your God, is striding ahead of you. He's right there with you. He won't let you down; he won't leave you.
DEUTERONOMY 31:6 MSG

Can plunder be retrieved from a giant, prisoners of war gotten back from a tyrant? But God says, "Even if a giant grips the plunder and a tyrant holds my people prisoner, I'm the one who's on your side, defending your cause, rescuing your children.
ISAIAH 49:24-25 MSG

I PRAY BECAUSE...

I pray because I can't help myself.
I pray because I'm helpless.
I pray because the need flows out of me
all the time—waking and sleeping.
It does not change God—it changes me.

C.S. Lewis

This brought Psalm 1:2 to mind. *"Delighting in the law of the Lord and meditating on it day and night."* seems to me to be a very beneficial way to live in these days of uncertainty and unrest. God is my strength and my only hope. I am thankful for like-minded friends and family members who offer added encouragement and prayers. Whenever I gather with them, it feels like we're having "church" because we invite God into our conversations and talk about things that matter in the eternal realm. My life and the way I live it is actually a prayer.

Pray all the time; thank God no matter what happens.
This is the way God wants you who belong to Christ Jesus to live.
I Thessalonians 5:17-18 MSG

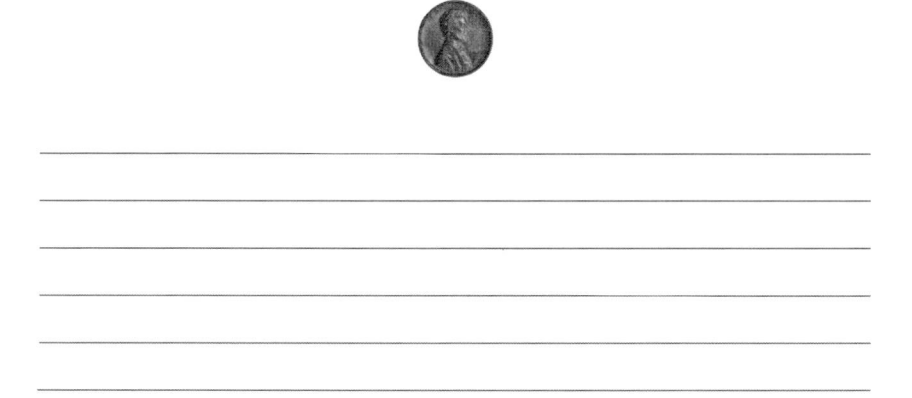

MIND RENEWAL IS CRITICAL

*The only way sin can control the way we live is
if we don't renew our minds after being born again.*

Creflo Dollar

Upon being born again, our spirit is in sync with God's Spirit, and our sins *are* forgiven. Will we continue to sin? Yes! Our soul, which is our mind, our will, and our emotions, is not born again. We have a lot of work to do to bring the soul into obedience to God's will for us. It is our responsibility to learn how to think the way God thinks, which alone is a big undertaking. Of course, the other two parts—what we want and how we handle our emotions—will also present similar challenges. When our commitment to the Lord is of utmost importance to us and His grace is fully understood and appreciated, we will think and act in ways that are acceptable to God. As a result, we will sin less and less and live a life of obedience to the One who gave us a new lease on life.

> *So what do we do? Keep on sinning so God can keep on forgiving?
> I should hope not! If we've left the country where sin is sovereign,
> how can we still live in our old house there? Or didn't you
> realize we packed up and left there for good?*
> ROMANS 6:1-2 MSG

GOD CARES, BUT...

Let God do His job.
Sometimes you follow your own will
because you think that God doesn't care for your problems,
but the truth is He is just waiting for you to surrender.

God cares, but He won't bust our boundaries. He never imposes His will on anyone's free will to do whatever pleases them. However, when we get tired of sitting on our own throne, unsuccessfully governing our own life, God is more than ready and able to respond when the white flag of *surrender* is raised. When we're prepared to stop snapping our fingers and ordering God to serve us and fulfill our desires, He will undoubtedly come in with great power on our behalf. It only takes voluntarily relinquishing our will and our being willing to serve Him.

Humble yourselves in the sight of the Lord, and He will lift you up.
JAMES 4:10 NKJV

BITS AND PIECES

C. S. Lewis wrote the following about the Bible, God's Word to us:
Each of us would like some bits of it (the Bible), but I am afraid very few of us would like the whole thing. We have all departed from that total plan in different ways, and each of us wants to make out his own modifications of the original plan itself. You will find this again and again about anything that is really Christian: everyone is attracted by bits of it and wants to pick out those bits and leave the rest. That is why we do not get much further and that is why people who are fighting for quite opposite things can both say they are fighting for Christianity.

Back in Deuteronomy 8:3, we were told that man does not live by bread alone. Later, Jesus reminded the people by saying:

*It is written, man shall not live by bread alone,
but by every word that proceeds from the mouth of God.*
MATTHEW 4:4 NKJV

Put away your black markers. Go for the whole truth—nothing watered down or wiped out. Guy Duininck talks about people who have a "Preferred Narrative" and look for Scriptures to fit their preference by sometimes warping and bending the Word to "say" what they want it to say. Anything running contrary to that is ignored. This is not a healthy practice for solid doctrines and Christian living. Make sure to search out Scriptures to balance Scripture rather than inventing a narrative to make your way of thinking the right way. That's a perilous strategy to implement.

Study this Book of instruction continually. Meditate on it day and night so you will be sure to obey everything written in it. Only then will you prosper and succeed in all you do.
JOSHUA 1:8 NLT

WORN OUT BIBLES

A Bible that's falling apart
usually belongs to someone who isn't.

Charles Spurgeon

I've always loved this image! Many homes have one or more Bibles, but they often still look pretty pristine, suggesting they don't get put to much use. People miss out on the best counsel and life coaching to live a great life when they neglect the precious nuggets available in the Word. It's time to pan for gold!

Picture this: My mom lived an extraordinary life into her 90s, with her Bibles held together by rubber bands. She experienced some hardships in her life, but she knew exactly where to go for counsel on how to get through them. She consulted the Bible for life tips all the days of her life. Imagine that, she didn't even consult TikTok or Instagram for any life hacks. If the Word was good enough for her, it's good enough for me.

> *All Scripture is God-breathed and is useful for teaching, rebuking, correcting and training in righteousness, so that the servant of God may be thoroughly equipped for every good work.*
> II Timothy 3:16-17 NIV

WHOSE WILL BE DONE?

> To pray "Thy will be done,"
> I must be willing,
> if the answer requires it,
> that my will be undone.
>
> Elisabeth Elliot

I always had a bit of a problem with the song *I Did It My Way*, because often, my way wasn't the best way to go. The Lord's Prayer is found in Matthew 6:9-13 and a shorter version in Luke 11:2-4, and there have been a great many messages that cover these few verses over the years.

I remember when I've been tempted to pray Matthew 6:10 like this: "*Thy kingdom come. MY will be done on earth as it is in Heaven.*" But I'm smart enough to know that my will and His Kingdom don't look the same, so wisdom tells me to renew my mind, will, and emotions to line up with God's perfect will. If mine does not line up with His, it must be undone. Case closed!

> *In this manner, therefore, pray:*
> *Our Father in heaven, hallowed be Your name. Your kingdom come.*
> *Your will be done on earth as it is in heaven.*
> MATTHEW 6:9-10 NKJV

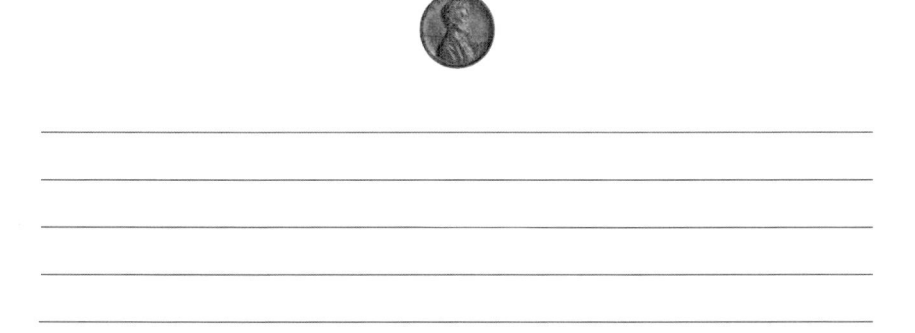

SPIRITUAL METABOLISM

*Our fellowship with God must be renewed day by day.
Our inner being metabolizes quickly,
and just one day of neglect
will bring on spiritual malnutrition.*

Joni Eareckson Tada

How true! We don't tend to ignore our bodies when the feeling of hunger comes. We fill up on whatever we crave. Sometimes we make bad choices and gorge on food that isn't very good for us. Consequently, we often pay the price when we experience chronic health issues. These can be fixed by choosing to feast on foods that are good for us. Sometimes we may even need to be prescribed medicines and other supplements that can bring us back into balanced health.

What then do we do when we are emotionally, psychologically, and spiritually hungry? Similarly, we might ignore filling up on the readily available Godly nutrition. Instead, the soulish "junk food" that we often seek floods us with dopamine further driving us back to brain-numbing habits such as excessive texting, Facebook surfing, gossip posting and self-loathing comparison scrolling—Pinterest anyone? These are not necessarily evil but, for the most part, lack any eternally nutritional value.

Maybe—just maybe—it's time to truly resolve to pursue a day-by-day renewal of your spirit and mind, giving time and first honor to the One who created everything from the galaxies to the individual hairs on your head. Developing a consistent relationship and being on a first-name basis with God Almighty trumps any other association or activity on this planet—or for that matter—any other planet in existence! He has a predetermined and—yes—a thriving, purpose-filled plan for your life.

*Therefore we do not lose heart.
Even though our outward man is perishing,
our inward man is being renewed day by day.*
II Corinthians 4:16 NKJV

BREAK THE CYCLE

Happy people don't go around intentionally making others miserable. They just don't. They don't tear down, or pick fights, or create drama where there is none to be made. They don't wish bad on others, or belittle, so it says something about people who are being awful right now.

Sad people do sad things. The end.

I used to love a clap back, and I used to think it was my job to "win" with people who'd been rude. I used to respond to negative comments, and I used to try to change people's minds, and then one day I thought "What the hell am I doing? I'm doing exactly what they want. This isn't revenge. This is me continuing the cycle."

I don't try to get back at people anymore. It's such a waste—of time, of energy, of my thoughts, and honestly, it's just not the right thing to do.

I'm gonna aim higher.

I'm gonna choose grace. I'm gonna chase gratitude. I'm gonna bring joy to the table. I'm gonna reach for hope. I'm gonna run with my arms wide open towards faith. I'm gonna guard my heart and I'm gonna protect my peace. I'm gonna dream and I'm gonna keep doing good and I'm gonna be kind. I'm gonna encourage and I'm gonna lift up and I can't do that if I get down on your level.

I'm gonna do what God's asked me to do and I'm gonna keep my thoughts on heaven, which is exactly where they belong.

I hope you'll follow suit and let it go because there is absolutely no happiness to be found in anger, bitterness, division, and hate. None. Maybe they really hurt you. Maybe they were really in the wrong and maybe they don't deserve goodness, but you do, and goodness is found in forgiveness. You deserve to let it go.

Life is so short, and it's so easy to waste it dwelling on nonsense. Spread light, and if other people don't like it, toss them some cheap sunglasses and just keep shining.

You have work to do, so you can't be distracted with all that.

The best way to get back at people is to want the best for them no matter what. Pray for them. They must be going through something, so you can either extend the arguing or you extend the mercy, but you can't do both.

Please don't jump in the ring. Don't play the game. Don't do that to your own heart. Don't do that to theirs. There's no glory there, and I know that's not who you are, and that's not what you do.

Break the cycle and go in a new direction. That's how you get ahead. You live above the fray, you live well, and you do it all with crazy doses of love and compassion.

Love, Amy

I don't know who Amy is, but I'd sure like to meet her. I think we'd sit down and have a very long conversation about stuff that matters to both of us. Breaking destructive cycles is undoubtedly on my short list of things that need to be addressed for such a time as this. What do you think?

Give your entire attention to what God is doing right now, and don't get worked up about what may or may not happen tomorrow. God will help you deal with whatever hard things come up when the time comes.
MATTHEW 6:34 MSG

TWO CENTS MORE

Your eyes are windows into your body. If you open your eyes wide in wonder and belief, your body fills up with light. If you live squinty-eyed in greed and distrust, your body is a dank cellar. If you pull the blinds on your windows, what a dark life you will have!
MATTHEW 6:22-23 MSG

THE YOKE IS ON YOU

When you sit still and trust Him, God works.
When you work and trust yourself, God sits still.
Which do you prefer?

Joseph Prince

My preference should be obvious. How about you? Don't worry—God will give you plenty to do. The key is sitting and waiting patiently for your assignment from Him rather than going off half-cocked on your own. Your own ideas and solutions are often incomplete and lack essential insights. It's always best to follow God's lead and work together with Him. God will be your best traveling companion for life; He will never steer you wrong.

Take My yoke upon you and learn from Me, for I am gentle and lowly in heart, and you will find rest for your soul. For My yoke is easy and My burden is light.
MATTHEW 11:29-30 NKJV

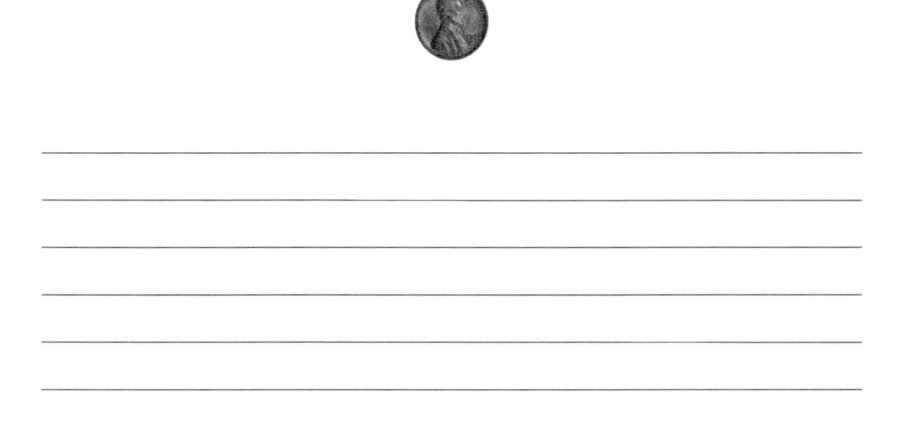

IT IS FINISHED!

When God forgives us, He blots out the record. It is clean.
It is just as though that which was forgiven had never taken place.
Not only does He blot out the record, but He blots it out from His own memory. He says that He will remember our sins no more.

Derek Prince

No—God isn't forgetful! When He remembers our sins no more, it means He won't bring them up to us over and over again by saying, *"Oh yeah, remember when you _____?" (fill in the blank)* He forgives perfectly, unlike us. We say we forgive others, but when a conflict of a different color comes up, we often throw the past "forgiven" event back into the mix. To truly forgive, it must be more than just a dismissive word flippantly spoken.

You might wonder about this though: If we are commanded to forgive others, are we also required to forgive ourselves? *No?* Go back to the original post. If God says that we, who love His Son, are totally forgiven, we are clean, and the offense—past, present, and future—is gone. If we say we have to forgive ourselves, in essence, what we are saying is that God's forgiveness isn't good enough. But what Jesus did on the cross is enough, once and for all. Why would we even want to bring it up and struggle with it repeatedly? The replaying of our screw-ups in our heads, wishing to erase the bad with good works, is a needlessly futile activity.

Here's what you *can* do—rather than working on forgiving yourself by trying to be "good enough" and never make those mistakes again, just *receive* His perfect forgiveness, thank Him, drop it and move on. His grace is sufficient. We must understand and appreciate this forgiveness by not continuing in our destructive behaviors. Come up higher! What did Jesus say? *It is finished!*

*For I will be merciful to their unrighteousness,
and their sins and their lawless deeds I will remember no more.*
HEBREWS 8:12 NKJV

TIME TO CHOOSE

*The key word for most people today is repent.
Stop fooling around and playing church and
being a little religious and get desperate.
Make a decision.*

Derek Prince

Being double-minded and playing it both ways depending on circumstances and who we're with makes for a very rocky ride in this life. Better buckle up! And when you decide to get serious, don't take the "Religious Route"—*I despise the religious mindset!* Religion is so legalistic and full of "thou shalt" and "thou shalt not" rules that require a personal impetus to follow and achieve. That takes too much effort, and it's simply unattainable. Jesus even recognized this in Matthew 5:20 when He said, "*Unless your righteousness exceeds the righteousness of the scribes and Pharisees, you will by no means enter the kingdom of heaven.*" His point was not that we should live sinfully but rather that we are to rely on the finished work of the Cross to compel us to a pure relationship with Him.

> *For He made Him who knew no sin to be sin for us, that we might become the righteousness of God in Him.*
> II CORINTHIANS 5:21 NKJV

I love having this unbreakable friendship with my Lord and Savior. My greatest desire is to be 100% committed to the One who has my best interests at heart. If I say I'm serious about being an authentic Christian, then I'm going to, unashamedly, *be one!* I'm not fooling around on this crucial issue. I have decided to follow Jesus—no turning back.

MORE FOCUSED UPWARD

*Draw near to God and He will draw near to you.
Cleanse your hands, you sinners;
and purify your hearts, you double-minded.*
JAMES 4:8 NKJV

TWO CENTS MORE

HARDENED "HEART-ERIES"

Some years ago, I heard a pastor begin his sermon talking about how high cholesterol can cause clogging and hardening of the arteries. He said that we can do something about that by the way we tend to our physical bodies and watch what we eat or ingest to sustain us. Then the pastor began to address the issue of arrogance and pride versus humility. His segue suggested that a lack of humility could create a blockage and harden one's heart.
It occurred to me that the presence of arrogance and pride results in clogging and hardening of the "heart-eries". It is so important to take as much (or even more) care when addressing spiritual issues. What we ingest spiritually needs to be carefully selected and ingested for optimal sustenance in a world that is running rampant on spiritual junk food.
A strong heart is the order of the day for Christians.

Rowgo

There has been growing turmoil across the globe today. A spiritual war is raging in the cultures and in the unseen realm. We are not wrestling against flesh and blood, but against principalities and powers and rulers of the darkness of this world and against spiritual wickedness in high places. (see Ephesians 6:12) And yet, there are so many people waging war and bringing verbal and physical resistance to anything that smacks of Christianity—God, Jesus, the Bible, and even believers gathering to praise and worship the Lord. Censorship is becoming all too familiar. We once could express ourselves without recrimination—you know, in America, free speech is guaranteed to us as a right.

On top of all that, I have noticed a troubling trend in some churches. A desire to please everyone and their political agendas have watered down the fundamental tenets and instructions God laid down in His Word. Pastors and church leaders must return to the basics and stop acquiescing to the craziness taking over the unrepentant world. People-pleasing has been taking precedence over pleasing God. Lost people don't need a weakened "feel good" message lacking power. They need the unadulterated truth. Churches should not be social clubs, seeking cash and catering to the rich and famous and social influencers; instead, they should be safe places to train up and fully arm the saints of God for battling in the spiritual realm where most have been ignorant. It is time to rise up and choose allegiances. As for me and my house, we will serve the Lord. (See Joshua 24:15)

> *For this nation's heart has grown gross (fat and dull), and their ears heavy and difficult of hearing, and their eyes they have tightly closed, lest they see and perceive with their eyes, and hear and comprehend the sense with their ears, and grasp and understand with their heart, and turn and I should heal them.*
> MATTHEW 13:15 AMP

WHO'S TALKING?

*When I pray, I talk to God,
but when I read the Bible,
God talks to me.*

Smith Wigglesworth

I love how Wigglesworth said this. So many people get a little testy when their friends tell them that God told them something. Yeah, right—God spoke to you! What makes you so special? Nothing really. God speaks to all of us—He is no respecter of persons. The Bible is His Word to us. All Scripture is God-breathed. When we read it, we read the words He has spoken to us. If we can wrap our brains around that, we will realize that God is always speaking to us. Let's have the good sense to read and "listen" to what He has to say on a daily basis.

*For the word of God is living and powerful,
and sharper than any two-edged sword, piercing even
to the division of soul and spirit, and of joints and marrow,
and is a discerner of the thoughts and intents of the heart.*
HEBREWS 4:12 NKJV

_____

_____

_____

_____

_____

THIS IS WRONG!

*A mother is a shooting star who
passes through your life only once.
Love her because when her light goes out,
you will never see her again.*

I just about came out of my chair when I read this post! I vociferously disagree with this message! My mom shot through life here on earth, and then she was gone. But she wasn't lost by a long shot. I know exactly where she is, and because we each made the most important decision in our life, I'll not only see her again—I'll be enjoying her company forever. It doesn't get any better than that!

Never see her again? *Pffft!*

> *We are confident, yes, well pleased rather to be absent from the body and to be present with the Lord. Therefore, we make it our aim, whether present or absent, to be well pleasing to Him. For we must all appear before the judgment seat of Christ, that each one may receive the things done in the body, according to what he has done, whether good or bad.*
> II Corinthians 5:8-10 NKJV

CORRIE TEN BOOM

During Corrie's presentations to audiences, she would often hold the wrong side of a piece of embroidery with hundreds of tangled threads hanging from it. Many wondered if she was holding up the wrong side by mistake. As she held up the messy side of the embroidery to the audience, she would ask:

"Does God always grant us what we ask for in prayer? Not always. Sometimes He says, 'No.' That is because God knows what we do not know. God knows all. Look at this piece of embroidery. This wrong side is chaos. But look at the beautiful picture on the other side—the right side." Triumphantly she would flip the cloth over and reveal an elaborately embroidered crown—symbolizing our crown of eternal life. The crown was intricately stitched and had threads of many colors, including gold, silver, and pearls.

"We see now the wrong side; God sees His side all the time. One day we shall see the embroidery from His side and thank Him for every answered and unanswered prayer."

In the late '70s, my mom and I had the incredible opportunity to meet this highly-respected woman of faith. For those unaware, Corrie and her family protected and hid many Jewish families in their home in the Netherlands during World War II, capturing much of the details in her book, *The Hiding Place*. When I think about the struggles endured by her family and those they protected, her message rings true: How we see things through our natural eyes and how God sees things through His omniscience vary considerably. It's all a matter of perspective. One day we will all be able to get the whole picture and understand why things happened the way they did. Clearly, Corrie now sees both sides of the cloth and is fully aware of the impact her trust in the Lord Jesus Christ has had on countless generations.

Sidenote: After I became a Christian over 50 years ago, I watched *The Hiding Place* film and added quite a few of Corrie's books to my library. She was so kind, gracious, and full of faith—one of my heroes. I admired her boldness and felt empowered reading about her life. After hearing her speak on two separate occasions, Mom and I approached and struck up meaningful conversations with her. I don't recall the subtleties of our talk, but we exchanged pleasantries—my mom even spoke a little Dutch with her. As I look back over my life experiences, these times with Corrie ten Boom, a modern woman of faith, rank high among my life's highlights.

> *Now we see things imperfectly, like puzzling reflections in a mirror, but then we will see everything with perfect clarity. All that I know now is partial and incomplete, but then I will know everything completely, just as God now knows me completely.*
> I CORINTHIANS 13:12 NLT

> *Therefore if any person is [ingrafted] in Christ (the Messiah) he is a new creation (a new creature altogether); the old [previous moral and spiritual condition] has passed away. Behold, the fresh and new has come!*
> II CORINTHIANS 5:17 AMP

ASK THE RIGHT QUESTION

The question isn't why would a loving God send people to hell?
The question is why would anyone choose hell over a loving God?

Exactly—ask the right question! It has never been about a loving God sending people to hell. The Message Bible states it clearly:

> *He is restraining himself on account of you,*
> *holding back the End because he doesn't want anyone lost.*
> *He's giving everyone space and time to change.*
> II PETER 3:9 MSG

But everyone can be sure of one thing. Our time here will run out eventually, and that's when we "pay the piper," so to speak. It's all about free choice—and being willing to live (and die) with that choice. Ever since Adam and Eve's failure, God's desire has been that *all* would accept the gift His Son gave at the cross to purchase our freedom and salvation. If we don't do that, we *will* suffer the consequences. For an account of what that would look like, grab a Bible and read Luke 16:19-31.

> *The Lord does not delay and is not tardy or slow about what He*
> *promises, according to some people's conception of slowness, but He*
> *is long-suffering (extraordinarily patient) toward you, not desiring*
> *that any should perish, but that all should turn to repentance.*
> II PETER 3:9 AMP

MORE THAN ENOUGH

You are more than…
>   your past
>   your financial situation
>   your job
>   your personality
>   your triumphs
>   your failures.
> You are a child of God.

This post refers to the people who have responded to John 1:12, which states, *"But as many as received Him, to them He gave the right to become children of God, to those who believe in His name."* Based on that verse, a condition must be met to be rightfully called a "child of God." Once that condition has been met, everything that God has to say about us is final. We are much more than the list that was posted. We *are* who God says we are—and we are more than enough.

> *But to as many as did receive and welcome Him, He gave the authority (power, privilege, right) to become the children of God, that is, to those who believe in (adhere to, trust in, and rely on) His name. Who owe their birth neither to blood nor to the will of the flesh [that of physical impulse] nor to the will of man [that of a natural father], but to God. [They are born of God!]*
> JOHN 1:12-13 AMP

GO IN ALL THE WAY

Max Lucado tells the story of a little boy who fell out of bed.
When his mom asked him what happened, he answered, "I don't know.
I guess I stayed too close to where I got in." That can happen with our
faith when we're tempted to stay where we got in and
never ever moved beyond the edge.

Developing four healthy habits may be the order of the day:
Give attention to an ever-increasing prayer life.
Increase giving—not just money—which will, in turn, increase joy.
Engage in personal Bible study which results in the idea of learning to learn.
Be loyal and faithful to a body of believers where the Word causes growth
and spiritual maturity.

Growth is the goal of the Christian. Maturity is mandatory.
Don't make the mistake of the little boy.
Don't stay too close to where you got in.
It's risky resting on the edge.

Max Lucado

When I shared this, one of my friends commented by saying that it's also possible to go so far in that there's a risk of going off the deep end on the other edge. There certainly is some truth in that statement. Brand-new Christians can become so excited about becoming a member of the "Family of God" that they can hardly wait to tell others all about it. In their zeal, they sometimes tend to blow people away and put them off.

When I first became a Christian, I wanted everyone to know how wonderful I felt about being in good standing with God. I certainly didn't want to be offensive. And I certainly didn't want to be critical or judgmental of others who had not decided to follow Jesus. I still am very excited about the decision I made over 50 years ago, and as I grow older and closer to relocating to heaven, I'm even more invested in sharing the Good News. I look forward to spending eternity with the people I love, but not all of them have chosen to go all in and accept the gift of salvation that is freely offered to everyone. Accepting the Lord is a choice available to everyone, but I must remember it is a free-will decision. I cannot make it happen, but I can pray for the best outcome for everybody. That's what I *can* do. Balance and being led by the Holy Spirit are key.

> *Let every detail in your lives—words, actions, whatever—*
> *be done in the name of the Master, Jesus,*
> *thanking God the Father every step of the way.*
> COLOSSIANS 3:17 MSG

LAYING BRICKS

*If you continue to carry the bricks from your past,
you will end up building the same house.*

My recommendation is to fire your old designer and hire the One who drew up your original blueprint. Totally discard the old bricks and carefully inspect the new materials you plan to use. Work daily with the Designer to ensure a solid foundation supports a structure of purpose that opens the door to a beautiful future.

> *"These words I speak to you are not incidental additions to your life; homeowner improvements to your standard of living. They are foundational words, words to build a life on. If you work these words into your life, you are like a smart carpenter who built his house on solid rock. Rain poured down, the river flooded, a tornado hit—but nothing moved that house. It was fixed to the rock. "But if you just use my words in Bible studies and don't work them into your life, you are like a stupid carpenter who built his house on the sandy beach. When a storm rolled in and the waves came up, it collapsed like a house of cards."*
> MATTHEW 7:24-27 MSG

GOD'S PLAN

God doesn't want us to have broken hearts, wounded emotions, and messed up personalities. He wants us to know who we are in Christ and to receive His unconditional love.

Joyce Meyer

If only—if only we would make it our highest priority to search out what God has to say about us, we could save ourselves a lot of heartaches and disappointments. Instead, too often we spend our time pursuing things that pull us away from God's plans for our lives. More than that, we tend to focus on who we aren't and why we aren't worthy to receive His unconditional love. If God has made His unconditional love crystal clear to us through His Word, our fickle feelings that diminish our self-worth need to take a hike. We *are* who God says we are, and that's final. God's love for us is indisputable.

> *For I am persuaded beyond doubt (am sure) that neither death nor life, nor angels nor principalities, nor things impending and threatening nor things to come, nor powers, nor height nor depth, nor anything else in all creation will be able to separate us from the love of God which is in Christ Jesus our Lord.*
> ROMANS 8:38-39 AMP

JUST BREATHE

There was a moment when Moses had asked God what His name is. God was gracious enough to answer, and the name He gave is recorded in the original Hebrew as YHWH.

Over time we've arbitrarily added an "a" and an "e" in there to get YaHWeH, presumably because we have a preference for vowels. But scholars and rabbis have noted that the letters YHWH represent breathing sounds or aspirated consonants. When pronounced without intervening vowels, it actually sounds like breathing. YH (inhale); WH (exhale).

So a baby's first cry, his first breath, speaks the name of God. A deep sigh calls His name—or a groan or a gasp that is too heavy for mere words. Even an atheist would speak His name unaware that their very breath is giving constant acknowledgment to God. Likewise, a person leaves this earth with their last breath, when God's name is no longer filling their lungs.

So when I can't utter anything else, is my cry calling out His name? Being alive means I speak His name constantly. Is it heard the loudest when I'm the quietest? In sadness, we breathe heavy sighs. In joy, our lungs feel almost like they will burst. In fear, we hold our breath and have to be told to breathe slowly to help us calm down. When we're about to do something hard, we take a deep breath to find our courage.

When I think about it, breathing is giving Him praise. Even in the hardest moments! This is so beautiful and fills me with emotion every time I grasp the thought. God chose to give Himself a name that we can't help but speak every moment we're alive. All of us, always, everywhere. Waking, sleeping, breathing, with the name of God on our lips. (Psalm 150:6)

Unknown

Upon doing a brief study of the name "Yahweh," I found the meaning of the name has been interpreted as "He Who Makes That Which Has Been Made" or "He Brings into Existence Whatever Exists"—though other interpretations have been offered by many scholars. When God revealed Himself to Moses, my Bible says that He said, "I AM WHO I AM."
The Amplified Bible says it this way:

And Moses said to God, Behold, when I come to the Israelites and say to them, The God of your fathers has sent me to you, and they say to me, What is His name? What shall I say to them? And God said to Moses, I AM WHO I AM and I WILL BE WHAT I WILL BE, and He said, You shall say this to the Israelites: I AM has sent me to you!
EXODUS 3:13-14 AMP

Just imagine—every breath we take is speaking God's name! It really doesn't matter whether or not we believe He exists. God knew what He was doing when He created us in such a way that His name would be spoken with every breath we take. I, for one, will be asking the Holy Spirit to remind me that God's name will be forever spoken by me no matter what joys or tribulations I may be experiencing for the rest of my life on this earth. It is comforting to me, as a Christian, to know that God's name—YaHWeH—will forever be spoken with every breath I take.

Let everything that has breath and every breath of life praise the Lord! Praise the Lord! (Hallelujah!)
PSALM 150:6 AMP

BALANCING THE SCALE

*Decisions become easier when your will
to please God outweighs your will
to please the world.*

Toby Mac

Remember the song *I Did It My Way*? Well—you can forget all about that. Do everything God's way for the win! There is way too much people-pleasing going on in the world today. People change their minds and rhetoric depending on their audience constantly. Rather than trying to fit in with everybody's agenda just to be accepted, it might be wise to pay attention to the standard God has established. When you understand what He has said about everything—and it matters to you more than anything else—decisions you make will be a piece of cake.

What does God say? Do that!

*For we speak as messengers approved by God to be entrusted
with the Good News. Our purpose is to please God, not people.
He alone examines the motives of our hearts.*
I Thessalonians 2:4 NLT

MIGHT AS WELL TAKE IT

God loves you whether you like it or not.

I LIKE IT! It would be perfection to complete the cycle and love Him back in the same manner He loves you. God would like that a lot. It would, no doubt, put a big smile on His face.

> *The Lord your God in your midst, the Mighty One, will save; He will rejoice over you with gladness, He will quiet you with His love, He will rejoice over you with singing.*
> ZEPHANIAH 3:17 NKJV

WOW—imagine that! In this instance, the translation for the word "rejoice" is "to dance." Picture this: God gets down off His throne and dances as He serenades you with joyful singing. God is crazy about you!

> *Your unfailing love, O Lord, is as vast as the heavens; your faithfulness reaches beyond the clouds. Your righteousness is like the mighty mountains, your justice like the ocean depths. You care for people and animals alike, O Lord. How precious is your unfailing love, O God! All humanity finds shelter in the shadow of your wings.*
> PSALM 36:5-7 NLT

WALKING ON LOGS

Before my dad was married, he lived with his parents and some of his brothers in the little village of Apgar, in Glacier National Park. My Uncle, his eldest brother Earl, had a cabin court just as you enter Apgar called "Moose Cabins." As a family, we spent a lot of time visiting and camping. My Dad was a fisherman. He would fish wherever there was water. One of his favorite spots was just up the old road to Kintla Lake, to a stream called "Fish Creek." That was the first place that I remember that he invited me as an 8-year-old to go fishing with him. It was a small stream that empties into Lake McDonald. In fishing it, you needed to cross the creek multiple times because of brush and overhangs. This included walking on logs that had fallen across the creek. Dad did this with no hesitation, and I was to follow. I hesitated, looking at the fast-moving stream under the log. My Dad would say, "Just walk across the log!" After some hesitation on my part, he would take off down the creek saying, "I'm going fishing downstream. Follow me if you want!" Out of fear, I learned to walk across a log with a rushing stream below me. As time went on, I did not hesitate to walk across the log because I gained confidence that I could do it. I did it without thinking. Confidence.

Since that time, I have had multiple opportunities to develop confidence. Life demands it of us. Life tends to beat us up. I've come a long way since that 8-year-old experience, but I have learned to walk many logs through my life.

I have turned to Psalm 27 many times when I am facing a challenge that is bigger than I am. Listen to the author as he tells us where he gains confidence. "The Lord is my Light and my salvation; whom shall I fear? The Lord is the defense of my life; of whom shall I be afraid?" (Think log walking).

When I am studying Scripture, I am always looking for key words. The Psalmist says, "The Lord is my light—". The New Testament speaks much about "light". It is not referring to some artificial light, but an inner illumination. It speaks of knowledge that can be attained beyond anything we may gain through cognitive study. Listen to Paul in I Corinthians 2:11; "For who among us knows the spirit of a man except the spirit of the man which is in him? Even so, the thoughts of God no one knows except the Spirit of God. We have received, not the spirit of this world, but the Spirit that is from God, that we may know the things freely given to us by God."

That is the light that the Psalmist speaks of; "the Lord is my light." So, if I have that "light," whom shall I fear? I see confidence building! The Psalmist then says, the Lord is also his salvation. The salvation he speaks of is not the salvation we receive from Jesus Christ, for Jesus had not yet been revealed. The word "Salvation" refers to the deliverance that the Psalmist has received by walking with God. Now, the Psalmist exclaims, "the Lord is the defense of my life…." In other words, the Lord has become a garrison or a fort around the Psalmist and he exclaims, "Whom shall I fear?"

Life is bigger than any of us. We face so many "logs" that need to be crossed, and we see the raging current of life that brings us fear. But the Psalmist is telling me that I have inner knowledge that he refers to as "light". This will be a beacon that will guide me through those raging currents of life. The Spirit of God within me keeps fear at bay, and I become aware that the Lord is indeed "the defense of my life" when the enemies of life seek to destroy my faith.

I see here the faith of the Psalmist. His life is built on the bedrock of what God has promised. He is not crossing the currents of life alone. His faith gives him strength to face what life brings. This faith comes from God alone. We must allow Him to become part of our life. Verse 4 states: "I have asked from the Lord that I may dwell in the house of the Lord all the days of my life." His life is interwoven with the very life of God; thus, he sees himself walking with God and not being alone. Note how he expresses this intimacy in verse 5. "For in the day of trouble He will conceal me in His Tabernacle, in the secret place of His tent He will hide me, He will lift me upon a rock" [I will not fall into the stream!].

Do you see his confidence? His focus is on God and his worship of God. His focus is narrow, "—one thing I have asked of the Lord."
I observe the confidence he has,
"…He will conceal me…"
"…He will hide me…"
"…He will lift me…"
He has found God to be his "light," his "Salvation," and his "defense."

This makes me ask myself, "Could it be that the reason I am so fearful, so anxious, so apprehensive, is because I have no God?" I ignore who He is and what He has offered me. So, I walk alone with my anxious thoughts and issues that want to consume me. The rushing water below the log on which I am attempting to walk absolutely consumes me. I do not see the strength of the log; all I see is the rushing water. I read with great interest what Jesus had to say to His apostle in Matthew 6. [I suggest you read the last half].
I want to walk with God, not just believe in Him.

Allow me to paraphrase verses 11-14 of this Psalm. "Point me down your highway, Oh God, direct me along the lighted street. Show my enemies whose side you are on. Don't throw me to the dogs, those lions who are out to get me, filling the air with their threat. I'm sure I will see God's goodness on this earth. Take heart; don't quit. I say it again; stay with God."

I ask myself three questions:
- What resources do you have to live life with?
   - Are they human or divine?
- What are your greatest fears?
   - There are three national fears:
     - loss of relationship
     - loss of acceptance
     - loss of fulfillment
- What is the focus of your prayers?
   - Do you listen to your prayers?

Robert Ross

This piece was written by Robert Ross and was published in the weekly, *Perspectives*, by Whitefish Assembly of God in Whitefish, Montana. I gained permission to print this from the author's son, Ron Ross, who was my choir director many years ago at First Assembly of God in Kalamazoo, Michigan.

I was so moved by how Robert connected his boyhood experiences of learning to gain confidence by walking logs to how the Psalmist learned to gain confidence and focus on God's provision and protection. We often lose perspective and focus on our troubles rather than turning to the One who promised to faithfully deliver us from all our fears. Has this ever happened to you—or am I the only one?

> *I sought the Lord, and he answered me;*
> *he delivered me from all my fears.*
> PSALM 34:4 NIV

TWO CENTS MORE

BLIND BELIEF AND OBEDIENCE

Faith is believing when you don't see it,
but it's also obeying when you don't understand it.

Rick Warren

Most of us like to figure stuff out on our own, and think that we know everything. And if we admit we don't know everything, we like to think we know enough. But sometimes, God is telling us to do something that clearly makes no sense at all. Our human nature would much rather prefer to do God's bidding only if it gels with our limited understanding. We had better get over ourselves. God doesn't owe us an explanation for why and how He wants things done. We won't always understand, but arguing with God is just plain stupid. Do what He says nonetheless—we cannot go wrong if we do.

*Now faith is the substance of things hoped for,
the evidence of things not seen.*
HEBREWS 11:1 NKJV

But be doers of the word, and not hearers only, deceiving yourselves.
JAMES 1:22 NKJV

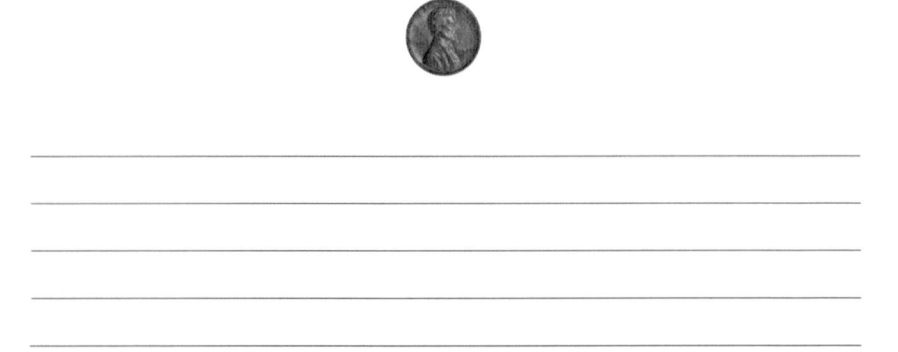

_____
_____
_____
_____

CONVERGENCE OF SCIENCE AND SCRIPTURE

Science and Scripture agree:
Your *mind* can and does contribute to both
cause and healing of whatever ails you.

According to the Bible, being thankful and correct thinking contributes to good health. "Stinking thinking" tends to erode and negatively affect healthy living. Scientific studies also agree that anxiety, depression, uncontrolled rage, and an assortment of other mental issues can cause physical ailments requiring medical attention. Here is a very descriptive picture of what that can look like:

> *A merry heart does good like a medicine,*
> *but a broken spirit dries the bones.*
> PROVERBS 17:22 NKJV

Remember that Proverbs arrived on the scene a considerable number of years before Mayo Clinic and Johns Hopkins. I'm so glad that the medical community agrees with God and His Word on this issue.

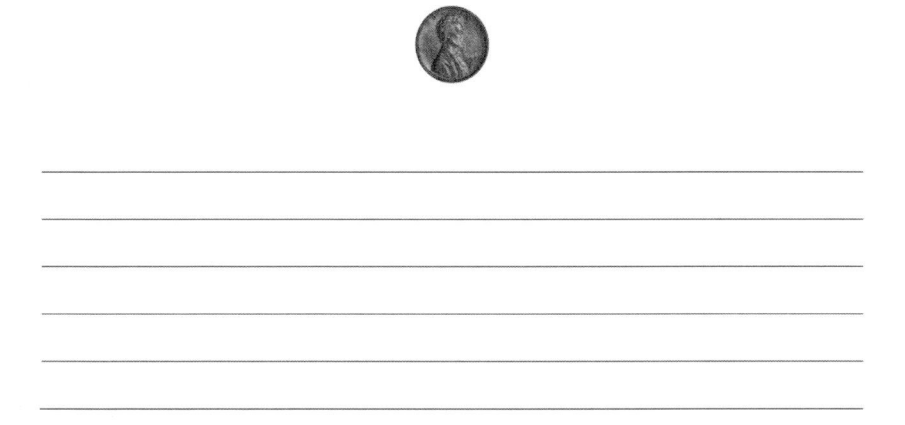

A GREAT INTERDEPENDENCY

God will take care of what you go through.
You take care of how you go through it.

Zig Ziglar

I depend on God, and He depends on me. This is an interdependency that I highly recommend. In fact, it is the only one that will work perfectly. God is very intentional as He goes about His business and is very careful to take us through whatever we face and bring us to safety. Our job is to trust God and keep a good attitude during our journey.

Fear not, for I am with you;
be not dismayed, for I am your God.
I will strengthen you, yes, I will help you,
I will uphold you with My righteous right hand.
ISAIAH 41:10 NKJV

TRIALS VERSUS WARFARE

*Don't confuse your trials with warfare.
When you do, you will resist the wrong spirit.
Yield to God in the trials. Resist the devil in the warfare.*

Jennifer LeClaire

In this world we will have trouble—that's a promise. Some of it will be of our own making, and some will appear out of nowhere. God allows us to go through some stuff so that we can grow, gain strength, and become more mature in the faith. When these times come, lean on the Lord and trust Him to bring us through our tough challenges, gaining wisdom as we reach the other side. It's best to work in harmony with God to overcome our trials.

On the other hand, Satan is in the business of committing heinous acts against all of us, and he would like nothing better than to wipe us out. Now that's what we call warfare, and the weapons of our warfare are not carnal—but they are mighty to the pulling down of strongholds (see II Corinthians 10:4). That's when we need to gird ourselves with the whole armor of God.

We must be able to differentiate between warfare and trials to properly discern the approach we are to take. But rest assured, His Word is our guide and exposes the enemy's tactics. Work with God to overcome every trial, and fearlessly resist the warring devil and kick his evil butt.

*Blessed is the man who remains steadfast under trial,
for when he has stood the test he will receive the crown of life,
which God has promised to those who love him.*
JAMES 1:12 ESV

For the weapons of our warfare are not carnal but mighty in God for pulling down strongholds, casting down arguments and every high thing that exalts itself against the knowledge of God, bringing every thought into captivity to the obedience of Christ, and being ready to punish all disobedience when your obedience is fulfilled.
II CORINTHIANS 10:4-6 NKJV

*Therefore submit to God.
Resist the devil and he will flee from you.*
JAMES 4:7 NKJV

HOLD ON TIGHT

When a father leads his four-year-old son down a crowded street,
he takes him by the hand and says, "Hold on to me." He doesn't say,
"Memorize the map" or "Take your chances dodging the traffic" or
"Let's see if you can find your way home." The good father gives the
child one responsibility: "Hold on to my hand."
God does the same for us.

Max Lucado

When challenges and tough times come, how come so many people are more apt to trust others rather than God? His promises to us are Yes and Amen (II Corinthians 1:20-22). As for me, I don't *ever* want to let go of His hand. God leads me where He wants me to go, shows me how to get there, and keeps me safe as I go. I must trust Him implicitly.

"For I, the Lord your God, will hold your right hand,
saying to you, 'Fear not, I will help you.'"
ISAIAH 41:13 NKJV

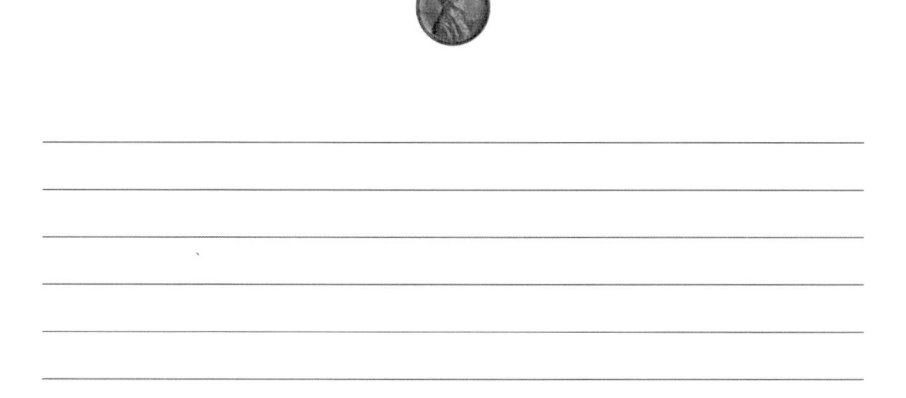

REV. HARPER AND THE TITANIC

The night the Titanic sank in 1912 on April 14th, 1,528 people went into the frigid waters. John Harper, after putting his only daughter on a lifeboat, was seen swimming frantically to people in the water leading them to Jesus before the hypothermia became fatal. Rev. Harper swam up to one young man who had climbed up on a piece of debris. Rev. Harper asked him between breaths, "Are you saved?" The young man replied that he was not.

Harper then tried to lead him to Christ, only to have the young man, who was near shock, reply "No." John Harper then took off his lifejacket and threw it to the man and said, "Here then, you need this more than I do—" and swam away to other people. A few minutes later, Harper swam back to the young man and succeeded in leading him to salvation.

Of the 1,528 people that went into the water that night, six were rescued by the lifeboats. One of them was this young man on the debris. Four years later, at a survivors meeting, this young man stood up and in tears recounted how John Harper had led him to Christ. Rev. Harper had tried to swim back and help other people, yet because of the intense cold, had grown too weak to swim. His last words before going under in the frigid waters were, "Believe on the name of the Lord Jesus, and you will be saved."

Does Hollywood remember the man? No. Oh well, no matter. This servant of God did what he had to do. While other people were trying to buy their way onto the lifeboats and were selfishly trying to save their own lives, John Harper gave up his life so that others could be saved.

John Harper knew what it meant to live life with urgency.

Unknown

This story from the tragic events surrounding the sinking of the Titanic stirs something deep within me. My closest friends and family members are aware of the sense of urgency that I have about facing the end of my life here. In fact, it was a topic of central importance to me over my birthday lunch in 2021 with my dear friend, Gloria Mihelich. I am passionate about being able to reunite with loved ones "in the blink of an eye"—read that chapter in *Two Cents*. At my level, there is *nothing* more important than that.

> *If you openly declare that Jesus is Lord and believe in your heart that God raised him from the dead, you will be saved. For it is by believing in your heart that you are made right with God, and it is by openly declaring your faith that you are saved.*
> ROMANS 10:9-10 NLT

SURRENDER IS THE KEY

God does not want you to try harder.
He wants you to trust Him deeper.
Stop trying. Start trusting.
This will change everything in you.

To trust Him deeper, you must humble yourself, become vulnerable and surrender who you are all the way to the root. Many people post the *"I'm gonna _____" (fill in the blank)* messages on their social media threads ad nauseum. The posts have a positive vibe and affirm what they're going to do, because they're so tired of the same stuff happening on repeat. Picture the hamster on a wheel going nowhere. Its intention is good and brimming with determination, but no real progress is made. Why? Because of who's sitting on the throne and who governs the rules of engagement. We try so hard to rule from a throne not intended for us. It's about as fruitless as waving our arms to direct traffic in Taiwan—from the comfort of our bedroom.

Instead, let God take charge and direct your path. Don't worry—He will give you plenty to do. You get to participate in your healing and growth, but you *must* wait on Him, trust Him, and follow His instructions to a tee. Don't Google anything and try to circumvent the process by posting "feel good" nonsense. It's best to keep this time of healing and dependence for maturity building. Spouting good intentions without following through and being able to show measurable results can cause real setbacks. It won't work unless you go root deep and trust God to do a work in you. It's time to fully surrender by letting go of control and trusting Him to handle everything you need. You are called to submit to God's will and do what pleases Him—pursuing truth and righteousness above all else.

*So humble yourselves under the mighty power of God,
and at the right time he will lift you up in honor. Give all your
worries and cares to God, for he cares about you.*
I Peter:6-7 NLT

*Trust in the Lord with your whole heart,
and lean not on your own understanding;
in all your ways acknowledge Him,
and He shall direct your paths.*
Proverbs 3:5-6 NKJV

FAITH HAS DIFFERENT DIRECTIONS

*Sometimes all you'll have going for you is faith.
Don't let go!*

Sandi Kradowski

We ALL have faith in something, but what direction does our faith take? Is our faith full of negativity, believing that nothing has ever turned out the way we wanted, so why should we ever think that things will ever change and get better? Have we adopted a victim-mentality faith and participated in countless pity parties? Or do we have the kind of faith that positively believes all things will work together for good and produce precisely what God has purposed for us?

> *And we know that all things work together for
> good to those who love God, to those who are
> the called according to His purpose.*
> ROMANS 8:28 NKJV

We must learn to hang on to the right kind of faith and not allow a mixture of unbelief to muddy the waters. Creflo Dollar has addressed this kind of faith many times. He teaches that *all* believers have enough faith, but we give more attention to the "yah but, what ifs" at times—and that kind of thinking dilutes our faith and gets in the way.

> *Don't copy the behavior and customs of this world,
> but let God transform you into a new person by
> changing the way you think. Then you will learn
> to know God's will for you, which is good
> and pleasing and perfect.*
> ROMANS 12:2 NLT

Truth be told, I struggle with this at times. I am guilty of developing a contingency plan just in case God "falls short" and doesn't follow *my* dream and deliver. The bottom line is that I have faith *and* unbelief simultaneously. Focus, Rowgo, focus! Renewing my mind is on my daily "To Do" list. Changing my stinking thinking and learning how to think the way God thinks will change my outlook and therefore, my life. It's all about perspective and exercising the right kind of faith.

> *Because of the Lord's great love we are not consumed,*
> *for his compassions never fail. They are new every*
> *morning, great is your faithfulness.*
> LAMENTATIONS 3:22-23 NIV

> *"You don't have enough faith," Jesus told them.*
> *"I tell you the truth, if you had faith even as small as a mustard*
> *seed, you could say to this mountain, 'Move from here to there,'*
> *and it would move. Nothing would be impossible."*
> MATTHEW 17:20 NLT

# IT'S CALLED "CONVICTION"

The Bible may hurt you with the Truth,
but it will never comfort you with a lie.

Here's the thing though—the Bible says many things that convict us regarding how we speak and act, hitting us right where we live. Those truthful words may hurt our fragile feelings but won't harm us. God is saying all of those things for our good. In fact, if we respond appropriately and make necessary adjustments to our words, thoughts, and behaviors, we will grow, heal, and become who we were created to be.

However, being "comforted" with a lie invites us to live a life contrary to God's will and His ultimate plan. How much comfort can there really be if we're living a life lacking integrity and truth?

Every part of Scripture is God-breathed and useful one way or another—showing us truth, exposing our rebellion, correcting our mistakes, training us to live God's way. Through the Word we are put together and shaped up for the tasks God has for us.
II TIMOTHY 3:16-17 MSG

HOPE FOR TOMORROW
BE LIKE DANIEL

My granny told me throughout my adolescent years—"Be like Daniel." As we ended our phone conversations, as I hurried off to school, before my Saturday track meets, as I walked out the door with my date, her words were an ever-present reminder. She had a way of taking the most profound thoughts and condensing them into the simplest of phrases. While I understood some of what she meant at the time, it's taken the last few years to come to fully value the depth of her wisdom.

The America I have known my entire life is no more. Driven by politics over relationships, we find the great tapestry of our Nation hanging on by a few worn-out threads. I am finding myself enraged by the actions of both sides. I am worried about what the future holds for my children. I am disheartened by all the noise. And I am broken over the divide we all find ourselves in.

This afternoon I wept as I watched the news. Is this really what America has become? Are we really allowing our country to be torn to shreds from sensational news coverage, social media posts, and a virus that has affected all of us in some way? Have we really allowed our nation to implode from within? The core of who we are—the UNITED States of America—utterly divided?

Tears ran down my face as I rocked my newborn son—how do I raise him and his sisters in such a tumultuous climate? What will life look like for them going forward?

As I continue to rock, my sweet Granny's southern tone filled my ears—"Be like Daniel." So I turned to Daniel 6. Daniel had just learned that his worship would sentence him to death in the lions' den. While many know this portion of Scripture from the Sunday School lessons, Daniel is saved from the lions, it is his response to the decree that warrants such a profound statement to serve as a reminder to us all.

"When Daniel knew that the document had been signed, he went to his house where he had windows in his upper chamber open toward Jerusalem. He got down on his knees three times a day and prayed and gave thanks before his God, as he had done previously." Daniel 6:10

"As he had done previously."
Be like Daniel, Arianna.

Daniel was guaranteed the consequences of going about life the same, yet he didn't waver in his commitment to worship. He didn't mourn the loss of his right to pray; he prayed as he had previously done. He didn't deny the punishment that was to come; he fixed his eyes on Jerusalem as he had previously done, remembering his identity as God's chosen people. He didn't fear death; he worshipped as he had previously done.

He remembered Who was in control.
He remembered Who alone he worshipped.
He responded by doing just as he had done previously.

Be like Daniel.

Friends, I don't know where you find yourselves tonight. There's a good chance that while we may all align differently on the political spectrum, we all find ourselves grieved by what has taken place today. Collectively, we mourn the state of our nation.

I don't know where you stand with Jesus Christ. I don't know what you believe and hold to. But I can tell you—my response going forward will be to do as I have previously done.

To raise my children to know and honor God, as warriors for His Truth, as soldiers of compassion and love for all made in His image, and as seekers of righteousness in a fallen world. To walk with my husband, hand-in-hand, proclaiming the Gospel in our words and deeds, creating a home that is a sanctuary of praise for our Father and a refuge of hope for those in need. To go about my days reading His Word, being refined by His Truth, transformed by His holiness, forever reminded that He holds our days in His hands.

I do not know what tomorrow holds. I do not know what life looks like ten years from now. I do not know how our nation will even go forward from here. But I can be like Daniel. Amid the dark news of today, I can respond by doing as I have always done—surrendered to the will of the Father, worshipping Him no matter what looms ahead. And in so doing, I can raise yet another generation to respond the same.

On the darkest of days.
When the world is more divided than ever.
When fear overwhelms.

Be like Daniel.

Fix your eyes on Him.
Fall on your knees before Him.
Pray, give thanks, and worship your God.
Just as you have done.

The God who shut the mouths of lions for Daniel holds the future in His hands. We need not fear. We simply must respond and do as we have previously done.

Arianna Freelen

January 6, 2021

I never knew my mom's mother—she went to be with Jesus long before I was born. But I'm thinking she would have been a lot like Arianna's granny. However, the simple phrases I frequently heard out of my mom's mouth have stayed with me over the years. I even shared a couple of them in *Two Cents:* "Do it because it's the right thing to do" and "Not tomorrow, but now!" Every day I also heard her declare with gusto, "Praise the Lord!" My mother was a genuine student of the Word and a bona fide prayer warrior. She was like Daniel—no matter what. Whenever troubles came, she did as she had done previously.

What can we learn from Arianna's post? My takeaway is to keep doing what we have always done even when the going gets tough, remembering our identity is with God and is defined by what He declares over us. He calls us His children, and we have everything He has promised us.

Arianna wrote about walking hand-in-hand with her husband. Many of us may live alone, without the benefit of another person nearby to bolster our courage when troubles hit. What then? The Word reminds us that we are never alone. God will never leave or forsake us, and His Word is always available. The Holy Spirit lives within believers to encourage and remind us that we have exactly what we need for whatever life or the devil throws at us.

> *This is my command—be strong and courageous!*
> *Do not be afraid or discouraged.*
> *For the Lord your God is with you wherever you go.*
> JOSHUA 1:9 NLT

No matter what is going on in the world, God is still on the throne and always will be. We may run around like chickens with our heads cut off, saying, "The sky is falling!" but God has a plan. He didn't consult us when He created the heavens, the earth, and all that went with it. He certainly doesn't need our help now. But there is something that would please God very much—that His children would trust Him, thank Him, have faith in His plan, be like Daniel, and pray and praise Him. If we jump on board and join God's team, we will be challenged by the enemy who seeks to destroy us, *but* we will win and be delivered from *all* our fears. We are already victors!

> *Don't be afraid, for I am with you.*
> *Don't be discouraged, for I am your God.*
> *I will strengthen you and help you.*
> *I will hold you up with my victorious right hand.*
> ISAIAH 41:10 NLT

THE CHASE IS ON

*If you chase Jesus as hard
as you chase the things you think you want,
you'll wind up with more than you'll ever need.*

Don't go on a wild goose chase. We grow up having hopes and dreams about our ideal life. *"If I got _____ , then I'd be happy."* Even the new car smell on the most expensive car will eventually fade—and a newer car will be desired. My go-to verse for this post is Matthew 6:33, *"But seek first the kingdom of God and His righteousness, and all these things shall be added to you."* What "things?" Simple—whatever you need. My son, Russ, wrote a song a few years back when he had been out of work for a spell that included the words—*Everything you need, He's (God) provided. Everything you need is in His hand.* That's more than wishing and hoping. It's even more than faith and trust in God's promises. It's *knowing*, pure and simple. Jesus *is* all we need, but He blesses us with much more as long as our priorities are in order. Make sure the first thing stays first!

*Steep your life in God-reality, God-initiative, God-provisions.
Don't worry about missing out. You'll find all your everyday
human concerns will be met.*
MATTHEW 6:33 MSG

GOD IS AN OVERACHIEVER

*Sometimes you can't see God in front of you
because He's got your back.*

Christine Caine

Quite often, we don't see or understand what's going on or what God is doing because He is working behind the scenes. He would like to think that we are carrying on and trusting in His care. In December of 2020, I wound up in the hospital with respiratory difficulties due to an earlier stint with Covid. I was told I would be there for five days, but 48 hours later, I was discharged. Two days passed very quickly, but while I was there, I had the beautiful opportunity to encourage a very weary and discouraged staff. I shared the Lord with them, and we laughed at my goofiness, cried, and prayed together. Later I discovered that my retirement organization paid 100% of all charges related to my Covid diagnosis—hospital, medications, doctors, tests, and *all!* And God was *behind* the whole thing! God had my back, and He proved Himself to be an Overachiever.

*Now to Him who is able to do exceedingly abundantly above
all that we ask or think, according to the power that works in us,
to Him be glory—*
EPHESIANS 3:20 NKJV

TWO CENTS MORE

A QUAFF FOR ATHEISTS

The first gulp from the glass of natural science
will make you an atheist, but at the bottom of the glass,
God is waiting for you.

Werner Heisendberg

Considered the Father of Quantum Physics

Lee Strobel, the author of *The Case for a Creator* and other case studies, became very aware of this the closer he came to the bottom of the glass. Everything his research chased after to prove that God was a crutch people leaned on in hard times turned out to be an undeniable truth and justifiable reality. Lee was intelligent—and choosing to not act the fool—he changed his mind and realigned his thinking. He is now fully convinced that God exists, and everything else in life depends on Him. Consider these words as starting points—they've been around a long time:

> *In the beginning God created the heavens and the earth.*
> GENESIS 1:1 NIV

> *But ask the animals what they think—let them teach you;*
> *let the birds tell you what's going on. Put your ear to the earth—*
> *learn the basics. Listen—the fish in the ocean will tell you their*
> *stories. Isn't it clear that they all know and agree that God is*
> *sovereign, that he holds all things in his hand—*
> *every living soul, yes, every breathing creature?*
> JOB 12:7-10 MSG

For ever since the creation of the world His invisible nature and attributes, that is, His eternal power and divinity, have been made intelligible and clearly discernible in and through the things that have been made (His handiworks). So [men] are without excuse [altogether without any defense or justification}.
ROMANS 1:20 AMP

ONE LIFE TO LIVE

You only live once, but if you do it right,
once is enough.

There are no do-overs with the one life you have been given here, and as the years accumulate, it becomes abundantly clear that time is running out. All of the things you thought about and planned to do but never got around to doing may still be on your bucket list. Live each day intentionally and finish your race with no regrets. There is still time to become all you were created to be, so go ahead—*do it!* As long as you have breath, it's never too late—life is an adventure! Just remember to do the first things first.

> *And just as each person is destined to die once and after that comes judgment, so also Christ was offered once for all time as a sacrifice to take away the sins of many people. He will come again, not to deal with our sins, but to bring salvation to all who are eagerly waiting for him.*
> HEBREWS 9:27-28 NLT

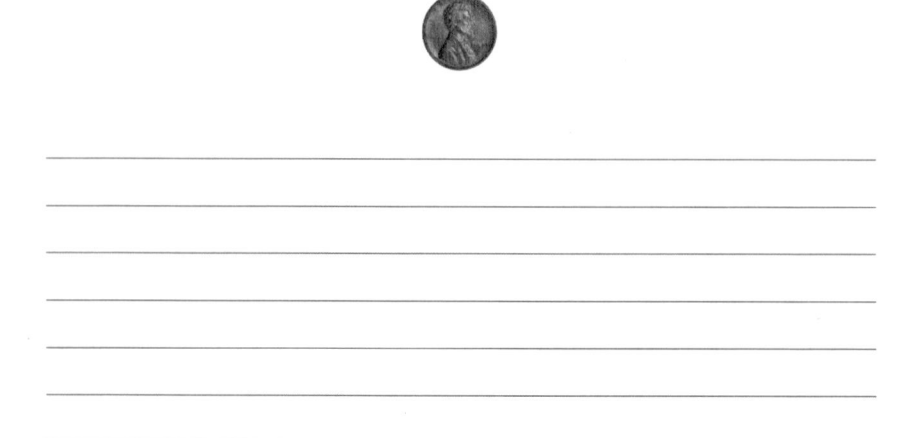

DO AS YOU'RE TOLD

People blame God for the suffering in the world when it's actually
the result of humanity doing the opposite of what God commands us to do.

The gift of life comes with instructions—a User Manual if you will. It's called The Bible. If you insist on jerry-rigging your life with baling wire and duct tape, figuring it all out alone doesn't always work out the best. We call this "user error," which is just plain stupid and can be avoided. Don't blame the Manufacturer for your foolishness.

Here it is in a nutshell: Just as one person did it wrong and got us in all this trouble with sin and death, another person did it right and got us out of it. But more than just getting us out of trouble, he got us into life! One man said no to God and put many people in the wrong; one man said yes to God and put many in the right.
ROMANS 5:18-19 MSG

Therefore you shall keep His statutes and His commandments, which I command you this day, that it may go well with you and your children after you and that you may prolong your days in the land which the Lord your God gives you forever.
DEUTERONOMY 4:40 AMP

THIS IS SO NOT TRUE!

Yes, I've made mistakes.
But you know what?
Life didn't come with instructions.

YES—IT DID! We just don't bother to read them—or prefer to do it our way first. What a cop-out! No more excuses and rationalizations. Truth be told, most of the time, we *do* know better; we just decide in our "infinite wisdom" not to do better. Instead, we choose to go our own way and do what "feels good" and pleases whatever our flavor of the day happens to be. We'd better get a grip. The Bible has been around for a long time, and God's Word contains all the instructions we need to live a great life.

> *All Scripture is inspired by God and is useful to teach us what is true and to make us realize what is wrong in our lives. It corrects us when we are wrong and teaches us to do what is right. God uses it to prepare and equip his people to do every good work.*
> II TIMOTHY 3:16-17 NLT

EXPAND THE GOAL

The goal isn't to get people to a church;
the goal is to get people to Jesus.

Then what? The church is a major vehicle used to introduce people to Jesus, but certainly not the only way. With modern technology, people can even virtually attend services held in churches worldwide—and get saved—while sipping coffee in the comfort of their homes. The world is full of those who have knelt beside their bed and asked Christ Jesus into their heart. The gift of salvation is available to everyone and can happen anytime, anywhere. The church building is not the only place where people get saved, but God encourages us not to forsake gathering together. Church attendance is one way that we can accomplish that goal.

It's important to know that salvation is only the beginning step. Accepting Jesus and making Him our Savior is huge, but making Jesus our Lord takes finding out who He really is. We need to grow in knowledge and wisdom—and pursue spiritual growth. God's Word will show us how to appropriate His promises of emotional, psychological, and physical healing.

Although there are churches striving to please itching ears that want to hear something that lines up with and agrees with their way of thinking, many still preach the unadulterated Truth found in the Bible. *Caution:* Yielding to the "self-made Christians"—how's that for an oxymoron?—may be "politically correct," but that's a significant departure from preaching God's knowledge and wisdom found in His Word.

Taking this next step is very important. As new Christians, we must be very cautious when searching out "the place" where we will receive teaching to grow and gain wisdom about our walk with the Lord. Growing in spiritual maturity will require finding a church that doesn't deviate from what God desires for and from us. When we're just getting started, we're spiritual babies and likely to latch on to anything that looks and sounds good. We need discernment, but that's a relatively new concept for new believers to understand. "Coming to Jesus" is a real high, and we tend to gravitate toward whatever "feels good." Proverbs encourages us to seek wise and mature counsel for all kinds of things and follow it. This certainly applies to finding a place to worship to grow. It must be our goal not to fall for the outer trappings of a church and get sucked into a place that preaches a faulty, incomplete Gospel. Find a church led by those not afraid to teach and preach the unadulterated truth found in God's Word. That's how Christians will heal, grow, and mature in this upside-down world.

Personal responsibility is required and must be embraced by *all* Christians. Growing in knowledge and wisdom calls for individual study as well as hearing the Word preached from the pulpit. One of my favorite ways to study and grow is to meet up with one or more friends on the same trip, pursuing God's plan for their own growth and spiritual maturity—becoming who they are created to be. That's a tiny church—but it *is* a church nonetheless.

God has always planned for believers to be in a relationship with Him *and* with others. He has a purpose for the church (the building)—and we are *the* Church (the people)—*together*.

> *Let's see how inventive we can be in encouraging love and helping out, not avoiding worshiping together as some do but spurring each other on, especially as we see the big Day approaching.*
> HEBREWS 10:25 MSG

MORE FOCUSED UPWARD

*For where two or three are gathered together in My name,
I am there in the midst of them.*
MATTHEW 18:20 NKJV

COMPULSIVE CHRISTIAN DISORDER

The DSM-V (Diagnostic and Statistical Manual of Mental Disorders) will never include the diagnosis of Compulsive Christian Disorder, but it is a term Creflo Dollar used on one of his broadcasts a few years ago. It describes Christian people who are still insisting on trying to figure everything out and coming up with their own formula for what only God can do and has already done—choosing to go down Flesh Avenue rather than trusting and following the Holy Spirit and God's Word.

Rowgo

Grace can never be fully experienced until self-effort is a thing of the past. Follow God's DSM—*THE DSM*—His final Word on everything. Compulsive self-effort will never, ever get the job done. The words "It is finished!" have already been spoken. Simply said—God's got this. That's why He's God, and we're not!

This is what the Lord says—
Israel's King and Redeemer, the Lord of Heaven's Armies:
"I am the First and the Last; there is no other God."
ISAIAH 44:6 NLT

FINISH STRONG

Someday we'll forget the hurt, the reason we cried and who caused us pain. We will finally realize that the secret of being free is not revenge, but letting things unfold in their own way and own time.

After all, what matters is not the first, but the last chapter of our life which shows how well we ran the race.

So smile, laugh, forgive, believe, and love all over again.

What matters the most? Being bogged down by memories of hurt and pain? Let go of all of that, so you can travel light. Put on your racing shoes and finish strong, but ensure you're running the right race. I'd love to see you at the finish line!

*I have fought the good fight, I have finished the race,
I have kept the faith.*
II TIMOTHY 4:7 NKJV

I HATE RELIGION!

> Morality is doing what's right, no matter what you are told.
> Religion is doing what you are told, no matter what is right.
>
> H.L. Mencken (1880-1956)

First of all, let me make one thing abundantly clear—*I hate religion!* But I do *love* the *relationship* I have with the Lord. This distinction makes all the difference.

Regarding morality, who or what gets to define this anyway? For me, I have decided that the Bible is my Guiding Light. It defines the following:

- right and wrong
- moral and immoral
- acceptable and unacceptable
- righteousness and sin

What some people call morality has nothing to do with what God has to say about it. What is right and moral in man's eyes is often a departure from God's will and purpose for us. Can people make up their own rules and define morality for themselves? Yes, I suppose they are free to do so, but at what price? I don't care whose opinion or mindset is defining morality; if it's contrary to what God has written in His Word, it's wrong. The kind of religion Mencken references is most likely the Pharisaical Laws of dos and don'ts that have nothing to do with God's loving instructions to His people.

In both of Mencken's premises, he fails to address how God will judge morality and, make no mistake about it, He will. We don't get to make it up as we go along. His Word will be final on the subject—so we'd better get to studying. We still have a thing or two to learn—and there is still time to adjust and renew our thinking.

*When people do not accept divine guidance, they run wild.
But whoever obeys the law is joyful.*
PROVERBS 29:18 NLT

*Where there is no vision [no redemptive revelation of God],
the people perish; but he who keeps the law [of God, which includes
that of man]—blessed (happy, fortunate, and enviable) is he.*
PROVERBS 29:18 AMP

*If people can't see what God is doing,
they stumble all over themselves;
but when they attend to what he reveals, they are most blessed.*
PROVERBS 29:18 MSG

FAULTY THINKING

You may think you can live fine without Christ,
but you cannot afford to die without Him.

Charles Spurgeon

That's the truth! The operative word is "think," but we all realize at some point that our thinking can be pretty messed up and create significant problems. Insert an oft-used phrase—*What was I thinking!?!?* A life without Christ can be very challenging; dying without Him is much, much worse. Better to be safe than sorry. Life works much better that way now *and* later.

*It's impossible to please God apart from faith. And why?
Because anyone who wants to approach God must believe both that
he exists and that he cares enough to respond to those who seek him.*
HEBREWS 11:6 MSG

BENEFITS FOR THE AGES

Age makes you old enough to know better,
but God makes you wise enough to do better.

Both parts of this statement are true. A relationship with God ensures that the Helper, the Holy Spirit, will constantly direct us to do the right thing. Once we are old enough to know better and wise enough to do better, it would be highly beneficial to follow through with whatever the Holy Spirit encourages us to do.

The law of the Lord is perfect, restoring the [whole] person;
the testimony of the Lord is sure, making wise the simple.
PSALM 19:7 AMP

NO SUBSTITUTE

Information about God is a poor substitute for intimacy with God.

It's all about relationships. I grew up in the church, and my family attended together regularly. Back in the day, before all of the distractions of all kinds of activities available to me and places to go easily, church was the big attraction that offered things to do for youth—like roller-skating and hayrides and endless potlucks for the general church population. Due to the religious exposure and activities, I heard a great deal about God—who He was, what He did, and how He dealt with His creation. I got a lot of information about Him and His Son, but not so much about the Holy Spirit. The third person of the Trinity was more often called the "Holy Ghost" at my church.

A little over fifty years ago, I got serious and entered into an intimate relationship with the One who loved me best and agreed to work on becoming all He created me to be. Being led by the One who put me on this planet has been such a blessing and so rewarding. Since that time, life has been an adventure of ups and downs, not unlike a roller coaster, but I have shared the ride buckled in on the same seat with my Father. We are traveling this life together, experiencing great safety and enormous blessings all the while.

> *[For my determined purpose is] that I may know Him [that I may progressively become more deeply and intimately acquainted with Him, perceiving and recognizing and understanding the wonders of His Person more strongly and more clearly], and that I may in that same way come to know the power outflowing from His resurrection [which it exerts over believers], and that I may so share His sufferings as to be continually transformed [in spirit into His likeness even] to His death, [in the hope] that if possible I may*

attain to the [spiritual and moral] resurrection [that lifts me] out from among the dead [even while in the body].
PHILIPPIANS 3:10-11 AMP

THERE IS ANOTHER OPTION

Instead of saying, "Lord, I don't know how I am going to do this,"
say, "Lord, I can't wait to see how you do this."

When we feel helpless, we really are *not* without help. Our concerns over the reality of our current situation is not a big deal if we accept and foster a real relationship with our Father who made the heavens and the earth and everything that exists therein.

God, you're such a safe and powerful place to find refuge!
You're a proven help in time of trouble—
more than enough and always available whenever I need you.
PSALM 46:1 TPT

CALL WAITING

Never put God on standby in your life—turn over your control to Him.
God will *never* steer you wrong.

Rowgo

Turning over control to God is an act of free will. There is no coercion or twisting of the arm, just an open invitation. This reminds me of the opening line of an old hymn: *Softly and tenderly, Jesus is calling.* If we answer that call, He can address all our needs and show us how to manage everything life throws at us. Unlike so many calls we make these days that have us on hold, listening to mind-numbing elevator music, God proves Himself to be an ever-present help in our time of need. His instructions are easy to understand and follow.

Once we connect with God, putting Him on hold would be pure folly. Our best ideas will never hold a candle to what God has already planned for our life. Telling Him to hold on a minute while we take the reigns and operate on our own is just plain foolish. We'll just wind up scrapping our big ideas that didn't work out and asking God to take the wheel.

> *By your words I can see where I'm going; they throw a beam of light on my dark path I've committed myself and I'll never turn back from living by your righteous order.*
> PSALM 119:105-106 MSG

HARD TRUTHS

People who die, young or old, don't become angels.
Not everyone who dies goes to heaven.
Jesus said there would be few in Matthew 7:14.
Dad may pray for you, but Dad can't put you in heaven.
You may join a church, but membership can't get you into heaven.
Being baptized won't get you into heaven.
A minister may speak at your funeral,
but a minister can't preach you into heaven.
Doing a lot of good things is great but won't gain access.
There's only one way for your journey on earth to end well.
Jesus said to him, "I am the way and the truth and the life.
No one comes to the Father except through Me."—John 14:6

Repent of your sin, believe on Jesus,
follow HIM and leave this world clinging to HIM in faith,
knowing HE has you in HIS hands. His grace is sufficient. Trust Him!

Unknown

Some of these statements sound pretty harsh and uncaring because we would all like to take comfort in many of these words when we have lost a loved one. I read through this post slowly and thoughtfully because, over my lifetime, I have lost many friends and family members who have been very near and dear to me at different times over my 78 years of living. The loss of each one has been difficult, and I miss all of them. At my age, I'm expecting losses to happen more frequently, and I'm aware that we have one final destination when our earth suit wears out. Our eternal destination is dependent on one thing only. John 14:6 spells it out, encouraging us to become a follower of Jesus and live a faith-filled life pleasing to God.

We are human *beings*, not human *doings!* Our good works, kind words, and prayers prayed over us by others won't do squat. God is all about relationships, and He wants one with every one of us. *Surrender!* Enter a *real* relationship with Him as your Father and with His Son, Jesus. Your eternal life, which we all have, depends on it.

Two songs came to mind as I read through this post and thought about how important it was to understand how salvation works. Remember *I'm Moving On Up*? That's *my* plan—I'm moving on up to the best time because the best is yet to come. My greatest hope is that my loved ones will join me by doing life God's way. Being a "good person" isn't enough.

The second song is *Lean On Me.* Trust in and lean on the Lord wholeheartedly. Don't lean on your own understanding. Acknowledge Him—which means to be constantly mindful of His presence in your life—and He will direct your path. These instructions can be found in Proverbs 3. Lean on God daily. Make Him an integral part of your life 24/7, and I'll surely see you later. To be continued...

> *God saved you by his grace when you believed. And you can't take credit for this; it is a gift from God. Salvation is not a reward for the good things we have done, so none of us can boast about it.*
> EPHESIANS 2:8-9 NLT

SING A NEW SONG

Silence is golden—unless you have a toddler.
In that case, silence is very, very suspicious.

This post brought back a precious memory. My daughter, Mara, was about 3 years old and had gone silently missing. My short search discovered her in our bedroom in front of the heat register. Her special blanket was laid out picnic-style on the floor, and all her dolls and stuffed animals were "seated" in front of her. They looked very much like a congregation that had gathered to have church. She was kneeling in front of them in her nightgown, eyes closed, hands reaching toward heaven, and sweetly singing as she led them in praise and worship to her Father.

Almost 50 years later, Mara still loves to worship and sing praises to her Papa. This seems to be a generational legacy handed down from generation to generation. Her great-grandparents on the Zichterman side of the family came from the Netherlands and were firm believers who lived out their Christian faith every day. They sang Dutch hymns in church and within the home. Mara's grandmother, Christine Zichterman Schrier, sang praise and worship songs until the day she relocated to heaven. I can only imagine what the heavenly chorus sounds like that she belongs to today. Mara's parents, her dad and I, enjoyed singing praises to God while being involved in the music ministry at the local church back in the day. And now, Mara's only sibling, Russ, has written many worship songs that he has played and sung to honor the Lord. The beat goes on—

Silence may be golden, but platinum is more durable than gold. I'd say making a joyful noise unto the Lord by singing praise and worship songs is priceless and has eternal value.

MORE FOCUSED UPWARD

*Oh, sing to the Lord a new song! Sing to the Lord, all the earth.
Sing to the Lord, bless His name; proclaim the good news
of His salvation from day to day.*
PSALM 96:1-2 NKJV

PUT ON YOUR LISTENING EARS

Pray, not until God hears you,
but until you listen to God.

Kelly's Treehouse

God hears you, but you'll need to be quiet at some point so He can get a word in edgewise. When you ask for something—even understanding—allow Him to answer your request.

If you don't know what you're doing, pray to the Father.
He loves to help. You'll get his help, and won't be
condescended to when you ask for it.
JAMES 1:5 MSG

If you need wisdom, ask our generous God,
and he will give it to you. He will not rebuke you for asking.
JAMES 1:5 NLT

This is God's Message, the God who made earth, made it livable and
lasting, known everywhere as GOD: Call to me and I will answer you.
I'll tell you marvelous and wondrous things that you could never
figure out on your own.
JEREMIAH 33:2-3 MSG

TELL PEOPLE THE TRUTH

Tell people the truth if you love them.
Everybody does not go to heaven.
Everybody is not resting in peace.
A lot of folks are in hell because they did not repent and accept
Jesus Christ as their Lord and Savior when they were alive.
The Bible says there is no peace for the wicked. (Isaiah 48:22)

Yes — hell is real and people go there every day.

"He is in a better place now." That statement does not
apply to everybody who died.

We can REST IN PEACE when we die, if we:
REPENT and turn back to God.
ACCEPT Jesus Christ as our personal LORD and SAVIOR
BELIEVE on His DEATH on the cross and on HIS RESURRECTION

Be ye saved while we are still alive.
Now is the time for salvation.

Priscilla Shirer

This is *not* a popular message, but it must be shared before it's too late. I know where I'm going—but I don't know who's going with me. That choice is up to every individual; it's not my call. So many times, I wish that it was. I pray that everyone who takes the time to read this will understand the truth of the message and take it very seriously. This is not a time to be nonchalant about eternity.

We are living in dire times, and we need all the help we can get with the assurance that we will be OK no matter what may come our way. Every one of us will die at some time. When our time on earth ends, our life will not be over. We will spend eternity in one of two places. According to the Bible, not everyone will "rest in peace"—some will not be in a better place at all.

> *There was a man of the Pharisees named Nicodemus, a ruler of the Jews. This man came to Jesus by night and said to Him, "Rabbi, we know that You are a teacher come from God; for no one can do these signs that You do unless God is with him."*
>
> *Jesus answered and said to him, "Most assuredly, I say to you, unless one is born again, he cannot see the kingdom of God."*
>
> *Nicodemus said to Him, "How can a man be born when he is old? Can he enter a second time into his mother's womb and be born?"*
>
> *Jesus answered, "Most assuredly, I say to you, unless one is born of water and the Spirit, he cannot enter the kingdom of God. That which is born of the flesh is flesh, and that which is born of the Spirit is Spirit. Do not marvel that I said to you, 'You must be born again.'"*
> JOHN 3:1-7 NKJV

CITIZENSHIP

You aren't a citizen of here working your way into heaven.
You're a citizen of heaven working His Way through here.

Ann Voskamp

The closer I get to relocating to my forever home, the more I realize how important the time I have left here is. That's why I'm writing so much and intentionally spending as much time as possible connecting with people who are interested in connecting with me.

> *Meanwhile, live in such a way that you are a credit to the Message of Christ. Let nothing in your conduct hang on whether I come or not. Your conduct must be the same whether I show up to see things for myself or hear it from a distance.*
> PHILIPPIANS 1:27 MSG

> *Set your mind on things above, not on things on the earth.*
> COLOSSIANS 3:2 NKJV

> *But we are citizens of the state (commonwealth, homeland) which is in heaven, and from it also we earnestly and patiently await [the coming of] the Lord Jesus Christ (the Messiah) [as] Savior.*
> PHILIPPIANS 3:20 AMP

_____
_____
_____
_____

VOICE RECOGNITION

You are defined by God and God alone.

Unless people are saying the same thing about you that God says, insert earplugs. Learn how to be a selective listener and shut out the harmful noise contrary to His viewpoint. After all is said and done, His assessment of who you are and how much He values you is the only one that counts. Listen for His voice and believe what He is saying about you. After all, God put you together in your mother's womb, and He knew how you would turn out from the very beginning.

Everything you have done and experienced in your life so far has not surprised God at all. He has nothing but good things to say to you about you. Sure, He may be giving you instructions on how to do things better that will help you enjoy your life more and bring about better success, but God will *always* be on your side and will tell you what you need to know. Just remember to thank Him for caring and *never* leaving you.

My sheep recognize My voice. I know them, and they follow Me. I give them real and eternal life. They are protected from the Destroyer for good. No one can steal them from out of My hand.
JOHN 10:27-28 MSG

WHO NEEDS TO BE FIRST?

*No matter what happens, my kids come first.
It's that simple.*

No—it really isn't that simple. I understand parents who will put the welfare and safety of their kids ahead of their own, but perhaps this statement can invite an expanded perspective. My comments are directed to the people who say their kids are their "world" and other similar over-the-top declarations. Let's be clear, I love my kids, grandkids, and great-grands, but they are *not* #1 in my life. *God is!* By putting God first, He puts everything else in proper order—His order.

I saw a post on Facebook a while ago that supports my sentiments to a tee: "Putting God first in our lives won't compete with our human relationships. It will protect them." Go ahead and love your kids "to the moon and back" and "a bushel and a peck," but never forget Who is to be in first place in your life.

*Seek the Kingdom of God above all else, and live righteously,
and he will give you everything you need.*
MATTHEW 6:33 NLT

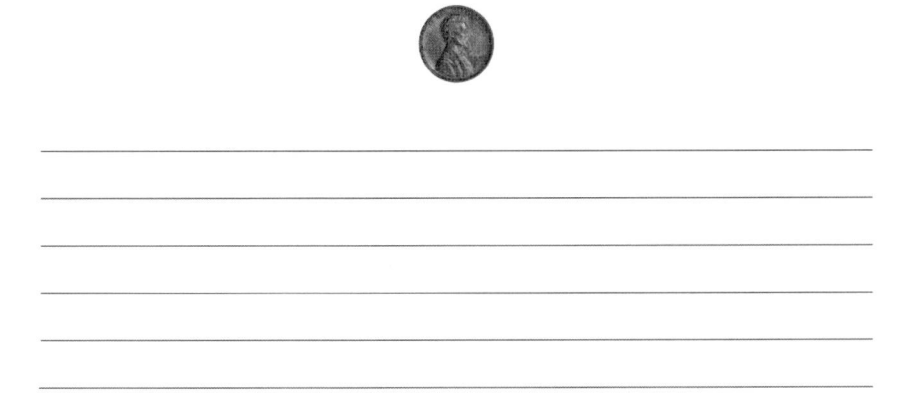

PRAY LIKE ELIJAH

Elijah, A Man Like Us

In an exhortation to pray from his epistle,
James offered believers a very encouraging insight.
Using Elijah as an example of a person who prayed effectively,
he did not write, "Elijah, the prophet, prayed and had great results."
Rather, he wrote, "Elijah, a man just like us, and subject to personal
challenges just like us, prayed and obtained great results."

James revealed that the heartfelt and earnest prayers of
normal, imperfect, human believers can "make much power
available that is dynamic in its working!"

Be encouraged! You don't have to be a prophet or a
perfect Christian to pray effectually! Pray fervently and
with faith! And expect to see great answers to your prayers!

Guy Duininck

I have never been the one to pray eloquent, beautifully phrased prayers. In fact, my prayers are often quite blunt and to the point. Let's face it—when I pray, I'm just talking to God, pleading with Him, pouring my heart out, and telling Him how much I love and appreciate Him. Don't ask me to pray an elaborate prayer at a big, fancy gathering because I will disappoint you. On the other hand, if you want me to pray to the heart of a matter, know that my words will come from my spirit and touch heaven. I, like everyone else, am a person with flaws who serves a mighty God. He listens to my prayers no matter how they come out, because He is deeply concerned and cares about everything on my heart.

*The earnest (heartfelt, continued) prayer of a righteous
man makes tremendous power available
[dynamic in its working].*
JAMES 5:16B AMP

RELIGION VERSUS JESUS

If your experience with Christianity
has left you with more guilt and less joy,
then you found religion, not Jesus.

Religion shackles and binds.
Jesus releases and frees.

Religion can bring guilt and shame.
Jesus brings forgiveness and joy.

Religion is about what you do for God.
Jesus is about what God did for you.

Pay attention and recognize the difference. I don't embrace religion at all. As a Christian, it's all about a relationship with the One who shows me how to become all I was created to be. Jesus is my best friend and has set me free from guilt and shame. He teaches me daily how to become who I was designed to be. Jesus paid the price for my salvation, and there is nothing I can do to repay what He did for me—except to love Him and others and keep His commandments. No guilt—no shame—just joy unspeakable and full of glory.

*I've told you these things for a purpose;
that my joy might be your joy, and your joy wholly mature.
This is my command: Love one another the way I loved you. This is
the very best way to love. Put your life on the line for your friends.
You are my friends when you do the things I command you. I'm no
longer calling you servants because servants don't understand what
their master is thinking and planning. No, I've let you in on
everything I've heard from the Father."*
JOHN 15:11-15 MSG

> "I've loved you the way my Father has loved me. Make yourselves at home in my love. If you keep my commands, you'll remain intimately at home in my love. That's what I've done—kept my Father's commands and made myself at home in his love."
> JOHN 15:9-10 MSG

DOES GOD LIMIT HIMSELF?

There is no limit on what God can do.

The operative word in this post is *can*. We've all heard it—God can do anything. But the bigger question is this: *Will He?* Sometimes our prayers beg Him to do things contrary to His Word. Can He answer our prayers the way we want Him to? Not really. He hears our prayers and answers them—but sometimes the answer is *no*. When we ask amiss, God will not violate His Word—because He is *the* God who *never* lies. He does put limits on Himself on what He's willing to do. His love for all of us is unconditional, and He is a good, good Father—so He will not do anything that is not in our overall best interest. We may argue about His decision, but we would lose that argument every time. Father knows best—always!

God will not violate or go contrary to what He has said. God's love is unconditional, but His responses to us and how He operates in His creation are conditional. God created boundaries, demonstrating to us how they are to be followed. He will not violate or ignore the boundaries He set for Himself. He wants us to follow His lead.

Back to the original post: "There is no limit on what God can do." That's a true statement—and it's a false statement. God *cannot* and *will not* do anything contrary to what He has said. If He did, He would be a liar—and He doesn't lie. God alone embodies the only power in and above creation great enough to willingly place this boundary limit on Himself; He did this to demonstrate that principled truth is more potent than raw might.

No, I will not break my covenant;
I will not take back a single word I said.
I have sworn an oath to David,
and in my holiness I cannot lie.
PSALM 89:34-35 NLT

So God has given both his promise and his oath. These two things are unchangeable because it is impossible for God to lie. Therefore, we who have fled to him for refuge can have great confidence as we hold to the hope that lies before us.
HEBREWS 6:18 NLT

RAMBLING WEE-HOUR TUTORIALS

A Run-On Memory

In October of 2016, I "enjoyed" another wee-hour tutorial with the Lord. I use quotation marks because the cold, hard truth is not always enjoyable—but it is beneficial if I choose to embrace it and act accordingly. The subject of this tutorial is all about relationships. Relationships are tricky, and God has been drawing correlations between my relationship with Him and my relationships with others. This will apparently become the main focus of my future writing as He reveals what His ultimate and perfect picture of friendships ought to be. He has already defined it in His Word, but now I get to experience some up-close-and-personal instruction.

During my very intense introductory time this morning, a phrase that my wise mom spoke to me many, many times came to mind. "Say what you mean and mean what you say." The Word says the same thing—Let your yes be yes and your no be no. Words are powerful and seem to come out of our mouths so hastily. We tend to say things—even meaning them at the time, but down the road, we have a change of heart or mind. Unmet expectations, or worse, promises, can cause trust to erode and break the bonds of friendship.

At my level, I cannot afford to communicate frivolously and be wishy-washy in my commitment to God or to people with skin on. I don't always say things well, but I speak the truth as I understand it—and hope that the people who know my heart will love me enough to extend God's grace my way. If necessary, I'm always willing to receive correction when I'm off base. Know this though—I will seek to say what I mean and mean what I say. Life is too short to play word games and do it any other way. I *will* make corrections and adjustments as needed.

This 2016 wee-hour tutorial was a much-needed lesson about relationships because God knew my desire to cultivate them in a safe and meaningful way. He emphasized the importance of being a woman of my word, making trust a foundational cornerstone for building relationships that would grow in maturity and wisdom and stand the test of time.

The Follow-Up
Fall 2021

Wow! This memory popped up from October 2016 and jarred my memory of this memorable encounter with the Lord. I'm thankful for this modern technology that preserves and triggers thoughts and possibilities for more growth and change. And yes, I'm still focusing my writing on how I can become the best version of myself that I can be. When God takes the time to reach out and teach me new things, even in the wee hours, I listen.

2021-2022: It seems like my focus is on the power and the value of connections now more than ever. Conversations have become more intense and meaningful. The heart of the matter and what *really* matters to me is flowing out of my spirit. As a result, a few of my heart connections have grown much more vital and gained much more value and momentum. I'm sure this growth has been due to the willingness to be honest and vulnerable in both directions and spend quality time together. Time is a crucial factor. Teeter-totter reciprocity is required to deepen a relationship, as it takes two "playing" to pray and grow together.

In recent years, some relationships that once appeared to be strong have lost their intensity. This can be due to changing belief systems, misalignment of life goals or even an unwillingness to discuss core relationship concerns. But that's OK; sometimes it has to be. However, it still saddens me to see people I love stepping away in varying degrees of withdrawal. I genuinely miss them, but the good news is, life goes on! I am celebrating my long-time *and* new safe friends willing to continue this journey with me. My goal is to live a quality, meaningful life and, hopefully, make a significant difference in the lives of others, with God leading all the way.

> *Let every detail in your lives—*
> *words, actions, whatever—*
> *be done in the name of the Master, Jesus,*
> *thanking God the Father every step of the way.*
> COLOSSIANS 3:17 MSG

MY THOUGHTS

'Twas ever so, where'er we go
In winter we encounter snow.
'Tis cold and raw the whole day long
And all winds sing a winter song.
O, may we stay and hope for spring
When sun again will melt the sting.
Yes, spring will come with flowers galore
And usher warmth from shore to shore.
And flowers burst from buds so firm,
And colors countless will confirm
That God is yet in charge over all
And that He will hear when we call
And guide us daily as we tread
Along life's pathway set by Him,
When we can cope with every whim
For all we must do is trust in Him.

Paul J. Schrier

My dad wrote this poem many years ago, around January of 1989. My sister found it shortly after he was diagnosed with lung cancer. His reference to winter in Michigan and looking forward to spring and new life suggests that it makes sense it was written at that time. I seem to recall that it might have been written even before that, but when it was written isn't what's important. It's what he wrote that spoke volumes to me. You see, I grew up in a religious household. My family went to church twice on Sunday and once on Wednesday. We sang the hymns, prayed the prayers, learned the Sunday school stories, sang in the choir, and even dropped money into the offering plate when it passed by. At home, we prayed before our meals and even read Bible passages to close out our family dinner time each night. And we certainly didn't cuss or treat one another disrespectfully without paying for it—the consequences were doled out with consistency. The boundaries in my home were well established and followed. That sounds pretty good, doesn't it?

But here's something that I think about all these years later. I grew up believing God was real, but He needed to be kept in His place—at church and around the dinner table. I always knew my mom had a very tender and personal relationship with the Lord. It wasn't so much about what she said but about who she was. On the other hand, my dad could be gruff and didn't often express his feelings. He was generally quiet around us until he got on the subject of politics or anything else he felt strongly confident about. But he definitely did *not* talk about the Lord. I know many of my parents' personality traits were handed down from their families of origin. My mom's family exuded joy, laughter, and generosity; my dad's family was quiet, stern, and lacking lively, fun conversations.

In the early 1970s, everything changed. My mom had a real awakening and experience with the third member of the Trinity—the Holy Spirit. Something broke loose in her, and she, already a devout God-fearing woman, blossomed with new life and openly prayed and praised the Lord daily. She voraciously read her Bible even more than ever before. I think my dad went into shock, and, of course, thinking she had gone off the deep end, he continued to be privately stoic about his feelings. I was married and out of the house, but I could see the change.

Intrigued by my mom's transformation, I investigated what happened to her, and soon after, joined her joy in this more profound spiritual journey. This God thing was no longer religion; it became a relationship. After going to church almost all my life and going through the religious motions, I became a for-real Christian—just like my mom.

Fast forward to September 1989, and now my dad's journey on earth was drawing to a close. I wondered then and had wondered until just recently whether my dad was a Christian and whether he would be spending eternity with the Lord. I knew he believed that God existed, but I wasn't sure that he *knew* God personally. He never said anything about it, even when my mom would pray over him in his final days. That really bothered me a lot. Knowing that God is real and has an excellent plan for my life and has blessed me with so much, I share my faith openly and freely. Why didn't my dad? I cannot even imagine not sharing the Good News. It was a significant Godwink when my sister recently discovered my dad's poem. It comforted me because I now know that he *is* with the Lord. I just wish that he had talked about his faith in the home as my mom did. Maybe in those days that Jesus stuff was left to the mother while the father went out and worked so he could bring home the bacon. I don't know. I'm grateful that my grown children and their spouses openly speak about their faith and how God continually impacts their lives. The Good News is proclaimed through generations!

My dad's reluctance to speak about his faith came up recently over brunch with my friend, Gloria Mihelich. Her parents were in the ministry and in church all the time, but there wasn't much spiritual talk in her home either. Christian music was often playing—her mom wrote and sang many songs about the Lord. Our dads seemed to hold their beliefs close to their chests; what they believed was between them and their God. Gloria gave me a fresh and great perspective relating to my concern about my dad. She said, "I think, back in those days, our parents were living their lives in such a way that would be good for us to follow." They were living honest, upright lives successfully so that we would see value in doing the same thing. Their lives honored God without talking about it. I figure the saying "actions speak louder than words" works quite well here. They were doing the *"Train up a child in the way they should go…"* thing—from Proverbs 22:6.

As my mom was getting ready to relocate to heaven, she told my sister, Deb, she was looking forward to seeing her "beloved Paul." She knew something that I wasn't sure of at the time. Now I am. As my time draws closer, I am convinced I will be reunited with *both* my parents—and it is well with my soul.

*But the Lord is in his holy Temple.
Let all the earth be silent before Him.*
HABAKKUK 2:20 NLT

THE IN-BETWEEN PLACE

Ruth Shriever wrote: I read this tonight and it almost took my breath away because it's exactly how it is while you're waiting for the Lord to call your loved one home.

"The fleeting moments that separate heaven and earth. The place where the pain of this world meets the glory of eternity above. The place of finally being Home.

This is the sacred place of the in between.

The place where breaths are shallow and slow, and the Spirit is worn and weary. When the fight has been fought and the race almost finished. The place where they lay and wait for their name to be called.

This is the sacred place of the in between.

The place hair is stroked and hands gently held. Hands held for the very last time.

This is the sacred place of the in between.

The place where hymns are sung and memories linger on like their presence in the room. Laughs come through tears, and silent sobs replace the words we try to say. But we can't find the words, can we? Because how do you fit a life's worth of memories into a few sentences?

This is the sacred place of the in between.

The place where heaven meets earth, the moments we wait for and dread all at once. The minutes we want to pass quickly, yet hang onto for dear life.

> *This is when the sacred place of the in between becomes the place of the most holy. The moment they see Jesus, and it takes their breath away."*
>
> Posted by *From Blacktop to Dirt Road.com*

So powerful and breathtaking! I remember when Gloria, my very special friend and caretaker of my mother, told me that Mom was straddling the fence and had one foot on earth and one foot in heaven. Heaven won, and those of us left here felt the loss.

Truth be told, my mom was the biggest winner as she peacefully slipped away to meet the Lord face-to-face and greet her precious family and friends who got to relocate before her. It wasn't a competition to see who could get there first, but she finished her race strong. She received her crown—and I'm pretty sure she laid it at Jesus' feet. One day we'll meet again—of this, I am very sure. As a matter of fact, anyone who calls Jesus their Lord and Savior can confidently proclaim to the masses, "I will be home someday and I hope to see you there." What a day that will be!

> *Yes, we are fully confident,*
> *and we would rather be away from these earthly bodies,*
> *for then we will be at home with the Lord.*
> II Corinthians 5:8 NLT

_____

_____

_____

_____

NOT TOMORROW, BUT NOW

God says, "Come to Me now."
not
"Come to Me when you have it all together."

When I was young, my mom would occasionally ask or tell me to do something. If I stalled or put her off, she would sing this little phrase—"Not tomorrow, but now." As I grew older, I learned to respond more quickly. My mom relocated to heaven in 2005, but I can still hear her singing that little ditty in my head whenever I'm procrastinating and not doing something that must be done right away.

Some time ago, I was talking with one of my granddaughters about getting serious about living her life in a way that was pleasing to God. She had asked Jesus into her heart earlier, but nobody could tell by the way she lived her life. Getting her foot just in the door, she wasn't ready to come all the way in and make herself at home, saying she had to get some stuff together first. She entirely missed the point. God's presence and leadership is available *so* we can get our stuff together.

Excuses, excuses—we hear them all the time, don't we? "I'm not ready." "I have other things to do first." "Living a life for Jesus is so limiting and boring." "I won't be able to have any fun anymore!" Really!?!? Are you serious? I've been a Christian for over 50 years and never had so much fun or felt so free. Life is an adventure filled with many blessings and great favor from God. Sure, there have been challenges and hardships too, but God has never wandered off—He has always been there for me.

I think there is one word that stops people in their tracks and keeps them from living the supernatural life that God has planned for them. The word is *surrender*. We hate to relinquish *our* control over things. Realize that God is not a dictator and will not force anyone to do anything they don't want to do. We all have the freedom to choose how we want to live our lives. Here is a powerful quote from Elisabeth Elliot that appears elsewhere in this book as well: "To pray 'Thy will be done,' I must be willing, if the answer requires it, that my will be undone." God will not impose His will upon us. No, it's up to us to willingly trade ours for His and follow Jesus unashamedly. Let's not continue sitting on our own throne of free will and be the sole conductor of our own lives. We can do that, but the price we pay is more than we can afford.

God sits on *The Throne*—with a capital *T*. There is one *God*—with a capital G, and we aren't Him. *Surrender!* He has a fail-proof plan for our lives, but He will not bust our boundaries and force it upon us without our consent. Our will must be freely surrendered to His so He can work wonders in our lives. *Do it*—not tomorrow, but now.

> *The word that saves is right here, as near as the tongue in your mouth, as close as the heart in your chest. It's the word of faith that welcomes God to go to work and set things right for us. This is the core of our preaching. Say the welcoming word to God—"Jesus is my Master"—embracing, body and soul, God's work of doing in us what he did in raising Jesus from the dead. That's it. You're not "doing" anything; you're simply calling out to God, trusting him to do it for you. That's salvation.*
> ROMANS 10:8-9 MSG

*With your whole being you embrace God
setting things right, and then you say it, right out loud:
"God has set everything right between him and me!"*
ROMANS 10:10 MSG

4

FINAL THOUGHTS

AFTERWORD

I AM SO GRATEFUL that you had a chance to meet my mother and hear her perspective seasoned by years of seeking to live for Christ. She would rightly say that even though we may have our flaws, our Savior speaks through us anyway, and we should not discount or apologize for the importance of our words when they line up with the Word of God.

I have prayed that the *Two Cents* series reaches much further than Mom ever dreamed. I'm confident it will. I find it refreshing that God uses our individuality and imperfections to successfully spread Kingdom principles through our circles of influence and then on to the far reaches of our world. Linda is fully aware of this truth and has sought to optimize her remaining time on this side of eternity in this pursuit—through writing and her preferred method of interaction, the "one-on-one."

If you ever happen upon Linda during your day, strike up a conversation. Don't be surprised if she is quick to identify herself not by her vocation, education, or social standing, but simply by her proximity to the wind of the Spirit. To her, this is what it's all about. I suggest we all strive to live likewise, as this is the only consistent place where *who we are* meets *who we can be.*

It is fitting to remember the unchanging nature of the Word of God as we live each day despite being within an environment naturally hostile to the Spirit of God. Although we cannot see what lies ahead, God can and has already been there with a willingness to strengthen us as we face our unknowns. Consider the following promises:

> *...I am with you always, to the end of the age.*
> MATTHEW 28:20 ESV

> *And the peace of God, which surpasses all understanding,*
> *will guard your hearts and your minds in Christ Jesus.*
> PHILIPPIANS 4:7 ESV

> *You make known to me the path of life;*
> *in your presence there is fullness of joy...*
> PSALM 16:11 ESV

Jeremiah gives us a picture of God's direction to His people regarding living captive in a foreign land in one of the most practical and down-to-earth applications of scripture we would do well to heed:

> *Build houses and dwell in them; plant gardens and eat their fruit. Take wives and beget sons and daughters; and take wives for your sons and give your daughters to husbands, so that they may bear sons and daughters—that you may be increased there, and not diminished. And seek the peace of the city where I have caused you to be carried away captive, and pray to the Lord for it; for in its peace you will have peace.*
> JEREMIAH 29:5-7 NKJV

Finally, as Linda has implored throughout, as God's children, we are *individually* responsible for aligning our thinking and behaviors with that of Christ Jesus. As we have spent a great time focusing our actions inward, outward, and upward, we now shift our focus *forward*. As we do this, I encourage you to wholeheartedly get to know God's heart and His perfect will for you. This can only be accomplished when you spend purposed time connecting with Him and applying His Word daily. Strengthening this relationship is the cornerstone to living life to the full and can be initiated with a declaration something like this:

> *God, I am deciding today that no matter what mistakes I've made in the past, I know Christ has already forgiven me when He laid down His life at the Cross. I believe that He was God's only Son and was raised back to life on the third day and is now seated with the Father in heaven. I now have unlimited access to speak to and hear from the Godhead—the Father, the Son, and the Holy Spirit. I am deciding today to relinquish control of my life and give it over to my now Lord and Savior Jesus Christ and lean fully on His understanding, and not on my own, to help me live out the Truth of His Word.*

As we part, consider that even though Abraham, Moses, and the apostle Paul were examples of those having checkered pasts, God was fully able to empower them to accomplish His great purpose. Their histories did not disqualify them, just as ours will not. As we focus forward on God's perfect will for us, consider Paul's encouragement:

> *Not that I have already obtained it [this goal of being Christlike] or have already been made perfect, but I actively press on so that I may take hold of that [perfection] for which Christ Jesus took hold of me and made me His own. Brothers and sisters, I do not consider that I have made it my own yet; but one thing I do: forgetting what lies behind and reaching forward to what lies ahead...*
> PHILIPPIANS 3:12-13 AMP

I am convinced that if you do this, you will encounter resistance, but build character, experience new enemies, but find safer friends, recognize subtle falsehoods, but learn to confront them with the principles you've come to know and trust. You've got this. Seek first the Kingdom!

Rusty

FINAL THOUGHTS

TOPICAL SCRIPTURE REFERENCE

Anxiety
  PHILIPPIANS 4:6, *32*

Authority
  ISAIAH 44:6, *368*
  JOHN 1:12-13, *327*

Avoiding Unsafe Conditions
  HEBREWS 5:11, *83*
  I CORINTHIANS 15:33, *108*
  II CORINTHIANS 6:14, *153*
  II TIMOTHY 4:3-4, *231*
  PROVERBS 12:26, *200*
  PROVERBS 13:19, *138*
  PROVERBS 13:20, *144, 198*
  PROVERBS 14:7, *57*
  PROVERBS 17:19, *221*
  PROVERBS 22:24, *74*
  PROVERBS 22:24-25, *200*
  PROVERBS 23:9, *161*
  PROVERBS 9:7-8, *60*

Bitterness
  HEBREWS 12:15, *91*

Boldness
  JOSHUA 1:9, *125*

Boundaries
  I CORINTHIANS 3:6-7, *146*
  I THESSALONIANS 4:11, *25*
  MATTHEW 10:12-15, *24*
  MATTHEW 10:13-14, *103*

Children
  PSALM 127:3, *195*
  PSALM 144:12, *195*

Choices
  DEUTERONOMY 30:19-20A, *63*
  II SAMUEL 22:26, *66*
  JOSHUA 24:15, *321*
  MATTHEW 6:22-23, *314*
  PSALM 37:27-30, *268*

Confidence
  II CORINTHIANS 5:8, *183*
  II CORINTHIANS 5:8-10, *323*
  II CORINTHIANS 5:8-9, *279*

Conflict
  ISAIAH 48:22, *383*

Consequences
  LUKE 16:19-31, *326*

Creation of God, The
  JOB 12:7-10, *360*

Deliverance
  PSALM 34:4, *339*

Dependence on God
  MATTHEW 6:33, *238*

Depression
  PSALM 34:17-18, *128*
  PSALM 34:18, *75*

Desire
  I CORINTHIANS 11:1, *248*
  PHILIPPIANS 2:13, *34*

Devotion
  I THESSALONIANS 2:4, *334*
  MATTHEW 6:21, *245*

Discernment
  EPHESIANS 4:14-15, *251*
  PHILIPPIANS 1:9-11, *26*
  ROMANS 1:20, *361*

Encouragement

413

HEBREWS 10:25, *366*
I THESSALONIANS 5:11, *152*
ISAIAH 41:10, *357*
ISAIAH 43:1B-2, *76*

Failure Recovery
LUKE 13:6-9, *101*
PSALM 37:23-24, *86*

Faithfulness
HEBREWS 11:1, *340*
II TIMOTHY 1:5, *214*
II TIMOTHY 4:7, *369*
LAMENTATIONS 3:22-23, *351*
MATTHEW 25:23, *289*
ROMANS 14:12, *213*

Family Leadership
COLOSSIANS 3:21, *151*
EPHESIANS 5:25-27, *147*
EPHESIANS 5:28, *148*
EPHESIANS 6:4, *226*
MATTHEW 6:33, *147*
PROVERBS 19:18, *219*
PROVERBS 22:6, *143, 178, 252, 399*

Fatherly Advice
II THESSALONIANS 4:11-12, *239*
PROVERBS 19:19, *240*
PSALM 32:8-9, *239*

Favor of God, The
II CORINTHIANS 12:9-10, *90*
REVELATION 21:4-5, *280*

Focus
COLOSSIANS 3:2, *385*
LUKE 10:38-42, *174*
ROMANS 12:2, *14*

Forgiveness
EPHESIANS 4:31-32, *175*
EPHESIANS 4:32, *194*

Foundation
MATTHEW 7:24-27, *330*

Freedom
I CORINTHIANS 10:31-33, *42*
II CORINTHIANS 3:18, *44*
JOHN 8:36, *154*

Friendship
I THESSALONIANS 5:11, *168*
PROVERBS 12:26, *190*
PROVERBS 18:24, *127, 142*
PROVERBS 27:17, *158, 193, 199*

Future, The
II TIMOTHY 3:1-5, *73*
MATTHEW 25:21, *262*

God's Word
DEUTERONOMY 8:3, *306*
HEBREWS 4:12, *322*
HEBREWS 4:12-13, *39*
II TIMOTHY 3:16-17, *131, 308, 352, 364*
JOSHUA 1:8, *272*
MATTHEW 4:4, *306*
PSALM 1:2, *303*
PSALM 119:105-106, *70*
PSALM 19:7-8, *233*
PSALMS 119:105, *38*

Goodness
ROMANS 12:9-10, *84*

Grace of God, The
EPHESIANS 2:8-9, *379*
HEBREWS 8:12, *317*
II CORINTHIANS 12:9, *125*
II PETER 3:9, *326*
JOHN 8:3-11, *111*

Guidance
II Thessalonians 3:5, *33*
Proverbs 29:18, *371*
Proverbs 3:11-12, *135*
Psalm 23:3, *7*
Psalm 25:3, *97*

Healing
Matthew 13:15, *321*
Proverbs 17:22, *341*
Psalm 147:3, *93*

Holiness of God, The
Habakkuk 2:20, *400*
Isaiah 55:8-9, *29*

Home, Our
II Corinthians 5:8, *402*
Philippians 3:20, *385*

Honesty
Proverbs 10:9, *203*
Proverbs 11:3, *203*
Proverbs 20:7, *30*, *196*

Hope
Hebrews 6:18, *393*

Humility
Ephesians 4:2, *156*
Ephesians 4:2-3, *145*
James 4:10, *305*
Luke 22:24-26, *207*
Proverbs 13:7, *217*
Romans 12:9-10, *218*

Integrity
Philippians 1:27, *385*

Jesus is the Way
John 14:6, *378*

Journey, The
Isaiah 43:18-19, *94*
Matthew 6:33, *358*
Philippians 1:6, *262*

Philippians 3:12-13, *411*
Proverbs 3:5-6, *278*
Psalm 37:23-24, *99*

Joy
I Thessalonians 5:16-18, *215*
Psalm 16:11, *68*, *410*
Psalm 30:5, *93*

Kindness
Ephesians 4:32, *150*
Proverbs 15:4, *105*

Leadership
Matthew 20:26-28, *207*

Life Planning
Jeremiah 29:11, *128*
Jeremiah 29:5-7, *410*
Matthew 6:20-21, *98*
Proverbs 16:1-3, *80*
Proverbs 3:5-6, *126*
Psalm 139:13-16, *275*

Living by Faith
Hebrews 11:6, *372*
Matthew 17:20, *351*

Love
Ephesians 3:19, *7*
I Corinthians 13:4, *156*
I Corinthians 13:4-7, *236*
I Corinthians 13:4-8, *65*
I John 3:1, *45*
I Peter 4:8, *130*
John 13:34-35, *222*
Matthew 5:44, *170*

Love of God, The
John 15:11-15, *390*
John 15:9-10, *391*
Romans 8:38-39, *331*
Zephaniah 3:17, *335*

Maturity
EPHESIANS 4:14-15, *249*
EPHESIANS 4:14-16, *186*

Name of God, The
EXODUS 3:13-14, *333*

New Life
GALATIANS 6:7-8, *123*
II CORINTHIANS 3:18, *134*
II CORINTHIANS 4:16, *311*
II CORINTHIANS 5:1-2, *182*
II CORINTHIANS 5:17, *286*, *325*
II CORINTHIANS 5:17-19, *56*
JOHN 1:12, *327*
JOHN 10:10, *225*, *294*
JOHN 3:1-7, *384*

Obedience
DEUTERONOMY 4:40, *363*
DEUTERONOMY 5:32-33, *257*
EPHESIANS 6:1-3, *160*
I JOHN 5:2, *18*
I SAMUEL 12:24, *35*
JAMES 1:22, *340*
JOHN 10:27, *267*
JOHN 14:21, *293*
JOSHUA 1:8, *307*
PHILIPPIANS 2:14-16, *216*
PROVERBS 16:20, *81*
PSALM 19:8, *63*
TITUS 2:12, *233*

Patience
I THESSALONIANS 5:14, *180*
II TIMOTHY 2:23-24, *230*
PSALM 27:14, *169*
PSALM 40:1, *266*
PSALM 40:1-2, *41*

Patience of God, The
II PETER 3:9, *326*

Peace
JOHN 14:27, *37*
JOHN 16:33, *299*
LUKE 10:5, *30*
MATTHEW 11:29-30, *315*
PHILIPPIANS 4:6-7, *95*
PHILIPPIANS 4:7, *410*
ROMANS 12:18, *24*

Perseverance
GALATIANS 6:9, *102*
JAMES 1:12, *343*
PHILIPPIANS 4:13, *291*

Power of God, The
GENESIS 1:1, *360*

Praise & Worship
EPHESIANS 5:19, *228*
HABAKKUK 3:17-19, *206*
PSALM 104:33, *228*
PSALM 139:14, *106*
PSALM 150:6, *333*
PSALM 96:1-2, *381*

Prayer
DANIEL 6:10, *354*
I THESSALONIANS 5:17-18, *303*
JAMES 1:5, *382*
JAMES 1:5-8, *79*
JAMES 5:16, *88*
JAMES 5:16B, *389*
JEREMIAH 33:2-3, *382*
LUKE 11:2-4, *309*
MATTHEW 6:9-13, *309*
ROMANS 8:26-27, *276*

Presence of God, The
DEUTERONOMY 31:6, *302*
I KINGS 19:11-12, *283*
ISAIAH 41:10, *342*
JOSHUA 1:8-9, *297*

Joshua 1:9, *356*
Matthew 18:20, *367*
Matthew 28:20, *410*
Proverbs 18:24, *177*
Psalm 139:7-10, *269*
Psalm 16:6-9, *234*
Psalm 46:1, *268*
Romans 8:9-11, *49*

Pride
James 4:16-17, *11*

Promises of God, The
II Corinthians 1:20-22, *345*

Provision of God, The
Isaiah 41:13, *345*
Matthew 6:33, *387*
Revelation 21:6-7, *281*

Purpose, Our
Isaiah 46:9-10, *285*
Jeremiah 29:11-13, *17*
Romans 8:28, *15*, *34*, *58*, *350*

Respect
Leviticus 19:32, *242*

Responsibility
Galatians 6:4-5, *92*, *229*
Galatians 6:4-6, *254*
Galatians 6:5, *104*

Reverence
Matthew 6:9-10, *309*

Righteousness of God, The
II Corinthians 5:21, *273*, *318*
Psalm 36:5-7, *335*

Safety
John 10:27-28, *386*
Proverbs 29:25, *210*

Psalm 46:1, *376*

Salvation
Hebrews 9:27-28, *362*
Romans 10:8-9, *404*
Romans 10:9-10, *347*
Romans 5:18-19, *363*

Seeking God
James 4:8, *319*
Matthew 6:33, *9*
Proverbs 18:15, *109*
Proverbs 3:5-6, *349*

Self-Discipline
Hebrews 12:11, *139*
II Timothy 1:7, *124*
Philippians 4:8-9, *28*
Proverbs 12:1, *224*
Proverbs 12:16, *202*
Proverbs 13:24, *62*
Proverbs 6:20-23, *165*

Selflessness
Hebrews 13:16, *201*
John 15:13, *122*
Luke 6:31, *121*
Matthew 7:12, *150*, *244*

Spirit of God, The
Corinthians 2:11, *337*

Spirit-Led Living
1 Corinthians 2:14, *298*
Acts 2:17, *166*
Ephesians 3:20, *359*
Ephesians 6:11-15, *271*
Galatians 5:16-18, *53*
James 1:19, *137*
Matthew 5:43-48, *171*
Philippians 2:13, *205*
Philippians 3:10-11, *375*
Proverbs 13:18-20, *191*
Proverbs 16:32, *61*
Psalm 51:10, *265*

PSALM 92:12-14, *107*
ROMANS 10:10, *405*
ROMANS 6:1-2, *304*

Spiritual Warfare
EPHESIANS 6:12, *320*
II CORINTHIANS 10:4, *343*

Strength
II CORINTHIANS 12:10, *46*
ISAIAH 49:24-25, *302*
PSALM 46:1-3, *296*

Surrender
DEUTERONOMY 6:5, *284*
I PETER:6-7, *349*
JAMES 4:7, *344*
PSALM 139:23-24, *72*
ROMANS 12:1, *13*

Thankfulness
COLOSSIANS 3:17, *288*, *329*, *396*
I THESSALONIANS 5:18, *77*
II THESSALONIANS 1:3, *209*

Thought Life
PHILIPPIANS 4:8, *69*
PHILIPPIANS 4:8-9, *243*
PROVERBS 16:3, *89*
ROMANS 12:1-2, *13*, *287*
ROMANS 12:2, *96*, *350*

Timing
ECCLESIASTES 3:1, *78*

Trust
MATTHEW 6:34, *313*
PSALM 118:8, *263*

Truthfulness of God, The
II CORINTHIANS 10:4-6, *344*
JOHN 8:32, *250*

PSALM 89:34-35, *392*

Vision
EPHESIANS 1:18-19, *47*
I CORINTHIANS 13:12, *22*, *325*
II CORINTHIANS 3:16-17, *43*

Wisdom
ECCLESIASTES 10:2, *19*
I CORINTHIANS 8:2, *22*
JAMES 1:5, *100*
JOB 12:12, *107*, *181*
PROVERBS 12:14, *113*
PROVERBS 12:15, *114*
PROVERBS 22:17, *27*
PROVERBS 4:11, *20*
PROVERBS 9:9, *12*
ROMANS 11:33-34, *19*

Words, Our
COLOSSIANS 4:6, *247*
EPHESIANS 4:31-32, *185*
II TIMOTHY 2:23, *189*
JAMES 3:3-5, *132*
JAMES 3:6, *133*
MATTHEW 12:34, *164*
MATTHEW 5:33-37, *204*
MATTHEW 5:37, *172*, *232*
PROVERBS 16:24, *162*
PSALM 19:14, *164*

Work Ethic
COLOSSIANS 1:10-12, *54*
COLOSSIANS 3:23, *290*
COLOSSIANS 3:23-24, *124*, *197*
EPHESIANS 5:11-13, *55*
GALATIANS 6:4-5, *71*
I TIMOTHY 5:18, *188*
II TIMOTHY 2:15, *50*, *212*
MATTHEW 5:16, *157*

INDEX

A

Ahemad, Niyaz, 245
Aitchison, Steven, 97
Andrews, Andy, 42, 154, 199
anxiety, 95, 124, 341

B

Beck, Madalyn, 161
Benge, Dustin, 297
Bergman, Ingmar, 134
Blame Game, 94, 109, 123, 211
boundaries, 27, 64, 66, 82, 103, 135, 154, 172, 184, 190, 197, 229, 232, 233, 234, 239, 253, 254, 292, 305, 392, 398
Boundaries, 82
Brown, Jeff, 192
Burchard, Brendon, 71

C

Caine, Christine, 273, 277, 359
Case for a Creator, The, 360
Changes That Heal, 82
Chodron, Pema, 12
Choice Theory, 85
Cloud, Henry, 113, 145
Coelho, Paulo, 74
confidence, 8, 72, 183, 198, 220, 237, 263, 279, 323, 336, 337, 338, 339, 393, 398, 402, 409
consequences, 38, 53, 123, 158, 253, 292, 326, 354, 398
Cooke, Tony, 139
Copeland, Gloria, 276
Corrie ten Boom, 324, 325
Cravens, Alex, 301

criticism, 8, 139, 191

D

Dion, Kalen, 213
disappointment, 34, 66, 84, 153, 159, 292
discernment, 26, 138, 179, 366
disobedience, 38, 344
disrespect, 71, 136, 159, 184, 185
Dobson, James, 178
Dollar, Creflo, 290, 304, 350
Duininck, Guy, 47, 100, 163, 189, 306, 388

E

earth suit, 134
Einstein, Albert, 19
Elliot, Elisabeth, 131, 309
Emerson, Ralph Waldo, 59
empathy chip, 16, 120, 213, 222

F

failure, 55, 90, 167
failure to thrive, 167
Feynman, Richard, 21
Freelen, Arianna, 355

G

Godwinks, 24, 119, 121, 293, 399
Goodwin, Paula, 235

H

Hades, Arch, 202
Harper, John, 346
healing, 30, 43, 49, 52, 75, 87, 101, 105, 136, 167, 186, 273, 276, 341, 348, 365
heartspace, 91

Heisendberg, Werner, 360
Hickson, William Edward, 90
Hiding Place, The, 324
Hill Sr., Rob, 82
Hoffman, Reid, 248
Hunt, Jim, 152

I

identity, 8, 15, 287, 356
ignorance, 10, 270
Instruction Manual, 262, 270, 363

J

JCLU Forever, 208

K

Kelly's Treehouse, 382
knowledge, 8, 21, 26, 27, 47, 224, 231, 237, 337, 344, 365, 366
Kradowski, Sandi, 350

L

LeClaire, Jennifer, 343
lessons, 67, 143, 208, 252, 353
Lewis, C.S., 166, 299, 303
LIFE-O-SUCTION, 206, 223, 229
love tank, 6, 152, 176, 223, 245
LovingMeAfterWe.com, 75
Lucado, Max, 8, 328, 345

M

maturity, 186
McClellan, Mara Allin, 82, 157, 280, 380
McGill, Bryant, 179, 191
Melton, Glennon Doyle, 62
Mencken, H.L., 370
Menk, Mufti, 69
Meyer, Joyce, 94, 331
Mihelich, Gloria, 347, 399, 402
Mind Journal, The, 128
mistakes, 10

Montagnes, Jim, 85
Moody, D. L., 55
Muller, George, 131
My Longest Day, 270
My Thoughts, 397
Myss, Caroline, 123

N

Narc-Wise, 36
negativity, 27, 73, 74, 91, 163, 246, 290, 350
Nutt, Justin, 6

O

obedience, 99, 287, 292, 304, 344
Okamuro, Deborah, vii, 120, 141, 155, 399

P

people picker, 149
Perseverance, 291
persistence, 90
Prayer of Salvation, 411
preferred narrative, 306
Prince, Derek, 316, 318
Prince, Joseph, 315

R

reciprocity, 70, 149, 192, 200, 203, 395
rejection, 15
relationship, 23, 26, 30, 34, 56, 58, 67, 70, 75, 84, 87, 93, 120, 128, 132, 136, 137, 140, 141, 147, 153, 169, 176, 182, 187, 190, 203, 213, 214, 217, 226, 232, 233, 235, 243, 246, 247, 249, 254, 285, 289, 292, 299, 318, 338, 353, 366, 370, 373, 374, 379, 387, 390, 394, 395, 398, 464

respect, 64, 71, 159, 226, 232, 242
responsibility, 10, 16, 25, 27, 35, 38, 51, 71, 87, 89, 92, 104, 112, 165, 167, 190, 211, 229, 254, 301, 304, 345, 366
Richardson, Cheryl, 52
Ride Podcast, The, 170
Roger Lee Quotes, 35
Ross, Robert, 338
Rowgo, Hope, 197, 227
Rowgo, Linda C., xxii, 23, 85, 135, 227, 261, 285, 320, 368, 377, 409, 410, 464
Rowgo, Rusty James, vii, xxii, 1, 141, 170, 280, 287, 358, 380, 411, 465

S

safe people, 57, 66, 144, 149, 208, 217, 230, 249
Safe People, 82, 200, 217
Sain Jr., Chris, 249
Schmidt, Barb, 211
Schrier, Brian, 119
Schrier, Christine, v, 380
Schrier, Paul J., 397
self-control, 35, 42, 124
self-talk, 106, 274
Shirer, Priscilla, 383
shoulding, 85, 112, 113, 143
Shriever, Ruth, 401
Silk, Danny, 232
Smyser, Mary, 141, 182
Spafford, Horatio, 295
Sparks, Rick, 264
Spurgeon, Charles, 308, 372
stinking thinking, 69, 341, 351
Stover, Stephen, 227

Strobel, Lee, 360
surrender, 12, 43, 291, 305, 403
Sweet tea was more than enough, 120
Swope, Renee, 141

T

Tada, Joni Eareckson, 310
Tawwah, Nedra, 64
TerKeurst, Lysa, 8, 29
thankful, 24, 77, 119, 126, 206, 208, 215, 271, 341, 395
thoughts, 2, 13, 27, 29, 69, 78, 80, 89, 95, 128, 162, 214, 276, 287, 312, 322, 337, 338, 352, 353, 395
Toby Mac, 334
tomorrow, 16, 237, 313, 355, 356, 403, 404
Townsend, John, 78, 87, 173, 223, 246
Tozer, A.W., 18, 270
transformation, 18
trust muscle, 56
Twain, Mark, 61
Two Cents, 1, 347, 356, 466

V

Victim Card, 109
Voskamp, Ann, 91, 385

W

Walking on Logs, 336
Warner, Ashleigh, 101
Warren, Rick, 340
Wigglesworth, Smith, 322
Wilde, Oscar, 194
wisdom, 19, 20, 47, 78, 100, 107, 138, 161, 170, 231, 233, 261,

297, 309, 353, 364, 365, 366,
  382, 395
Wolfe, David "Avocado", 109
Wooten, Linda, 124
Workingwomen.com, 153
worry, 31, 79, 95, 238, 315, 348,
  358

Y
You Are Special, 8

Z
Zantamata, Doe, 77
Zichterman, Herman, 270
Ziglar, Zig, 27, 342

FINAL THOUGHTS

FOCUSED FORWARD JOURNAL

As you steady your gaze forward and focus toward the land God is directing you, we thought it fitting to provide some fresh journaling papers for the journey.

As you lean more fully into the work of the Holy Spirit, you will hear His steadfast counsel penetrate through the noise to a greater degree. Expect this. The Word of God is alive and will leap off the pages speaking directly to your unique situation and bear witness with the voice of the Spirit as you spend time with Him in prayer. It is of great value to archive what the Lord is saying; whether you use these pages or other methods, we encourage this. They are a reminder and will testify to God's continual presence and faithfulness during the difficult times.

Remember—you've got this. Every solution you seek is found in your partnership with Christ; He is as close as a whisper and Lord over all!

TWO CENTS MORE

TWO CENTS MORE

TWO CENTS MORE

TWO CENTS MORE

FOCUSED FORWARD JOURNAL

TWO CENTS MORE

TWO CENTS MORE

FOCUSED FORWARD JOURNAL

TWO CENTS MORE

TWO CENTS MORE

FOCUSED FORWARD JOURNAL

TWO CENTS MORE

FOCUSED FORWARD JOURNAL

TWO CENTS MORE

TWO CENTS MORE

FOCUSED FORWARD JOURNAL

TWO CENTS MORE

TWO CENTS MORE

TWO CENTS MORE

TWO CENTS MORE

TWO CENTS MORE

TWO CENTS MORE

FOCUSED FORWARD JOURNAL

TWO CENTS MORE

TWO CENTS MORE

FOCUSED FORWARD JOURNAL

ABOUT THE AUTHORS

Linda C. Rowgo grew up in Kalamazoo, Michigan, and though technically a part of the "silent generation," she is anything but. Still residing in the city of her youth, she is a Christian, mom, grandma, and, most importantly, friend. Vocationally, Linda has worn the hat of schoolteacher, limited license psychologist, high school counselor, and small group leader over her nearly 80 years on planet earth.

In 2006, Linda retired but likes to refer to the time since as her *refirement*. She continues to cherish times spent with friends and family, talking about the things that matter and building solid and priceless relationships. Teaching, counseling, encouraging, and loving others will continue to be the beat that goes on as long as Linda lives this side of eternity.

Her prayer has always been that after relocating to heaven she will have left warm memories and lots of smiles behind. Beyond that, she hopes to see everyone again and likes to part with the words, *"To be continued..."*

ABOUT THE AUTHORS

Rusty James Rowgo resides in Greensville County, South Carolina and is married to the wife of his youth. A proud homeschooling father of two and professionally active in the information technology field, Rusty has balanced his creative pursuits between the corporate world and lay ministry endeavors of fathering, worship leading, lifestyle podcasting, and writing. As host of *The Ride Podcast*, he is driven by the desire to create environments where the Spirit of God is given the freedom to speak to our moment and empower us to make needed changes.

WHERE IT ALL STARTED

Linda has been sharing hope with many through her years of life-affirming counseling in the high school, individual, and group settings. Her first book, *Two Cents*, was birthed to share the hope of Christ with future generations desperate to apply consistent and time-proven principles to the challenges of everyday living.

TWO CENTS

Generational Wisdom Without All the Fuss

Instant gratification has inundated our culture. Consequently, we have permitted a great many distractions to steal our attention from the meaningful now. Linda is aware of this troubling trend and is armed with a dry wit and earnest desire for us to slow down our thought life and think about what we are thinking about.

Two Cents is a wake-up call for us to focus on the areas of our lives that need addressing and to seek help from the outside when we realize that we don't have it all together. Much more than just another book on self-discovery, you will find a trustworthy friend alongside to help confront the real issues and approach them with a God-directed plan for success.

You can find Linda's books at online retailers and her publisher page at

store.bookbaby.com/book/two-cents